Gender, Justice and Legal Feminism

Volume 3

The Series Gender, Justice and Legal Feminism seeks to harness the diverse and innovative work within and across the boundaries of jurisprudence and gender studies, with a specific attention to approaches inspired both by traditional and more recent feminist movements (e.g., both by difference feminism and LGBTQ+ streams – with their different conceptualizations of identity and neutrality). Sexual difference can be considered as one of the characteristics that differentiate individuals (like for instance age, or ethnic belonging) and such difference plays a focal function in issues of equality, justice, discrimination, as the philosophical concept of "différence" as properly shown. Such difference is indeed linguistic, logica, theoretical and must be studied in all its aspects. Through the lense of the difference, the series aim to publish works engaging with the intrinsic bond between justice and gender studies (through language and psychoanalysis), encouraging perspectives that can be defined as feminist according to the various meanings attributed to such term. For example, like in the meaning attributed to the term by the project of Feminist Legal Judgments, which demonstrated that legal practice can be "rewritten" and re-imagined from a point of view that includes diverse subjectivities and does not consider the male subject as the dominant and principal subject of the law. The main objective of the series is to build on theories on gender and feminism in order to propose a different perspective on legal science and method. In pursuing these tasks, the series aims to engage with the connections between gender identity, gender relations and political systems, and with all the societal aspects interacting in the construction and depiction of gender through language and human action. Such type of inquiries challenges the positivist view of law and constitutes a privileged critical point of observation. The series welcomes proposals – be they edited collections or single-authored monographs – emphasizing the conflicts and connections between justice, gender, and law, proposing critical approaches to law and feminist studies, offering analyses in areas such as jurisprudence, legal theory, gender studies, legal semiotics, law and language.

Keywords: Justice, Law, Feminism, Gender Studies, Jurisprudence, Equality, Language, Symbolic Order, Difference Feminism, Abuse, Violence, Stereotypes, Neglection, Vulnerability, Welfare, Mental health and Social Care, Anti-Discriminatory/Affirmative Actions, Human Rights, Freedom of Expression and Choice, Resilience, Queer studies, LGBTQ+ studies

Unique Selling Points:

- Challenges traditional approaches to gender and law through the unique lense of feminist discourses
- Combines the insights from legal theory, legal feminist, semiotics of law, law and language and is strongly interdisciplinary
- Proposes a new interdisciplinary field bringing together well established and young, innovative research

Sharon Duignan

Transforming Justice for Women

Springer

Sharon Duignan
School of Business
Atlantic Technological University
Galway, Ireland

ISSN 2948-1651 ISSN 2948-166X (electronic)
Gender, Justice and Legal Feminism
ISBN 978-3-031-82454-8 ISBN 978-3-031-82455-5 (eBook)
https://doi.org/10.1007/978-3-031-82455-5

This Springer imprint is published by the registered company Springer Nature Switzerland AG
The registered company address is: Gewerbestrasse 11, 6330 Cham, Switzerland

Contents

Chapter 1
Introduction

1.1 Background

The economic instability caused by the demise of the Celtic tiger created a more unsettled society with increasing recidivism and growing concerns over prison overcrowding. This compelled Irish policymakers to search for community-based sanctions to alleviate systemic pressures and to deal with the surge in short-term incarceration rates. Legislative reforms which encouraged alternatives to custodial sentences for terms of less than twelve months marked a significant shift towards reducing dependence on imprisonment.

The Irish government's penal policy can be better understood within the broader socio-economic and political landscape that prompted the adoption of a prison diversion strategy in the early 2010s. Although there was a shift towards non-custodial sentences, this approach overlooked the unique circumstances and needs of women offenders. This is troublesome, as women represent a smaller, often marginalised group within the criminal justice system, whose specific challenges are frequently disregarded in broader penal reforms. Without a qualitative assessment of how these policies impact women, one can only infer their effects from quantitative data, such as the rise in women receiving short-term prison sentences (STPS). Experience in other jurisdictions, such as Scotland and England & Wales, highlight that penal policies which do not address the needs of minority populations often fail to effectively support those cohorts.[1]

The Irish government's penal policy emerged as a response to the exacerbated issue of prison overcrowding following Ireland's economic crisis. To mitigate the increasing incarceration rates, the government promoted community-based alternatives and enacted legislation aimed at reducing the prevalence of STPS, particularly

[1] Jean Corston (2007).

S. Duignan, *Transforming Justice for Women*, Gender, Justice and Legal Feminism 3, https://doi.org/10.1007/978-3-031-82455-5_1

those under twelve months.[2] However, this strategic shift towards non-custodial sanctions did not sufficiently consider the specific needs and circumstances of female offenders. Women, constituting a smaller and frequently marginalised segment of the offending population, have seen their unique challenges largely overlooked in the broader application of these reforms.

1.2 The Role of Gender in Justice

The role of gender in justice has often been neglected by penal policymakers, but it is an important consideration when addressing the unique needs and circumstances of female offenders. Women constitute around ten percent of offenders in the criminal justice system, representing a minority who are frequently marginalised within the penal system. Traditional, male-focused approaches have not adequately addressed their distinct needs and circumstances. However, there is a need for gender-responsive practices that recognise and address the distinct realities faced by women. Such approaches can include trauma-informed care, mental health support, and programs designed to maintain family connections. By adopting these targeted approaches, the system can better support women in building stability and resilience, ultimately improving their chances of reintegrating successfully and reducing reoffending.

Now as a prominent member of the international community, the Irish government has been increasingly required to consider gender in its policy decisions.[3] Research has been undertaken in neighbouring jurisdictions on the different pathways into offending taken by women, and it is universally acknowledged that a greater understanding is needed of the types of penal sanctions appropriate for this cohort.[4]

In general, women are less likely to pose a significant risk of harm to the public and therefore most female offenders can be managed more effectively through non-custodial sanctions.[5] However, both male and female offenders are sentenced to short-term prison sentences[6] (STPS) in the same manner, without differentiation. The Irish sentencing system dictates that certain overarching structural principles be

---

[2] Criminal Justice (Community Service) (Amendment) Act (2011); Fines (Payment and Recovery) Act (2014).

[3] Department of Justice and Equality (2018);United Nations Rules for the Treatment of Women Prisoners and Non-custodial Measures for Women Offenders: Vienna: UNODC(2011)2010. United Nations Office on Drugs and Crime (UNODC); Equality Department of Children, Disability, Integration and Youth (2017).

[4] Jean Corston (2007); Carlen (1983); Carlen (1988); Carlen and Worrall (1987); Irish Penal Reform Trust (2021)

[5] Handbook on Women and Imprisonment (2014) Vienna, p. 122.

[6] Short term prison sentences (STPS) in this work refers to prison sentences for twelve months and under.

uniformly applied, which can sometimes lead to the neglect of individual offenders' unique characteristics.[7] This is particularly evident in the busy lower courts where most STPS are issued.

Despite this, Ireland has pledged to enhance the use of non-custodial measures for women offenders.[8] This commitment involves promoting the implementation of non-custodial sanctions, especially for those who do not present a significant risk to public safety, thereby decreasing the dependence on imprisonment as a means of punishment for female offenders.[9]

International standards advocating for the humane treatment and effective reintegration of female offenders also emphasise the importance of considering the specific experiences of women, including their roles as primary caregivers, their increased vulnerability to mental or physical health issues, and their histories of abuse or trauma.[10]

1.3 Penal Policy in Context

As a response to Ireland's ever evolving socio-economic landscape, the country's penal policy has undergone significant transformations. Historically, the government has approached penal reform using draconian measures like increased imprisonment. Incarceration and the promotion of community-based sanctions have been notably influenced by economic turmoil and the later recovery periods policies, leading to fluctuating priorities. In recent decades, the government has tried to address prison overcrowding using initiatives such as the introduction and encouragement of Community Service Orders ('CSO's) and legislation aimed at reducing STPS for fine defaults and other minor offending. These initiatives aim to divert offenders from incarceration, signifying a shift towards more progressive, rehabilitative strategies. However, implementation has often lacked a unified guiding philosophy, leading to mixed outcomes and unintended consequences. Paradoxically, however, the imprisonment rate for female STPS recipients increased, contrary to the policy's goals.[11]

In the early 2000s, the Irish government, faced with rising incarceration rates, prioritised the financial stability of the state.[12] This approach aimed to reduce costs by reducing the number of STPS recipients (male and female).[13] However, as

[7] Law Reform Commission(1996), 3.13.

[8] Bangkok Rules.

[9] Kelly and Bogue (2014).

[10] Bangkok Rules, Rule 61.

[11] Irish Prison Service; O'Hara and Rogan (2015).

[12] 'Ireland' or 'Irish' refers to of the geo-political territory and the individuals of the Republic of Ireland (ROI).

[13] STPS refers to sentences of committal to prison for 12 months and under.

statistics were published together, the small, but growing, cohort of female STPS recipients were overlooked.[14] Historically, this group has been under-researched and has evaded reform efforts, due to its small size and the low level of criminality associated with its members.[15]

As a member of the Council of Europe, the Irish state has a duty to regularly report to the European Committee for the Prevention of Torture and Inhuman or Degrading Treatment or Punishment (CPT).[16] In its 2006 Report to the Irish government, the European Committee for the Prevention of Torture and Inhuman or Degrading Treatment or Punishment (CPT) issued a compelling recommendation to the Irish authorities: they were "strongly encouraged to invest the necessary resources into the existing prison estate to ensure that all prisoners are kept in appropriate conditions of detention."[17] Fast forward five years to the Committee's 2011 Report, and the situation had taken a troubling turn. The prison population had "expanded considerably"[18] since the CPT's last visit, and by 2010, with no substantial investment in new facilities, the CPT observed:

> Imprisonment is not achieving its purpose in respect of these people. Instead, more might be achieved through devising programmes for such persons to serve their sentences in the community.[19]

In 2006, the emphasis was on ensuring adequate space for detainees. The government's response to this was to reaffirm its commitment to building a new prison campus at Thornton Hall, designed to accommodate over two thousand prisoners across various security levels.[20] By 2010, however, overcrowding had become the central issue. At the time of this visit, the country was in the grip of economic austerity and this expansion plan was shelved. Ireland had transitioned from the economic boom of the Celtic Tiger era to a period of financial hardship. Employment fell from 2.1 million in 2008 to 1.9 million in 2009, social welfare expenditures rose to 15.6% of gross national income (almost double from a decade earlier), and theft and related offences had increased steadily from 2004 to 2009.[21]

---

[14] Sharon Duignan (2023)

[15] Irish Penal Reform Trust (2013a), p. 3.

[16] This obligation involves regular inspections and assessments of Ireland's detention facilities, including prisons, police stations, and psychiatric institutions. The CPT's role is to ensure that these institutions follow the European Convention for the Prevention of Torture and Inhuman or Degrading Treatment or Punishment. Ireland must provide detailed reports on the conditions and treatment of individuals within these facilities, responding to any recommendations made by the CPT to improve standards and rectify any identified issues. This process ensures transparency and accountability in the treatment of detainees, promoting adherence to human rights standards and the humane treatment of all individuals in custody.

[17] CPT (2007), p. 16.

[18] CPT (2011).

[19] Ibid, paragraph 24.

[20] Ibid, paragraph 23.

[21] Central Statistics Office (2010).

Rather than constructing more prisons, the government opted to implement another CPT recommendation: reducing the inmate population serving shorter sentences to allocate resources more effectively. At the publication of the 2010 Irish Prison Service Report, Alan Shatter, the then Minister for Justice, Equality, and Defence, remarked that it was clear from the 2010 Annual Report that the greatest challenge facing the Irish Prison Service was 'the increasing number of prisoners being committed to custody'.[22] This led to the enactment of the Criminal Justice (Community Service) Act 2011 ('the 2011 Act'), which amended the Criminal Justice (Community Service) Act 1983 ('the 1983 Act'). The 2011 Act aimed to decrease the use of STPS and promote the use of the Community Service Order (CSO) as a direct alternative to incarceration. Section 2 of the 2011 Act substitutes Section 3 of the 1983 Act:

> Where a court, by or before which an offender stands convicted, is of opinion that the appropriate sentence in respect of the offence of which the offender is convicted would…be one of imprisonment for a period of 12 months or less, the court shall… consider whether to make …a community service order.[23]

The 2011 Act mandates that courts consider CSOs as alternatives to imprisonment for minor offences that would typically result in prison sentences of up to twelve months. However, while the legislation outlines guidelines for imposing CSOs, it falls short in providing strategies to effectively reduce the reliance on STPS. This challenge is compounded by the structure of the Irish criminal justice sentencing system. The District Court, which issues the majority of female STPS, operates as all other courts, under the principle of proportionality. However, it is also the court where judicial discretion is most exercised and, thus, where sentencing inconsistencies are most often observed.[24]

1.4 The Hidden Demographic

Research suggests that government and judicial efforts to divert offenders from STPS may have disadvantaged female offenders.[25] By treating men and women equally in this context, the distinct needs of women have been overlooked, exacerbating the challenges they face in their communities.[26] In 2011, the Irish Inspector for Prisons published the Standards for the Protection of Prisoners—'Women Prisoners' Supplement,[27] in which he stated that treating women offenders the

---

[22] Department of Justice (2010).

[23] Criminal Justice (Community Service) (Amendment) Act (2011), s2, as substituted by s3.

[24] Carr and Maguire (2017); Maguire (2016).

[25] Hedderman and Gunby (2013).

[26] Carol Hedderman (2004);Jean Corston (2007).

[27] Inspector of Prisons (2011).

same as men 'is not tantamount to achieving equality of gender'.[28] Citing the Office of the High Commissioner for Human Rights, he noted:

> [T]he concept of equality means much more than treating all persons in the same way. Equal treatment of persons in unequal situations will operate to perpetuate rather than eradicate injustice.[29]

The Prisons Act 2007 provides for the appointment of the Inspector of Prisons by the Minister for Justice. The Act outlines the functions and powers of the Inspector, including the authority to enter and inspect any prison or place of detention and allows the Inspector to make recommendations to the Minister for Justice on the improvement of prison conditions and the treatment of prisoners. The Inspector of Prisons ensures that prison conditions comply with relevant EU Law and international frameworks.[30]

The legislation also mandates the production of an annual report, while also allowing the Inspector to issue added reports on specific matters as needed. These reports are essential for ensuring oversight and transparency within the Irish prison system. Thematic reports may address specific issues such as healthcare provision, mental health services, or the treatment of vulnerable prisoners, providing in-depth analysis and targeted recommendations.[31]

The Women Prisoner's Supplement makes explicit reference to the international standards for the treatment of women in prison and the management of women's prisons, detailing standards for healthcare, safety, and security.[32] It also includes guidelines on maintaining family contact, staff training, and the treatment of pregnant women and mothers with children in prison. The aim is to highlight the challenges and needs of incarcerated women and offer recommendations to improve their treatment and overall prison experience.[33] However, the implementation of these measures requires additional resources and a clear policy commitment from the State to meet these standards, which potentially clashes with the government's cost-cutting and decarceration approach driven by austerity measures.

As a response to this, the Irish Prison Service and the Probation Service introduced the Joint Strategy 'An Effective Response to Women Who Offend' in March 2014.[34] This strategy outlined how the two organisations would collaborate while recognising the distinct pathways, characteristics, and offences of women. Whilst

[28] Ibid, p. 6.

[29] Ibid, paragraph 2.8 Citing Office of the High Commissioner for Human Rights, "Fact Sheet No. 22- Discrimination against Women: The Convention and the Committee", Geneva, undated as accessed at http://www.ohchr.org/Documents/Publications/FactSheet22en.pdf.

[30] Convention for the Protection of Human Rights and Fundamental Freedoms (1950) European Court of Human Rights; European Committee for the Prevention on Torture (CPT);Rule 9 - European Prison Rules(2020)Council of Europe; Bangkok Rules.

[31] Prisons Act (1970), s31.

[32] Inspector of Prisons (2011).

[33] Bangkok Rules, paragraph 2.11.

[34] Joint Probation Service - Irish Prison Service (2014).

the government had promised to ensure that 'the rights of women and men to equality of treatment and to participate fully in society'[35] would be upheld, the domestic policy of the Fine Gael Labour government had shifted its focus towards national recovery measures.

> We will ensure that violent offenders and other serious offenders serve appropriate prison sentences, while at the same time switching away from prison sentences and towards less costly non-custodial options for non-violent and less serious offenders. This will result in a reduction in the prison population and alleviate overcrowding.[36]

However, the Irish penal system has been slow to adopt these principles comprehensively, resulting in systemic biases and insufficient support for women. There are only two female prison facilities in Ireland: the Dóchas Centre and Limerick prison's female wing and both grapple with severe overcrowding and limited rehabilitation opportunities. Currently, the Dóchas Centre, once a pioneering facility, is severely overcrowded, restricting its ability to offer meaningful rehabilitation. Unlike male prison facilities that feature multiple security levels, female facilities are limited to a single medium-security level. Additionally, the absence of step-down programs and non-custodial measures tailored to women makes the government's diversion programs unsuitable for female offenders.

Advocacy groups like the Irish Penal Reform Trust underscore the necessity for non-custodial measures and community-based programmes specifically designed for women.[37] They argue that a one-size-fits-all approach fails to meet the distinct needs of female offenders, who frequently encounter additional challenges related to trauma, mental health issues, and caregiving responsibilities.[38] Thus, reform is essential to ensure that female offenders receive fair, rehabilitative treatment, facilitating their successful reintegration into society.

Law

Convention for the Protection of Human Rights and Fundamental Freedoms (1950)
United Nations Rules for the Treatment of Women Prisoners and Non-custodial Measures for Women Offenders: Vienna: UNODC (2011)
Rule 9 - European Prison Rules (2020)
Handbook on Women and Imprisonment (2014)
Prisons Act (1970)
Criminal Justice (Community Service) (Amendment) Act (2011)
Fines (Payment and Recovery) Act (2014)

---

[35] Programme for Government (2011), p. 48.
[36] Ibid, p. 48.
[37] Irish Penal Reform Trust (2013b).
[38] Irish Penal Reform Trust (2021).

Online Resource

Central Statistics Office, 'Statistical Yearbook of Ireland, Chapter 7 'Crime" <https://www.cso.ie/en/media/duplicatecsomedia/newmedia/releasespublications/documents/statisticalyearbook/2010/Chapter_7_Crime.pdf>

Department of Justice, 'Publication of Irish Prison Service Annual Report' <http://www.justice.ie/en/JELR/Pages/PR11000171 >

Programme for Government, *Government for National Recovery 2011 - 2016* (2011)

Irish Prison Service, *Sentenced Committals Classified by Sentence Length & Gender from Years 2007 to 2020 - Irish Prison Service/Home/Information Centre/Statistics & Information/Yearly Statistics* (Irish Prison Service)

References

Book

Carlen P (1983) Women's imprisonment: a study in social control. Routledge & Kegan Paul, London

Carlen P (1988) Women, crime, and poverty. Open University Press Milton Keynes

Carlen P, Worrall A (1987) Gender, crime and justice. Open University Milton Keynes

Maguire N (2016) Sentencing. The Routledge handbook of irish criminology. Routledge

Journal Article

Carr N, Maguire N (2017) Pre-sentence reports and individualised Justice: consistency, temporality and contingency. Irish Probat J 14:52

Hedderman C (2004) The "Criminogenic" needs of women offenders. Women who offend 227

Hedderman C, Gunby C (2013) Diverting women from custody. Probat J 60:425

Joint Probation Service - Irish Prison Service (2014) An effective response to women who offend

Kelly J, Bogue J (2014) Gender differences in criminogenic needs among irish offenders. Irish Probat J 11:87

O'Hara K, Rogan M (2015) Examining the use of community service orders as alternatives to short prison sentences in Ireland. Irish Probat J 12:22

Report

CPT (2007) Report to the Government of Ireland on the visit to Ireland carried out by the European Committee for the Prevention of Torture and Inhuman or Degrading Treatment or Punishment. Strasbourg

CPT (2011) Report to the Government of Ireland on the visit to Ireland carried out by the European Committee for the Prevention of Torture and Inhuman or Degrading Treatment or Punishment (CPT) from 25 January to 5 February 2010. Strasbourg

Department of Children E, Disability, Integration and Youth (2017) National Strategy for women and girls 2017-2020: Creating a better society for all.

Department of Justice and Equality (2018) National Strategy for women and girls 2007-2016: Progress report as of 01/05/2015, Gov.ie/Gender Equality/Department of Children, Equality, Disability, Integration and Youth

Inspector of Prisons (2011) Standards for the Inspections of Prisons in Ireland-Women Prisoners' Supplement

Irish Penal Reform Trust (2013a) Position Paper 10- Women in the Criminal Justice System: Towards a non-custodial approach

Irish Penal Reform Trust (2013b) Women in the Criminal Justice System: Towards a Non-Custodial Approach. Dublin

Irish Penal Reform Trust (2021) Progress in the Penal System (PIPS)- The Need for Transparency. Dublin

Jean Corston B (2007) The Corston Report: A report of a review of women with particular vulnerabilities in the criminal justice system. London

Law Reform Commission (1996) Report on Sentencing. Dublin

Thesis

Duignan S (2023) Evaluation of the effect of Irish Penal Policy on female short-term prison sentence recipients: the need for gender-specific policy. University of Galway

Chapter 2
Historical Context of Penal Policy

2.1 Introduction

This chapter offers a comprehensive analysis of the Irish government's penal policy within its historical context, focusing on the developments that led to the implementation of the prison diversion policy in the early 2010s. This policy emerged as a response to the exacerbated issue of prison overcrowding following Ireland's economic crisis. To mitigate the increasing incarceration rates, the government promoted community-based alternatives and enacted legislation aimed at reducing the prevalence of short-term prison sentences, particularly those under 12 months. However, this strategic shift towards non-custodial sanctions did not sufficiently consider the specific needs and circumstances of female offenders. Women, constituting a smaller and frequently marginalised segment of the prison population, have seen their unique challenges largely overlooked in the broader application of these reforms.

2.2 Rehabilitative Ideals and Retributive Realities

Women's experiences in Ireland, both as offenders and as subjects of penal policy, were largely shaped by imported legislative measures rather than any tailored approach, reflecting the specific social context of Ireland. Instead, there was a reliance on British models of criminal justice which often ignored the distinct needs and circumstances of women, perpetuating a system that was not fully responsive to gender-specific issues.

O'Donnell describes how the "early years of the Irish state, after its foundation in 1922, were characterised by a parsimonious approach to imprisonment with a low

S. Duignan, *Transforming Justice for Women*, Gender, Justice and Legal Feminism 3, https://doi.org/10.1007/978-3-031-82455-5_2

level of interest in penal affairs."[1] In terms of creating new legislative policies, policymakers often looked to Westminster for direction, especially where a problem arose in Ireland which had not been addressed before. This was particularly the case in the area of criminal justice. If a solution was thought to be appropriate for common law in Britain, it would be assimilated into Irish law without too many debates on the subject.[2] The adoption of Community Service Orders in Irish penal policy is a prime example of the transference of legislative measures from England and Wales to Ireland in the tradition of legislative 'cross fertilisation.'[3]

Early criminal justice legislation in Ireland reflected rehabilitative ideals, as seen in the Probation of Offenders Act (1907), the Prevention of Crime Act (1908), and the Children Act (1908). Despite this, there was often a disconnect between policy and legislation, leading to a lack of coherence in Irish penal policy. Rogan notes that:

> [d]evelopments in penal policy…often surfaced as a political response to emerging issues or crises while at other times penal policy has been driven more by a culture of 'drift' rather than a single cohesive approach.[4]

External social control extended beyond the formal criminal justice system, blurring the line between morality and criminality. Institutions such as Mother and Baby Homes and the Magdalene Laundries, which were retributive in both nature and effect, operated well after Ireland gained independence. In July 2011, the government established an initial Committee to investigate the facts of State involvement with the Magdalene Laundries.[5] Additionally, the Commission of Investigation into Mother and Baby Homes and certain related matters was established in February 2015 to provide a full account of the treatment of vulnerable women and children in these institutions from 1922 to 1998. The final report was submitted in October 2021 and is also known as the McAleese Report.[6]

These institutions served to 'normalise' the incarceration of women until relatively recently in Ireland. Although most residents had not been convicted of any crime, conditions inside were prison-like. 'Redemption' often involved coercive measures such as shaven heads, institutional uniforms, bread and water diets, restricted visiting, supervised correspondence, solitary confinement, and physical abuse.[7] Thus, an older sense of retribution persisted concerning incarcerated women, even as rehabilitative discourse gained prominence in Irish politics as a new language of reform, correction, and normalisation.[8] Unmarried mothers, alcoholics, and

[1] O'Donnell (2008), p. 253.
[2] Riordan (2009), p. 124.
[3] O'Mahony (2002), p. 6.
[4] Rogan (2011), Chapter 1.
[5] Department of Justice (2013).
[6] Department of Children Equality Disability Integration and Youth (2021).
[7] Blakemore (2019).
[8] Rogan(2012), p. 10.

the mentally ill were subjected to social control regimes that were often more extensive and open-ended than those applied to convicted criminals.[9]

Welfare institutions formed a significant part of the Irish penal system, with many individuals confined in places like industrial schools, hospitals, and homes for unmarried mothers rather than traditional prisons. These institutions, especially those affecting women, often conflicted with the rehabilitative intentions suggested by the legislation inherited from Britain.

When the Irish Free State was established on December 6, 1922, all existing laws in Ireland, including those enacted by the Westminster parliament, became part of Irish law. This ensured legal continuity from the British government to the Free State government. Even after the 1937 Irish Constitution was enacted, the Westminster statutes remained in force and were amended as necessary.

In the 1960s, a young Minister for Justice, Charles Haughey, began advocating for the importance of rehabilitation. An inter-departmental committee was established and began engaging in activities characteristic of 'penal-welfarism'. Following the enactment of the Criminal Justice Act 1960, the Prisoners Temporary Release Rules 1960[10] were formulated to provide detailed guidelines on how a scheme of temporary release from prison would be administered. However, at that time, temporary release from prison was not initially conceived as a method to enhance offender rehabilitation, as it is understood today.

2.3 The Evolution of Temporary Release and Rehabilitation in Ireland

Section 2(1) of the Criminal Justice Act 1960 ('the 1960 Act'), which introduced temporary release, was not initially designed as a measure to save prison space. In the late 1950s, as preparations for the Bill that would eventually become the 1960 Act were underway, numerous prisoners petitioned the Minister for Justice for brief releases to visit critically ill family members or attend funerals. These requests were approved, and it seems that the prisoners adhered to the conditions by returning to prison after the allotted time.[11]

Nonetheless, the Minister was informed that while he had the authority to grant early release, those granted it were not legally required to return to prison since this could be seen as 'remission' which effectively concludes a sentence.[12] The Oireachtas debates on the Criminal Justice Bill clarified that the intention behind

[9] Mulcahy(2007), p. 8.

[10] Prisoners (Temporary Release) Rules (1960).

[11] O'Malley (2010), p. 6.

[12] 'Remission' is one type of early release and is outlined in Rule 59 of the Prison Rules 2007 to 2014. Once granted remission, the individual's custody concludes, and they are released from prison without any conditions or supervision, meaning they cannot be arbitrarily returned to

the legislation was to allow prisoners to return home for short periods for compassionate reasons.[13] Although this type of temporary release was not originally intended to manage prison overcrowding and was used for more humanitarian purposes, it would later become used as an important tool in government policy to reduce prisoner numbers as the decade progressed.

O'Malley states that "in Ireland, unofficial 'back-door release' mechanisms have been used as a 'covert way of limiting the prison population without… attracting much media or judicial attention'".[14] The legislative basis for temporary release is set out in the Criminal Justice Act 1960, as amended by the Criminal Justice (Temporary Release of Prisoners) Act 2003,[15] and all applications for temporary release are assessed by the Irish Prison Service on a case-by-case basis.

The safety of the public is paramount when decisions on temporary release are being made. Before a final determination is made, various factors are considered, including:

- the nature and gravity of the offence to which the sentence relates.
- the sentence concerned and any recommendation made by the Court in relation to the sentence imposed.
- the person's previous criminal record.
- the potential threat to the safety and security of the public should the person be released.
- the risk that the person might commit an offence during any period of temporary release.
- the risk of the person failing to comply with any of the conditions of temporary release.[16]

Notwithstanding its humanitarian basis, the 1960 Act was increasingly used as a "safety valve for the system,"[17] where it acted to "keep population numbers at manageable"[18] levels of committals from the courts, and its use was increasingly viewed as bringing the system into disrepute.[19]

In the 1970s, Irish media began to reflect a shift towards rehabilitation, emphasising that the focus had moved from punishing offenders to attempting to cure them of the 'disease of crime.'[20] These narrative changes culminated in the Prisons Act 1970, which declared rehabilitation as the official aim of the Irish Prison

prison if they reoffend. In contrast, 'temporary release' involves supervision, and the individual may be returned to prison if they violate the terms of their licence.

[13] Minister for Justice (Mister Traynor) (1999).

[14] O'Malley (2008), p. 9.

[15] Criminal Justice (Temporary Release of Prisoners) Act (2003).

[16] Ibid, s 2(a)-(f).

[17] Irish Prison Service.(2006), p. 17.

[18] Ibid p. 17.

[19] Department of Justice.(2022), p. 51.

[20] (1967).

system and officially renamed prisons as 'places of detention'.[21] The ambitious Minister for Justice at the time saw himself as a new type of European 'penal imaginary.'[22]

The Prisons Act 1970, particularly Section 2, laid the groundwork for open prisons by providing for "the rehabilitation of offenders…in places of detention other than prisons."[23] Open prison facilities, with fewer restrictions on prisoners' movements and activities, aimed to prepare inmates for reintegration into society. Three open prisons were established for male prisoners: Shanganagh Castle in 1968 (closed in 2002), Shelton Abbey, and Loughan House, both opened in 1972.[24] However, Kilcommins et al. note that the rationale of rehabilitation was neither "enthusiastically embraced nor despondently abandoned in Ireland as in other jurisdictions".[25]

2.4 The Move Towards Tougher Penal Measures in the 1980s

The 1980s in Ireland saw a significant shift towards a more punitive approach to imprisonment, driven by escalating concerns about security and crime rates. As more offenders were committed to prison, the earlier focus on rehabilitation, prominent in the 1970s, began to diminish. Courts increasingly handed down prison sentences, which contributed to a burgeoning prison population. MacBride's report highlights how welfare services and training programmes were limited to a small number of prisoners and were generally inadequate.[26]

By 1980, the optimistic rehabilitative discourse of the 1970s had largely disappeared. A 1981 report on prisons and places of detention starkly described the primary purpose of imprisonment in Ireland as containment rather than rehabilitation.[27] This shift was further fuelled by public fear and political responses to rising crime levels, leading to calls for more structured and integrated penal policies. The National Economic and Social Council's 1985 report criticised the piecemeal approach to criminal justice reform and advocated for a cohesive decarceration strategy.[28]

---

[21] Prisons Act (1970), s2.

[22] Armstrong and McAra (2006).

[23] Prisons Act (1970), s2.

[24] In 1976, a rehabilitative training unit was opened in the Mountjoy campus known as St Patrick's Training Unit. This facility closed in 2013.

[25] Shane Kilcommins and others (2004), p. 188.

[26] MacBride Commission Report(1980), p.13.

[27] Prisons Act (1970); Eoin Guilfoyle and (2016), p. 52.

[28] (1985), p.19.

The increasing crime rates during this period generated significant public concern, particularly in urban areas. Politicians echoed these fears, highlighting the need for effective measures to combat crime. In a 1983 address to the Dáil, Minister Gerard Brady highlighted the critical need to address the escalating crime rates, reflecting a pressing public concern over societal safety and security.[29] In 1985, the Dáil debated a motion condemning the government's failure to provide adequate and secure prison accommodation, underscoring the political pressure to adopt a 'tough on crime' stance.[30]

This era was characterised by political instability, economic challenges, and social upheaval. The government faced three general elections within 18 months, substantial cuts in public spending, high unemployment, and a devalued currency.[31] These factors compounded the crisis in the criminal justice system, where increasing imprisonment was seen as a necessary response to societal fears, despite the lack of substantial rehabilitative measures.

Despite the more punitive turn, the criminal justice system straddled a hybrid approach, balancing elements of penal welfarism with a strong emphasis on control and punishment. The Irish state closely observed developments in England and Wales, where Community Service Orders were introduced in 1972, following the recommendations of the Wootton Report.[32] This report advocated for a new sanction requiring offenders 'to engage in some form of part-time service to the community.'[33]

The CSO which had been introduced in England and Wales in 1980 was not simply confined to being an 'alternative to custody' to address rising incarceration levels; it was also utilised as "a reformative tool."[34] The legislation governing CSOs did not limit their application solely to cases where custodial sentences were the alternative, providing flexibility to impose CSOs in various circumstances, including those not leading to imprisonment. This flexibility characterised the English CSO's use.

2.5 Introduction of the Community Service Order

Ireland introduced the Community Service Order 11 years after this development in England and Wales, in 1980. While the legislation in Ireland mirrored the British model, discussions and application of the sanction differed. Kelly argues that it was "simply one more example in the ignominious parade of legislation masquerading

[29] (1983).

[30] (1985).

[31] Rogan (2011), p. 135.

[32] Wootton (1970).

[33] Ibid, p. 26.

[34] Guilfoyle (2017), p. 191.

under an Irish title ... which is a British legislative idea taken over here and given a green outfit with silver buttons to make it look native."[35]

In the same year as the first CSO was made, the Taoiseach Garret Fitzgerald commissioned the Committee of Inquiry into the Penal System, chaired by the distinguished Irish economist and public servant, Dr. Whitaker. Whitaker led the committee in a thorough review of the penal system in Ireland, aiming to identify areas for improvement and make recommendations for reform. The resulting Whitaker Report considered that prison could be beneficial in reforming and deterring offenders but should only be used "if the offence is such that no other form of penalty is appropriate."[36] The report emphasised the preference for community-based interventions and recommended capping prison capacity at 1500 places to avoid excessive reliance on incarceration. It also recommended that prison should be used "as a sentence of last resort" and advocated for the expanded use of community-based penalties due to the "substantial net gain in using non-custodial methods of disposal of offenders as distinct from sending them to prison."[37]

When the CSO was introduced in Ireland through the Criminal Justice (Community Service) Act 1983[38] ('the 1983 Act'), the Dáil debates did not definitively resolve whether the CSO would serve exclusively as an alternative to imprisonment or if its primary aim would be punitive, requiring offenders to forfeit their free time by engaging in unpaid work. Thus, the precise punitive objectives of CSOs remained somewhat ambiguous within the Irish legal framework, as the purpose of CSOs had not undergone comprehensive deliberation regarding penological philosophy, unlike the thorough consideration by the Wootton Committee in England.[39] The Minister for Justice at that time, Michael Noonan, sagely observed that the CSO, lacking a specific guiding philosophy, could potentially lead to an increase in imprisonment rather than achieving a reduction.[40]

> If, for example, the CSO is used often as an alternative penalty to a fine, or as a rehabilitative measure in lieu of a probation order, but at the same time a custodial sentence is regularly being imposed for breach, the result could easily be an increase rather than a reduction in the population of penal establishments... Ambivalent policies can produce consequences which satisfy no one.[41]

Despite these concerns, Minister Noonan proceeded to endorse the Bill to the Dáil, highlighting a key distinction between the Irish CSO and its English and Welsh counterpart.[42] In the Irish version, a CSO could only be imposed as an alternative to a prison sentence. A Home Office Study had shown how over half of the CSOs in

---

[35] Wootton (1970).

[36] Department of Justice (1985).

[37] Ibid, p. 11.

[38] Criminal Justice (Community Service) Act (1983).

[39] Wootton (1970).

[40] (1983).

[41] Ibid.

[42] Ibid.

England and Wales were imposed as an alternative to other non-custodial sanctions, limiting the sanction's impact on the prison population.[43] In Ireland, it was clear that the main objective behind implementing the CSO was to decrease the prison population rather than considering it as an independent sanction. However, there was still an acknowledgment of the potential advantages that this alternative could offer. Although these benefits were not extensively discussed or analysed as they had been in England, there was hope that similar advantages would apply in the Irish context.[44]

Within the Dáil, external developments sparked intense discussions regarding the true implications of the CSO as outlined in the Community Service Bill of 1983. The debates primarily revolved around whether the CSO aimed to incorporate 'reparation and restitution'[45] as integral aspects of Irish criminal policies or if it simply served as a cost-effective substitute for prison sentences to address prison overcrowding:

> This Bill puts the foot in the door of opening to us access to that resource so that we can help the people in prisons to rediscover what the essence of rehabilitation is, the discovery of meaning in their lives. It is only if people are afforded the opportunity of meaningful or useful work or educational access…that they will get off the treadmill of crime.[46]

This discussion emphasised the ideology that underscored probation policy and practice ab initio.

2.6 The Shifting Culture of the Community Service Order

Community service practices began to emerge within the Irish penal system but, as Guilfoyle correctly notes, Ireland had not experienced "anywhere near the same rise in the ideology of 'community' as had been experienced in England and Wales, nor did it have the same extensive history of successful community service practices within the penal system."[47] A definitive probation policy emerged later in Ireland than in England and Wales. This delay could be attributed to Ireland's smaller jurisdiction and corresponding lower crime rates, or possibly due to a lack of extensive discussion on the matter. However, it is always relevant to consider England and Wales due to their proximity to Ireland and the legislative similarities, stemming from the significant amount of legislation that Ireland inherited upon gaining independence.

The Probation Service history in England and Wales had been an evolving practice, beginning around the turn of the twentieth century.[48] It began from

---

[43] Ibid.

[44] Ibid.

[45] (1983).

[46] Ibid.

[47] Guilfoyle (2018), p. 45.

[48] Harris (1995); Raynor and Robinson (2005).

missionary-style work, trying to persuade those regarded as 'sinners' to reform. Commentators have described this work as having "a clearly religious ethos with a harm reduction objective."[49] In general, probation activities were perceived as rehabilitative, with a successful outcome defined as transforming the offender into "a respectable, self-supporting, abstinent citizen."[50] The goal was the offender's spiritual welfare, and a successfully rehabilitated offender was regarded as "reformed."[51]

David Garland notes that during this time, the reformation of offenders gained significant momentum, leading to an increase in the assessment and classification of offenders.[52] Reformative efforts were largely seen as the domain of voluntary organisations and charities rather than the government. The pursuit of salvation and the exercise of mercy were perceived as matters for individual choice rather than public policy.[53] The Probation of Offenders Act 1907 ('the 1907 Act') in Britain and Ireland created a new cohort of professionals within the criminal justice system, known as probation officers. Their role was based on the work which court missionaries had previously fulfilled, however many of these professionals quickly "aspired to a more secular, professional and 'scientific' standing."[54]

In Britain in the late 1980s, a "populist punitiveness"[55] impacted the practices and identity of probation interventions. A new emphasis was placed on risk and public safety. Rehabilitation was increasingly justified, not so much by its beneficial effect on the lives of offenders, but by improvements in the safety of potential future victims.[56] Where traditionally the offender in probation was perceived as a 'sinner' who could receive redemption through moral reform in the 1970s and 1980s, they now became ultimately depicted as a 'patient' who might be cured through 'treatment'. During this period however, there was a further reconfiguration of the subject of rehabilitation, so that the offender was now perceived as "a risk-bearing subject: one whose risks must be assessed and then managed and, where possible, reduced."[57]

David Garland considers the 1950s and 1960s to be an exemplary period in criminal justice policy, during which the Probation Service adhered to its ideology of duty to "advise, assist, and befriend."[58] However, some experts believe that the management of perceived risk signalled the decline of the penal welfare approach.[59]

---

49 Geiran (2016); McNally (2007).

50 McNally (2007).

51 Ibid.

52 Garland (1985).

53 Booth (1890), p. 58.

54 Raynor and Robinson (2005), p. 51.

55 Bottoms(2006); Anthony Bottoms and others (2004).

56 Raynor and Robinson (2009).

57 Feeley and Simon (1992), p. 29.

58 Garland (2001), p. 177.

59 Cohen (1985); Hough et al. (2003).

The preoccupation with 'risk' and its containment significantly influenced the changes within the Probation Service. Observers have noted that the service began to enhance its supervisory role in the community by implementing measures such as curfews and electronic tagging. They also point out that the service increasingly focused on administering these more punitive measures, thereby moving away from its original mission statement of advising, assisting, and befriending offenders.[60]

There is a school of thought which argues that the new rehabilitative interventions earned legitimacy by virtue of their contribution to the broader goal of risk management.[61] The objectives of imprisonment and supervisory penalties shifted away from solely reforming or rehabilitating offenders. Instead, the promise of rehabilitative interventions came to signify a step towards the broader aim of managing societal risk. Effective rehabilitation became equated with effective risk management, introducing a moral dimension to successful rehabilitation. The focus shifted towards regulating individual conduct and "helping maintain order and obedience to the law by binding individuals into shared moral norms and values."[62]

It is also possible that the development of community-based sanctions and alternatives to prison in Ireland emerged from internal pragmatic necessities. By the late 1960s, rising crime rates and diminishing public tolerance for such behaviour created a need for effective solutions beyond traditional imprisonment. Between 1968 and 1981, the number of indictable offences in Ireland surged nearly fourfold, from 23,104 in 1968 to 89,400 in 1981.[63] Non-indictable offences rose at a similar rate.[64]

A combination of the political response of 'zero tolerance', which represented this 'new punitiveness',[65] and the resultant prison system, which had become weighed down with low-level offenders serving STPS,[66] led to the fore-fronting of a novel discourse which discussed 'risk and public protection.'[67] Research later notes how concerns for accountability, value for money, and management of those deemed 'risky' contributes to an ideological shift from 'rehabilitation and welfare to risk assessment and offender management.'[68]

As noted earlier, it is also possible that debates in the United Kingdom influenced the structure of community-based sanctions in Ireland.[69] While there were calls in the Dáil for more severe penalties, such as mandatory minimum sentences and

---

[60] Cohen(1985); Hough et al. (2003).

[61] Garland (2004).

[62] Clear et al. (2001).

[63] (1977) Dublin: Stationery Office, p. 3; (1981) Dublin: Stationery Office, p. 3.

[64] O'Donnell and O'Sullivan (2001), p. 23.

[65] Ibid.

[66] (1985), p. 152.

[67] McNeill (2004), p. 33.

[68] Richardson (2008), p. 5.

[69] McNeill (2004).

increased use of consecutive sentences,[70] it was argued that the demand for sterner penalties would likely have worked against the introduction of the CSO.[71] Throughout its evolution, the CSO was never presented as a more punitive measure than imprisonment, and reviews of the CSO were generally positive.[72]

When addressing the rising crime and prison issues in Ireland, policymakers often looked to Britain for legislative solutions.[73] In the early 1970s, England and Wales faced a similar prison crisis, and the implementation of the CSO in those jurisdictions had yielded favourable outcomes.[74] As risk management became a central focus, it was hoped that the Irish equivalent (the 1983 legislation) to the English legislation (the 1972 legislation)[75] would be equally successful.

Like England and Wales, the Irish Probation Service underwent a transformation, shifting its focus from primarily the offender to prioritising public well-being. Moving away from its mission statement to "advise, assist and befriend,"[76] the 2006 Strategy Statement detailed the restructuring of the Service's mission, strategic goals, objectives in strategy statements, and work plans.[77] Kilcommins noted how Ireland's criminal justice system was "showing signs of drifting in the direction of an 'assembly-line' model of justice in which the State–individual balance is increasingly tipped in favour of the former."[78]

This shift was also accompanied by a change in terminology. The service previously known as "The Probation and Welfare Service" was rebranded as "The Probation Service". The language used also shifted: "clients" became "offenders," "pre-sentence reports" turned into "risk assessments," and "supervision" of clients was now termed "offender management."[79] Irish penal policy became entrenched in the discourse of risk, increasingly perceiving probation supervision as an action performed by the probation officer upon the supervisee. This trend reflected a notable shift towards more punitive strategies in managing offenders and risk. The

---

[70] Dáil Debate, col. 169, 3 May (1983) "The public want to know [if the Minister] will introduce mandatory minimum sentences for mugging elderly people, for housebreaking, robbery with violence and assault. They want to know will he . . . perhaps have mandatory sentences for unlawful possession of firearms and explosives. They want to know will he tighten up on the conditions of bail and provide for consecutive sentences The Community want to see that the punishment fits the crime and is seen to fit the crime. At present they see too many criminals getting off too lightly."

[71] Guilfoyle (2017).

[72] Ibid.

[73] Guilfoyle describes the "well-established practice of legislative transference from Britain to Ireland, particularly in the criminal justice system. So, in seeking a solution to the prison crisis and the rising crime rate, politicians in Ireland did as their predecessors had done many times before and looked to England and Wales." Guilfoyle (2017), p. 194.

[74] Pease and others (1975); Pease et al. (1977).

[75] Criminal Justice Act (1972).

[76] Probation of Offenders Act (1907).

[77] The Probation Service (2006).

[78] Kilcommins (2011), p. 69.

[79] Ibid.

probation role now encompassed punishment, behavioural modification, support, and supervision of offenders.[80]

Then, in 2009, the Probation Service committed to "re-launch Community Service ... as an effective court sanction adding value to communities and enriching reparation by offenders."[81] This initiative aimed to increase the Service's capacity to manage larger numbers of CSOs from the courts. This development mirrored government policy to promote the use of CSOs and included the piloting of the "Community Return" programme in 2011.[82] Now academic scholarship has recognised a prevailing trend in many Western jurisdictions where community-based punishments are more common than imprisonment in traditional facilities.[83]

2.7 Early Release and Its Impact on Prison Overcrowding in Ireland

The issue of prison overcrowding in Ireland is closely tied to the use of early release mechanisms. These mechanisms, when employed strategically, can provide significant benefits to the criminal justice system by incentivising good behaviour among prisoners and reducing the duration of incarceration. Early release has also been described as 'an effective approach to bring the prison population within safe custody limits'.[84]

However, early release effectively acts as a form of re-sentencing, altering the original sentence and allows unofficial movement through what is often referred to as the 'prison back-door.' This practice has sparked concerns about the executive branch's involvement in the sentencing process and prompted a reassessment of the delicate balance between public safety and the goals of rehabilitation and reintegration.

As governments have limited control over judicial sentencing decisions, some administrations might view unofficial executive release mechanisms as a discreet and convenient way to reduce prison populations without attracting significant media or judicial attention. However, while this form of early release can have certain benefits, it also risks encroaching on the judicial sentencing domain.[85] Thus, policies quite benignly aimed at improving prison management and promoting prisoner rehabilitation can unofficially modify judicially imposed sentences despite the constitutional prohibition on encroaching upon judicial sentencing outlined in Article 37.1. O'Malley notes that unofficial 'back-door release' mechanisms have

[80] Ibid.

[81] The Probation Service (2009).

[82] The Probation Service (2011).

[83] McNeill and Beyens (2013).

[84] Irish Penal Reform Trust (2012), p. 2.

[85] Beth Weaver and others (2012).

been used as a 'covert way of limiting the prison population without... attracting much media or judicial attention'.[86]

In the early 1980s, Irish prisoners were increasingly released from their sentences early to facilitate the incoming committals because of overcrowding.[87] In 1983, a provision in the 1947 Prison Rules that required prisoners to be kept in single cells was removed to increase the capacity of prisons. This change made prisons appear less overcrowded, but conditions deteriorated further. The overcrowded conditions in prison overflowed into the community, as temporary release was used to make room in the overwhelmed prison facilities.[88] Rogan noted how temporary release was used in a way that was "unsupervised and without prior planning."[89] She suggests that the introduction of the release facility known as "home leave" made an unstructured system even more chaotic.

Unofficial release mechanisms were sometimes engaged by prison authorities to manage the increasing prison populations. One such mechanism was known as the "home leave" system in 1983. In 1980, 891 prisoners were released to make way for new committals, with the figure rising to 1298 in 1982.[90] This was implemented as a supervised alternative to unsupervised temporary release which became known as 'shedding'.[91] Despite its name, this system enabled prisoners serving sentences for minor offences to remain out of prison, providing they regularly check in at a local Garda (police) station. This strategy offered a monitored option to traditional imprisonment for those convicted of less severe crimes.

Rogan argues that because the State had taken this laissez-faire approach to prison policy in the 1980s, policy was largely "moribund and inert."[92] She notes that the 1980s were "one of the bleakest periods in the history of Irish prisons."[93] The system was becoming overburdened and is described in grim terms:

> Unprecedented levels of overcrowding, a system unable to cope with an influx of drugs and those addicted to drugs, poor industrial relations and a high level of deaths in custody all led to the point where the state would have to take a stance and show the public that it was still in control.[94]

With offending rates at an all-time high in the mid-1980s and prisons overcrowded, the state had no policy and no funds to create policy.[95] The early part of the decade had been marked by economic stagnation, high unemployment, and a rapidly increasing national debt. These issues were compounded by the global recession

[86] O'Malley (2008), p. 9.

[87] Rogan (2013).

[88] Dáil Debates Vol 339 Col 373, (1983).

[89] Rogan (2013), p. 5.

[90] Dáil Debates, vol 339, col. 373, February 8, 1983.

[91] Mary Rogan (2013), p. 5.

[92] Ibid, p. 3.

[93] Ibid, p. 3.

[94] Ibid, p. 3.

[95] Stolz and Wedow (2013).

and high inflation rates. By 1987, the country's debt-to-GDP ratio had surged to over 120%, and the economy was on the brink of crisis.

However, by the late 1980s, following a series of fiscal adjustments and economic reforms, Ireland saw a reduction in its debt-to-GDP ratio and a return to economic growth. The country's fiscal policies, coupled with a favourable international environment, laid the foundation for what would later be known as the 'Celtic Tiger' era of the 1990s, characterised by rapid economic expansion and significant improvements in living standards.[96]

2.8 Prison Building

In 1997, the then Minister for Justice, Nora Owen, announced what she termed "the greatest prison building programme since the foundation of the State," which aimed to provide around 800 extra prison places.[97] This ambitious plan emerged in the wake of significant events, namely, the shooting of journalist Veronica Guerin and Garda officer Jerry McCabe in 1996, which O'Donnell describes as triggering a "moral panic" in its aftermath.[98] This period of social unrest coincided with a booming economy, as Ireland began to prosper alongside its EU neighbours.[99] The government seized this opportunity to prioritise prison expenditure, a policy direction it had intended since the 1980s. As Rogan noted, "the fiscal limits on the political desire to build prisons present in the 1980s were no longer acting as brakes on action."[100]

Mountjoy Prison, Dublin's main prison, first opened in 1850 and was described by one of its former governors in his memoir as "Dickensian" and "unfit for purpose."[101] In January 2005, lands were purchased in North County Dublin, and the Minister for Justice, Equality and Law Reform, Michael McDowell, announced plans to build a proposed new prison that would house 2200 prisoners.[102] The proposed new prison at Thornton Hall was designed to relieve the pressure on the existing facilities.[103] The government had hoped that the new facility would solve

[96] Ibid

[97] The Irish Times (1997), The spaces to be provided in St Patrick's (30), Castlerea (25), Limerick (55), the Curragh (60) and the new remand centre to be built at Wheatfield (400).

[98] O'Sullivan and O'Donnell (2003).

[99] Murphy (2000).

[100] Ibid, p. 7.

[101] Lonergan (2010).

[102] Department of Justice (2009).

[103] Irish Penal Reform Trust (2011a).

both the overcrowding and deteriorating condition problems, but at the time of writing, this has still not come to fruition.[104]

While the development of a new prison at Thornton Hall would have created more prison spaces, this would not have addressed the underlying issues affecting minority groups within the overcrowded prison system. When the government developed its STPS reduction policy, there is no evidence that it considered the full spectrum of groups within this cohort. Similarly, increasing the number of prison spaces would not necessarily have adequately provided for minority groups like women in the smaller-scale prison facilities. Critics of the new development note "how building extra prison places can become a self-fulfilling prophecy which will provoke changes in policy that lead to more people being imprisoned."[105]

The discussion surrounding the new prison at Thornton Hall exemplified the prevailing trend in Irish penal policy over the previous decade. The focus remained on increasing the number of prison places and detaining more individuals, while neglecting to explore or implement alternative sentences that could more effectively address the personal and social issues faced by those who appear before the courts.[106]

The CPT committee, during its 2010 visit, had already expressed "serious misgivings" about the plans the Irish government was making to expand the prison estate at Thornton Hall.[107] The Committee recognised that expansion of the penal estate alone would not adequately address the prison overcrowding problem. They also recommended changes to the prison itself and the treatment of prisoners, particularly minority populations that were escaping the reform radar.[108] Criminal justice statistics from 2011 to 2020 consistently show that women accounted for a small proportion of short-term prison sentence recipients, comprising just 18% of the total over these years.[109]

The Committee also reported that Irish prisons were overcrowded and commented that "the ill-treatment of detained persons is not acceptable and will be the subject of severe sanctions."[110] In particular, the CPT referenced a lack of

[104]Conor Murphy (2021) accessed 05/08/2022 Almost 17 years after the plans were first drawn up for the construction of Thornton Hall, the prison facility has yet to be constructed. The site has remained vacant since an agreement with a private developer collapsed 12 years ago. Despite a series of 'on-again', 'off-again' rumours, no definitive announcement has been made, and the site remains under the control of the Department of Justice. In 2019, the department offered some of the site to the Land Development Agency to build homes to ease the housing crisis.

[105]Irish Penal Reform Trust (2008), p. 3.

[106]Jesuit Centre for Faith & Justice (2007).

[107]European Committee for the Prevention of Torture and Inhuman or Degrading Treatment or Punishment (2011).

[108]Ibid, In relation to women: p. 25 No.42, p. 28 No.51, p. 52 101; In relation to juveniles: p.15; In relation to persons with intellectual disabilities: p. 69.

[109]Irish Prison Service Annual Report (2021), p. 39; (2020), p. 35; (2019), p. 32 cf.

[110]CPT (2011), p. 71.

resources and facilities and recommended that the Irish authorities "invest the necessary resources into the existing prison estate to ensure that all prisoners are kept in decent conditions of detention, pending the construction of Thornton Hall prison complex."[111]

Initially, the political response to these criticisms was "limited."[112] After the Whitaker Committee, it appeared there was a lack of political will to implement the recommendations.[113] However, the first female death by suicide in Mountjoy in 1995 and the appointment of a female Minister for Justice in 1993 marked a turning point in political attitudes. The more economically successful 'Celtic Tiger' years that followed led to an expansion in the prison system. In 1994, the Management of Offenders Plan was drawn up.[114] This five-year plan contained fifty-three recommendations, not specific to any one institution but referring to initiatives for the entire prison service.

It proposed the construction of a dedicated facility for women within 5 years. This plan gained momentum, and in 1996, the state-commissioned Study of Irish Female Prisoners was published. Conducted by Carmody and McEvoy,[115] the study explored family dynamics, health, psychiatric history, and substance misuse profiles of female prisoners. It aimed to provide insights for the design of the new female prison. The study involved interviews with one hundred female committals entering Mountjoy Prison over a six-week period.

The findings unearthed the predominant characteristics that were present in the cohort of women. They revealed that a significant portion of the female prisoner population had a history of opiate use, were mothers, and came from disadvantaged backgrounds. The study also highlighted their resistance to drug treatment. These predominantly occurring characteristics, whilst although not distinct from male offenders, highlights the specific needs of female offenders in the criminal justice system.

2.9 Inequalities in Women's Prisons

Prison management is guided by a set of legal standards that encompass various international agreements and principles. These standards form the foundation of universally applicable principles which govern prison systems worldwide, aiming to ensure fair treatment and protection for all prisoners, whatever their gender.

---

[111] Ibid, p. 72.

[112] Rogan (2011), p. 156.

[113] Carroll (2011).

[114] Government of Ireland (1994).

[115] Carmody and McEvoy (1996).

These standards include the Convention against Torture and Other Cruel, Inhuman or Degrading Treatment or Punishment,[116] which requires states to take effective measures to prevent such acts and establishes mechanisms for monitoring compliance. The United Nations Standard Minimum Rules for the Treatment of Prisoners, or the Mandela Rules[117] provide comprehensive guidelines on the treatment of prisoners, including basic principles of respect for their inherent dignity, prohibition of torture, and the need for proper living conditions, healthcare, and access to legal representation. The Body of Principles for the Protection of All Persons under any form of Detention or Imprisonment[118] outline fundamental rights for all individuals under any type of detention or imprisonment and emphasises the right to be treated humanely. They also delineate the right to be informed of charges, to have legal counsel, and to access fair and prompt trials.

The Basic Principles for the Treatment of Prisoners stress the need for the humane treatment of prisoners, focusing on their rehabilitation and social reintegration. They promote respect for prisoners' dignity and the prohibition of discrimination. The Code of Conduct for Law Enforcement Officials provide guidelines for the ethical conduct of law enforcement officials, emphasising respect for human rights, the use of force only when strictly necessary, and accountability for misconduct.[119] The United Nations Rules for the Treatment of Women Prisoners and Non-custodial Measures for Women Offenders (the Bangkok Rules)[120] address the specific needs of women in the criminal justice system. These rules advocate for gender-specific measures, including healthcare, safety, and rehabilitation programs tailored to women offenders.

However, despite the presence of frameworks intended to uphold standards, policies can and do still evidence discriminatory tendencies towards female prisoners. This bias primarily stems from the fact that prisons and their associated systems are predominantly designed to meet the needs of the majority, which, in most instances, refers to the male prison population.[121]

Following Carmody & McEvoy's study, a new purpose-built facility for women offenders was opened in 1999 in Dublin's Mountjoy campus. The opening of the Dóchas Centre[122] marked a significant milestone in the development of women's imprisonment in Ireland and served as a model for women's prisons worldwide.

---

[116] European Convention for the Prevention of Torture and Inhuman or Degrading Treatment or Punishment, 26 November 1987, ETS 126(1987).

[117] United Nations Standard Minimum Rules for Non-Custodial Measures (The Tokyo Rules) (1991).

[118] Body of Principles for the Protection of All Persons under Any Form of Detention or Imprisonment (1988).

[119] Code of Conduct for Law Enforcement Officials(1979).

[120] United Nations Rules for the Treatment of Women Prisoners and Non-custodial Measures for Women Offenders: Vienna: UNODC(2011)2010. United Nations Office on Drugs and Crime (UNODC).

[121] Irish Prison Service (2007–2017).

[122] Dóchas means 'hope' in Gaelic.

However, over the years, the high standards initially set by the facility have been undermined by the persistent issue of overcrowding. This detrimental effect has not gone unnoticed by prison visiting committees, established under international and European legal standards.[123] The CPT Report urged the government to revisit the issue of overcrowding, stating:

> Since the CPT's 2006 visit the prison population has expanded considerably; as was the case in 2006, the de facto overcrowding, combined with the conditions in certain of the old and dilapidated prisons, raises real concerns as to the safe and humane treatment of prisoners.[124]

The Dóchas Visiting Committee also expressed regret, having to "draw the Minister's attention to a greatly deteriorated prison environment".[125] The report highlighted:

> Overcrowding continues to be a problem in the prison. Dóchas Visiting Committee wish to draw attention to the numbers of prisoners being held at the prison which peaked at 150 with three babies in a prison designed for 85 women.[126]

According to the daily prisoner population figures published on the Irish Prison Service website, it is evident that the Dóchas Centre consistently exceeds its bed capacities.[127] The Dóchas Centre, originally designed to accommodate 85 prisoners, frequently houses more individuals than its intended capacity. This highlights the need for appropriate measures to address this issue and ensure the well-being and safety of incarcerated women.

Considered pioneering at the time, the Dóchas Centre was originally designed with seven house blocks to accommodate 85 women. In 2012, the facility expanded to house an additional twenty women. This operates as a closed, medium security prison for female adults and operates as the committal prison for females committed on remand or sentenced from all courts outside the Munster area. In 2024 it has an operational capacity of 146.[128] Over the past two decades, there has been a significant shift in the profile of women in Irish prisons. Most women committed to prison are committed on a short-term basis for non-violent offences.[129]

Statistics show that the issue of overcrowding remains unresolved, and due to unmanageable committals from the courts, overcapacity continues to limit what the women at Dóchas can access in education, training, and purposeful activity.[130] This

---

[123]CPT(2011) made its fifth visit to Ireland from 25th January to the fifth February 2010, pursuant to Article 7 of the European Convention; (2010).

[124]CPT(2011), 1. Preliminary Remarks(a) Overcrowding.

[125]The Visiting Committee (2010).

[126]Ibid, p. 3.

[127]Irish Prison Service.

[128]Ibid.

[129]Irish Penal Reform Trust (2022) Women in Prison: The data 2.1 Committals of women to prison, p. 20.

[130]Irish Prison Service.

has significantly impacted the prison's ability to maintain safe regimes and provide adequate levels of meaningful activity.[131]

In contrast to male prison facilities, which include multiple security levels such as high security in Portlaoise, medium security in Mountjoy, and low security in Shelton Abbey, the women's prison facilities consist solely of a medium security level.

International standards state that all prisons should be managed within an ethical framework developed to protect the human rights of prisoners and to ensure that prisoners' treatment aims to facilitate their social reintegration as a priority.[132] However, there are no step-down facilities available for women who are at the end of their sentence, as "female prisoners do not have a dedicated lower-security, or open, prison where they could spend the end of their sentences in preparation for release."[133] Low-level security prisons are also important so that women who commit less serious offences and who are sent to prison for short periods do not become "traumatised" by "unacceptably violent and dangerous places" as evidenced by the "poor mental health, drug use, and the perennial problems of overcrowding, poor physical environments in ageing prisons, and inadequate staffing."[134] Covington et al. note that "addressing the realities of women's lives through gender-responsive policy and programs is fundamental to improved outcomes at all criminal justice phases."[135]

The only other facility for women in the Republic of Ireland besides the Dóchas centre in Dublin is the female-only wing at Limerick, which is predominantly a men's prison, built in 1815. Jewkes describes the accommodation in grim terms:

> The accommodation there is poor, with all prisoners held in catacomb-like cells, with tiny, heavily barred windows and poor ventilation. Access to natural daylight is scarce and the exercise yards are small concrete spaces with high walls topped with razor wire.[136]

G-wing of the male prison in Limerick has been used to accommodate female prisoners since the early 2000s. Initially, the women were housed in a section of the prison that was criticised for being cramped and inadequate. The conditions in this section were subpar, with overcrowding and limited facilities, which led to significant tension and frustration among the inmates.[137] In 2023, however, this wing underwent a reconstruction which the Irish Prison Service claimed was based on "a trauma-informed Scandinavian model which aims to foster rehabilitation and thereby reduce recidivism."[138] The purpose of this initiative was to provide female

---

[131] Jewkes and others (2019), p. 5.

[132] Handbook on Women and Imprisonment (2014) Vienna United Nations Office on Drugs and Crime (2014), p. 24.

[133] Council of Europe Development Bank (2019), p. 10.

[134] HM Inspectorate of Prisons for England and Wales (2016).

[135] Bloom et al. (2004), p. 21.

[136] Jewkes and others (Jewkes 2019), p. 5.

[137] JCFJ (2008).

[138] Dunphy(2023)

prisoners from the western region of Ireland with the chance to be housed closer to their homes and to address the shortage of accommodation by doubling the capacity of cells (which are known as "rooms"), thereby alleviating the strain on Dóchas. However, O'Sullivan and O'Donnell note that

> Prison cells are often held out by politicians as an antidote to crime. It is suggested that a kind of hydraulic relationship exists whereby if imprisonment rates are forced up, crime rates will inexorably be pushed down.[139]

Although there have been some improvements in both prison facilities for women, the conditions for female prisoners are still considered to be unsuitable, and as a minority group, they have been neglected in terms of political attention.[140] This neglect has continued at a political level and, while there has been no large-scale review carried out on women offenders to determine their needs either in prison or the community prior to creating diversion policies, a comprehensive report was carried out by the Irish Penal Reform Trust from 2016-2022.This report reviews the progress in the Irish penal system and notes how

> [T]here continues to be a lack of information on the availability and use of gender-sensitive community sanctions, and a general lack of research on the experience of women in the criminal justice system.[141]

Despite a Strategy Statement issued by the Department of Justice, Equality and Law Reform indicating an awareness of the obligation "to promote equality of opportunity between women and men through the development, implementation, and monitoring of appropriate policies," when creating the Thornton Hall Review Report,[142] at the time of writing no separate penal or prison policies have been made for women in the criminal justice system.

2.10 Conclusion

The economic challenges of the 1980s influenced a shift towards more punitive measures. The introduction of CSOs was intended to alleviate the strain on prisons. Yet, due to a lack of a clear guiding philosophy, the implementation of CSOs sometimes led to unintended consequences, including an increase in imprisonment rather than the desired reduction. Early release was used to control prison populations. Whilst this helped address overcrowding, it raised concerns about the impact on judicial sentencing and public safety. The government also proposed expanding prison facilities, a solution which, at the time of writing, remains controversial.

---

[139] O'Sullivan and O'Donnell (2003), pp. 33–64, p. 37.

[140] Irish Penal Reform Trust (2022), p. 41.

[141] Irish Penal Reform Trust (2021), p. 44. This report has been updated in 2022.

[142] Irish Penal Reform Trust (2011b).

The chapter highlights the pressing need for gender-responsive policies, in line with international standards like the Bangkok Rules, to guarantee humane treatment for female offenders. The Dóchas Centre, once seen as a pioneering institution, now grapples with severe overcrowding, significantly hindering its ability to offer effective rehabilitation. Unlike their male counterparts, who have access to various security levels, female prisoners are confined to a single medium-security level. Moreover, the absence of step-down programs and lack of non-custodial measures tailored to women's needs makes STPS diversion unsuitable for female offenders in the Irish justice system.

Law

Criminal Justice (Community Service) Act (1983)
United Nations Rules for the Treatment of Women Prisoners and Non-custodial Measures for Women Offenders: Vienna: UNODC (2011)
European Convention for the Prevention of Torture and Inhuman or Degrading Treatment or Punishment, 26 November 1987, ETS 126 (1987)
Code of Conduct for Law Enforcement Officials (1979)
Body of Principles for the Protection of All Persons under Any Form of Detention or Imprisonment (1988)
United Nations Standard Minimum Rules for Non-Custodial Measures (The Tokyo Rules) (1991)
Handbook on Women and Imprisonment (2014)
Probation of Offenders Act (1907)
Prisoners (Temporary Release) Rules (1960)
Prisons Act (1970)
Criminal Justice Act (1972)
Criminal Justice (Temporary Release of Prisoners) Act (2003)

Online Resource

JCFJ, 'Ireland's Women's Prisons'
Dáil Debate, vol 341, No.7, 20th April 1983
Dáil Debate, vol 343, No. 4, 8th June 1983
Dáil Debates, Vol 342, Col 1476, 20th April 1983
Dáil Debates, vol 359, col 1110, 11 June 1985
Dáil Éireann debate -Tuesday, 11 Feb Vol. 474 No. 6 1997
Dáil Éireann Debate, Wednesday - 16 February 2005
Seanad Debates 1999 (July 13, 1960) 1999
Irish Prison Service, *Daily Prisoner Population*

Irish Prison Service, *Persons Committed to Prison by Age and Gender* (Irish Prison Service Information Centre 2007-2017)

References

Book

Armstrong S, McAra L (2006) Perspectives on punishment: the contours of control. In: Girling E (ed) European identity, penal sensibilities, and communities of sentiment. Oxford University Press

Booth W (1890) In darkest England and the way out. The Salvation Army

Cohen S (1985) Visions of social control: crime punishment and classification

Garland D (1985) Punishment and welfare: a history of penal strategies. Gower, Aldershot

Garland D (2001) The culture of control. Oxford University Press, Oxford

Harris R (1995) Probation round the world: origins and development. Probation round the world: a comparative study. Routledge

Kilcommins S and others (2004) Crime, punishment and the search for order in Ireland. Institute of Public Administration

Lonergan J (2010) The governor. Penguin

McNeill F, Beyens K (2013) Offender supervision in Europe. Springer

O'Donnell I, O'Sullivan E (2001) Crime control in Ireland: the politics of intolerance. Cork University Press

O'Mahony P (2002) Criminal justice in Ireland. Institute of Public Administration

Pease K, Billingham S, Earnshaw I (1977) Community service assessed in 1976. HM Stationery Office

Raynor P, Robinson G (2005) Rehabilitation, crime and justice. Palgrave Macmillan

Rogan M (2011) Prison policy in Ireland: politics, Penal-Welfarism and political imprisonment. Taylor & Francis

Journal Article

Bloom B, Owen B, Covington S (2004) Women offenders and the gendered effects of public policy. Rev Policy Res 21

Bottoms A and others (2004) Towards desistance: theoretical underpinnings for an empirical study. Howard J Crim Just 43:368

Bottoms A (2006) Desistance, social bonds, and human agency: a theoretical exploration. The explanation of crime: context, mechanisms and development. Cambridge University Press, Cambrige p 243

Clear TR, Rose DR, Ryder JA (2001) Incarceration and the community: the problem of removing and returning offenders. Crime Delinq 47:335

Council of Europe Development Bank (2019) Doing more with less: Prisoner rehabilitation in Ireland

Feeley MM, Simon J (1992) The new penology: notes on the emerging strategy of corrections and its implications. Criminology 30:449

Garland D (2004) Beyond the culture of control. Crit Rev Int Soc Pol Phil 7:160

Guilfoyle E (2017) What exactly is a community service order in Ireland? Irish Probat J 4:189

Jewkes Y and others (2019) Designing 'healthy' prisons for women: incorporating trauma-informed care and practice into prison planning and design. Int J Environ Res Public Health 16:3818
McNally G (2007) Probation in Ireland: a brief history of the early years. Irish Probat J 4:5
McNeill F (2004) Correctionalism, desistance and the future of probation in Ireland. Irish Probat J 1: 28
Mulcahy A (2007) The Governance of Crime and Security in Ireland. UCD Geary Institute Discussion Paper Series; WP/32/2007 https://www.ucd.ie/geary/static/publications/workingpapers/gearywp200732.pdf
O'Donnell I (2008) Stagnation and change in Irish penal policy. Howard J Crim Just 47(2):121
O'Sullivan E, O'Donnell I (2003) Imprisonment and the crime rate in Ireland. Econ Soc Rev 34
Raynor P, Robinson G (2009) Why help offenders? Arguments for rehabilitation as a penal strategy. Eur J Probat 1:3
Richardson M (2008) Risky business: an examination of probation officers' attitudes towards risk assessment. Dissertations 9
Rogan M (2012) Rehabilitation, research, and reform: prison policy in Ireland. Irish Probat J 9:6
Rogan M (2013) Prison policy in times of austerity: lessons from Ireland. Dublin Inst Technol 5
Stolz SM, Wedow M (2013) Keeping banks afloat: public lifelines during the financial crisis. IEEP 10:81
Weaver B and others (2012) The failure of recall to prison: early release, front-door and back-door sentencing and the revolving prison door in Scotland. Eur J Probat 4:85

Media

Blakemore E (2019) How Ireland turned 'fallen women' into slaves. History
Dunphy L (2023) 'It's a great move forward for society': Limerick Prison opens new luxury women's wing. Irish Examiner (https://www.irishexaminer.com/news/arid-41250700.html 18th October 2023
Murphy AE (2000) The 'Celtic Tiger': An Analysis of Ireland's Economic Growth Performance
Murphy C (2021) Plans for 'Substantial' Prison on Thornton Hall Site Back on Agenda. The Irish Times. https://www.irishtimes.com/news/crime-and-law/plans-for-substantial-prison-on-thornton-hall-site-back-on-agenda-1.4478375 8th February 2021

Report

Carmody P, McEvoy M (1996) A study of Irish female prisoners. Dublin
CPT (2011) Report to the Government of Ireland on the visit to Ireland carried out by the European Committee for the Prevention of Torture and Inhuman or Degrading Treatment or Punishment (CPT) from 25 January to 5 February 2010. Strasbourg
Department of Children Equality Disability Integration and Youth (2021) Executive summary of the Final Report of the Commission of Investigation into Mother and Baby Homes. .https://www.gov.ie/en/publication/22c0e-executive-summary-of-the-final-report-of-the-commission-of-investigation-into-mother-and-baby-homes/
Department of Justice (1985) Report of the Committee of Inquiry into the Penal System (The Whitaker Report). Dublin
Department of Justice (2013) Report of the Inter-Departmental Committee to establish the facts of State involvement with the Magdalen Laundries

Department of Justice (2022) Criminal Justice Policy Review of Policy Options for Prison and Penal Reform 2022-2024, gov.ie/en/collection/
European Committee for the Prevention of Torture and Inhuman or Degrading Treatment or Punishment (2011) Report to the Government of Ireland on the visit to Ireland carried out by the European Committee for the Prevention of Torture and Inhuman or Degrading Treatment or Punishment (CPT) from 25 January to 5 February 2010. Strasbourg
Government of Ireland (1994) Five year action plan for the management of offenders
HM Inspectorate of Prisons for England and Wales (2016) Annual Report 2015-2016. London, UK
Hough M, Jacobson J, Millie (2003) A The decision to imprison: Sentencing and the prison population
Irish Penal Reform Trust (2008) Thornton Hall IRPT Position Paper 1. Irish Penal Reform Trust/ Irish Penal Policy/IRPT Position Paper-1-Thornton Hall
Irish Penal Reform Trust (2011a) Briefing Paper: Women in Detention
Irish Penal Reform Trust (2011b) Report of the Thornton Hall Project Review Group
Irish Penal Reform Trust (2012) Position paper 9- Reform of remission, temporary release and parole
Irish Penal Reform Trust (2021) Progress in the Penal System (PIPS)- The Need for Transparency. Dublin
Irish Penal Reform Trust (2022) Progress in the Penal System
Irish Prison Service (2006) Capital Expenditure Review
Irish Prison Service Annual Report (2019)
Irish Prison Service Annual Report (2021)
Jesuit Centre for Faith & Justice (2007) Thornton Hall Prison: Solution or Problem? https://www.jcfj.ie/article/thornton-hall-prison-solution-or-problem/
MacBride Commission Report (1980)
The Probation Service (2006) Strategy statement 2006-2007
The Probation Service (2009) Strategy Statement 2009–2011
The Probation Service (2011) Community Return Programme
The Visiting Committee (2010) Report of the Visiting Committee, Dochas Centre to the Minister for Justice, Equality and Law Reform
Wootton B (1970) Report on Non-Custodial and Semi-Custodial Treatment of Offenders (Probation). Penal Advisory Council Sub Committee on Non-Custodial Treatment

Conference Paper

Geiran V (2016) Customer, Consumer or Client? Putting the Service-User Centre-Stage in Probation Work
Kilcommins S (2011) Where is our criminal justice system going?. In: 4th Annual Martin Tansey Memorial Lecture
O'Malley T (2008) Principles of sentencing: towards a European conversation. The Limits of the Criminal Law
O'Malley T (2010) Time Served: The Impact of Sentencing and Parole Decisions on the Prison Population

Thesis

Carroll E (2011) An examination of the criminal justice policy processes behind the building of the Dóchas Centre. Dublin Institute of Technology

Guilfoyle E (2018) An examination of the community service order in Ireland: recommendations for change. University of Limerick

Riordan D (2009) The role of the community service order and the suspended sentence in ireland: a judicial perspective. Ph.D. University College Cork

Chapter 3
The Diverted Female Offender

3.1 Introduction

The Irish government initiated its penal policy of diversion away from custody in the 2010s. The 'diversion policy,' as implied by its name, refers to legislation aimed at diverting recipients of STPS away from prison custody. This legislation instructed courts to use CSOs instead of STPS, and fine defaulters were given CSOs instead of STPS.[1] However, this is quite a broad policy which encompasses a diverse range of offenders with varying levels of offences and different genders.[2] Most female offenders diverted from an STPS typically fall at the lower end of the STPS spectrum, as their sentences generally do not reach the upper limit of 12 months required for STPS substitution.[3]

This highlights the need for a more nuanced approach within the diversion policy to address the specific needs and circumstances of the two different cohorts, particularly women, to ensure effective rehabilitation.[4] Although a review was conducted in 1996 regarding the needs of women prisoners in Ireland, no review was carried out to assess the needs of women in the broader criminal justice system before implementing the diversion policy. Carmody & McEvoy's report detailed the necessary features for a new women's prison, but no report was commissioned to address the needs of women in the community when the diversion policy was created.[5]

---

[1] Criminal Justice (Community Service) (Amendment) Act (2011); Fines (Payment and Recovery) Act (2014).

[2] Irish Penal Reform Trust (2013a).

[3] Criminal Justice (Community Service) (Amendment) Act (2011), s3.

[4] Irish Penal Reform Trust (2013b), p. 3.

[5] Carmody and McEvoy (1996).

S. Duignan, *Transforming Justice for Women*, Gender, Justice and Legal Feminism 3, https://doi.org/10.1007/978-3-031-82455-5_3

3.2 The Corston Report

In 2007, the Corston Report, officially titled "A Review of Women with Particular Vulnerabilities in the Criminal Justice System",[6] was a significant government-commissioned report published in England. Led by Baroness Jean Corston, the report focused on the issues faced by women in the criminal justice system and made recommendations for reforms. The report recognised that women in the criminal justice system often have unique and specific vulnerabilities, including histories of abuse, mental health problems, substance misuse, and caring responsibilities. The Corston Report highlighted the inadequacies of the existing system in addressing these needs and argued for a distinct approach to women offenders. One of the key findings of the report was the ineffectiveness and disproportionate impact of short-term custodial sentences on women. It emphasised that imprisoning women for minor offences often had negative consequences, disrupting families, causing trauma, and hindering rehabilitation.[7]

The report recommended a significant reduction in the use of short-term sentences for women, particularly for non-violent and low-risk offenders. Instead of short-term imprisonment, the Corston Report advocated for a holistic and gender-responsive approach.[8] It proposed the development of community-based alternatives, such as women's centres and residential units that provide support, guidance, and specialised interventions to address the specific needs of women offenders. These alternatives aimed to address the root causes of offending, promote rehabilitation, and facilitate successful reintegration into society. The Corston Report also emphasised the importance of collaboration and coordination among various agencies and services involved in the criminal justice system. It called for improved partnerships between the criminal justice sector, health and social care agencies, housing providers, and community organisations to ensure a comprehensive and cohesive response to women's needs.[9] The findings of the Report were summarised in an article which called female prisons 'Our Social Dustbins'.[10]

> The extent of those 'particular vulnerabilities' are laid out starkly in the report: more than half of women prisoners have suffered violence at home. One in three have experienced sexual abuse. One quarter have been in local authority care. Two-thirds have a psychological disorder, such as depression or anxiety. Women prisoners have a much higher rate of severe mental illness such as schizophrenia: 14% compared with less than 1% in the general population. Over a third of women who are imprisoned will already have attempted suicide.[11]

---

[6]Jean Corston (2007).

[7]Ibid, p. 2.

[8]Ibid, p.3.

[9]Ibid.

[10]Lyon (2007).

[11]Jean Corston (2007), p. 6.

Labelling female prisons as 'social dustbins' suggests that female institutions serve as a dumping ground for women who have often endured a range of traumatic experiences and face multiple disadvantages. This term suggests that society's response to these women is one of neglect and marginalisation, rather than addressing the underlying causes of their involvement in the criminal justice system. The Corston Report emphasised how custody, even in the short term, has 'resulted in women in the criminal justice system persistently being marginalised',[12] leaving their needs unmet.

In The Standards for the Inspection of Prisons in Ireland, Women Prisoners' Supplement, Judge Michael Reilly, the then Inspector for Prisons, echoed the sentiments of Baroness Corston, acknowledging that "women prisoners must be treated differently to male prisoners in certain respects".[13] He referred to the Corston Report when he noted that, due to the small number of women prisoners, prison rules and regimes were formulated, in most cases, with the male prisoner in mind. The Inspector concluded that "it is now accepted that a gender-specific approach is required for women in prison."[14]

Despite the Irish government's policy of diversion, women continue to be committed to prison for non-violent offences, such as non-payment of fines.[15] They tend to come from 'a background of social disadvantage and poverty, and often suffer from mental health problems, substance dependency, accommodation problems and poor family relationships.'[16] Women are predominantly committed to prison for offences against property, theft, and road traffic offences: Eighty-seven percent of the women committed under sentence in 2021 were convicted of non-violent offences.[17] Women also play an important role in caring for dependent relatives. Women who are imprisoned can no longer fulfil their caring responsibilities, and the consequences of this may lead to familial breakdown and even intergenerational offending. Incarceration, however brief, can interrupt the family support structure, which may, in turn, prevent desistance and increase the likelihood of future involvement in the criminal justice system.

Andrews and Bonta explained the concept of a criminogenic need:

> Many offenders...have a variety of needs. They need places to live and work and/or they need to stop taking drugs. Some have poor self-esteem, chronic headaches or cavities in their teeth. These are all 'needs'. The need principle draws our attention to the distinction between criminogenic and non-criminogenic needs. Criminogenic needs are a subset of an offender's risk level. They are the dynamic attributes of an offender that, when changed, are associated with changes in the probability of recidivism.[18]

---

[12] Ibid.

[13] Inspector of Prisons (2011).

[14] Ibid, p. 3.

[15] Irish Penal Reform Trust (2013b), p. 5.

[16] Ibid, p. 5.

[17] Irish Prison Service.

[18] Andrews and Bonta (1998).

Examining women who have been diverted from custody poses significant challenges due to their dispersion throughout the community. There is a notable lack of large-scale qualitative research on women who receive community alternatives in Ireland. This shortfall may be attributed to the limited number of worksites or Community-Based Organisations (CBOs) where qualitative interviews can be conducted.[19]

3.3 The Female STPS Recipient

The female prisoner has a unique set of needs that demand tailored responses. The Bangkok Rules emphasise that "account shall be taken of the distinctive needs of women prisoners" and that the provision of these needs to accomplish gender equality "shall not be regarded as discriminatory."[20] While studies have been conducted on the characteristics of Irish prisoners in prison,[21] there is a scarcity of research on female prisoners, and this is mostly because they tend to receive shorter sentences and thus spend less time in prison.

In the absence of a comprehensive large-scale review specifically targeting women diverted into the Irish community, studies from similar jurisdictions, such as England & Wales and Scotland,[22] shed light on the various challenges concerning Irish female STPS recipients. These studies provide valuable insights into their reintegration into the community, the challenges they encounter, the support mechanisms that facilitate successful transitions, and potential pathways to reducing recidivism.[23]

In series of interviews with women prisoners at Scotland's Cornton Vale prison, Carlen found how "the pains of imprisonment" were felt more acutely by women than men. She attributed this to several factors specific to womanhood, such as isolation, dependency creation, infantilising effects, heavy discipline, the expectation of excellence in domestic duties, denial of status as real criminals or real women, and the absence of a 'woman-wise' penology.[24]

[19] Walsh and Sexton (2000).

[20] United Nations Rules for the Treatment of Women Prisoners and Non-custodial Measures for Women Offenders: Vienna: UNODC (2011)2010. United Nations Office on Drugs and Crime (UNODC).

[21] O'Mahony (1997).

[22] Jean Corston (2007); Barry and McIvor (2008).

[23] This author's doctoral research examined the experiences and outcomes of a small cohort of women who had been diverted into the community in Ireland. This gave insight into the unique challenges faced by female STPS recipients and highlighted issues related to trauma, addiction, mental health, and caregiving responsibilities, which are frequently overlooked in standard criminal justice approaches.

[24] Carlen (1983).

However, Carlen's theory faced criticism for overlooking the resistance strategies employed by incarcerated women. Critics argue that by concentrating solely on the structural factors contributing to women's imprisonment, Carlen's theories neglect the ways in which these women actively resist and assert their agency within the prison system. Liebling, for example, contends that an exclusive focus on women's 'pains' risks essentialising them as victims and ignores their resilience and agency within the prison environment.[25]

Despite these critiques, Carlen's theory provides an important framework for understanding the gendered dynamics of punishment and the specific challenges faced by incarcerated women in the context of 'prison's overwhelming power to punish'.[26] It is recognised that certain characteristics are more prevalent among women offenders compared to men, which can intensify the adverse effects of punishment and result in additional harm.[27]

3.3.1 Motherhood

A high proportion of women offenders are mothers.[28] In line with global trends, there has been a significant increase in the number of women in prison in Ireland in the last two decades, with the numbers more than doubling from 2000 to 2022.[29] This points to a corresponding increase in the numbers of children impacted by the imprisonment of their mother. A former Governor of the Dóchas Centre noted how 'women have a unique problem; [there are] very few residential treatments for women and some of the women have children.'[30] Female STPS recipients may also be mothers and may be the primary or sole caregivers for their children.[31] For the mother who is taken into custody, this may lead to familial breakdown because of the difficulties associated with maternal incarceration, however brief.[32] Several studies have highlighted the differences in outcomes for children of incarcerated mothers, versus fathers.[33] For instance, research shows how children of incarcerated mothers tend to experience more exposure to parental criminal activity, arrest, and sentencing, which can lead to higher levels of behavioural problems, compared to children of incarcerated fathers.[34] Maternal incarceration has also been linked to an

---

[25] Liebling and Arnold (2005).

[26] Carlen (1994), p. 137.

[27] Carlen (2002).

[28] Minson (2014).

[29] World Prison Brief.

[30] Gataveckaite and others (2019).

[31] Irish Penal Reform Trust (2021), p. 44.

[32] Minson (2014); Irish Penal Reform Trust (2021), p. 7.

[33] Dallaire and Wilson (2010).

[34] Melinda Tasca and Zatz (2011).

increased likelihood of youth offending, and children of incarcerated mothers 'were found to be are two and a half times more likely to be incarcerated themselves as adults.'[35] Additionally, incarcerated mothers are more likely to experience intergenerational and interfamilial incarceration, and imprisonment has been identified as a pathway to lone motherhood.[36]

Although separation from children typically affects incarcerated women more, the effects of the STPS and its associated fragmentation has a noticeable impact on the lives of all women. Even where women are diverted into the community, the challenges and consequences related to motherhood persist. The STPS, with its requirements and disruptions, is likely to contribute to a certain fragmentation experienced by women. This fragmentation could refer to the strain on maintaining relationships, the difficulties in fulfilling parenting responsibilities, or the overall disruption to their lives caused by diversion.

Understanding the specific challenges faced by STPS recipients who are also mothers is important to develop effective support and interventions. These interventions should address the unique needs of women and promote positive outcomes for both the women and their children. Research by Byrne and Trew has shown that women's alcohol use and offending behaviour are often linked to the responsibilities of motherhood. Additionally, they found that certain emotional and mental health problems are associated with the burdens of motherhood.[37] Women who abuse substances face greater stigma than men[38] and often experience motherhood in isolation, with minimal support for childcare when seeking treatment. Additionally, the fear of having their children taken away is a significant barrier to seeking treatment or disclosing their drug use.

3.3.2 Homelessness/Economic Need

Scholarship consistently highlights the complex needs of women prisoners who 'tend to come from a background of social disadvantage and poverty.'[39] Roberson and Radford also found that many women prisoners in Northern Ireland relied on social security benefits prior to their imprisonment.[40] Circumstances like these can increase the likelihood of women engaging in criminal activities as a means of basic

[35] Dallaire (2007).

[36] O'Reilly (2016).

[37] Byrne and Trew (2008).

[38] Guidelines on Drug Prevention and Treatment for Girls and Women (2016) https://www.unodc.org/documents/drug-prevention-and-treatment/unodc_2016_drug_prevention_and_treatment_for_girls_and_women_E.pdf.

[39] Irish Penal Reform Trust (2013a); Convery (2009); O'Neill (2011).

[40] Roberson and Radford (2006).

survival. Studies frequently highlight a connection between offending and the need to meet essential requirements.

The results of a survey conducted in 2005, which randomly sampled 241 prisoners in the Dublin metropolitan region, revealed that more than half of the participants had experienced homelessness at least once before their imprisonment.[41] Furthermore, the survey found that one quarter of the sample population were homeless at the time they were committed to prison. Their results indicate that the risk of ending up in the criminal justice system is greater for homeless women than for those with stable accommodation. The Irish Prison Service Joint Strategy Report found that those 'who are homeless upon release are more likely to reoffend'.[42] Research in the UK has identified a significant risk of homelessness among women offenders:

> Many have lived on state benefits, few have been in paid employment, many have large debts, about one in ten will have experienced homelessness and around two in five will have experienced foster or other state care prior to imprisonment. In a study that examined a random sample of 50 women prisoners, it was discovered that 33% of them were homeless at the time of their imprisonment.[43]

These findings suggest that women offenders are particularly vulnerable to experiencing homelessness. Furthermore, the study found that while women constituted less than one-fifth of the overall homeless population, they accounted for over two-fifths (43%) of homeless individuals referred to Probation services. The sample size was small, so these results should be interpreted with caution. However, the implications are that homeless women may be more likely to encounter the criminal justice system compared to non-homeless women. This highlights the intersectionality of homelessness and involvement in the criminal justice system among women, emphasising the need for targeted support and interventions for this vulnerable population. Gelsthorpe et al. note that

> as far as dynamic risk factors are concerned, financial difficulties are perhaps the most significant risk factor leading to offending by women, and women's acquisitive offending can be seen as a rational response to restricted opportunities for legitimate income generation.'[44]

Data from the Central Statistics Office illustrates that almost half the women in Ireland were at risk of poverty in 2017.[45] While poverty itself is not a direct criminogenic factor that can be addressed directly, it contributes significantly to the likelihood of reoffending.

---

[41] Seymour and Costello (2005).

[42] Irish Prison Service (2019), p. 9.

[43] McIvor et al. (2004).

[44] Hedderman (2004).

[45] Central Statistics Office (2019).

3.3.3 *Mental/Physical Health/Addiction*

Other issues which have been shown to particularly impact female offending behaviour include mental health problems, substance dependency, and poor family relationships.[46] In 2010, the Visiting Committee noted how 'a visiting psychiatrist attends on occasion.'[47] This is clearly not a habitual or regularised practice. Ten years later, reports fail to present a more optimistic picture. The Dóchas Chaplaincy Annual Report in 2020 noted how:

> Increasingly, prisoners are being sent to the Dóchas with pre-existing mental illness. Prison is not a suitable place for a mental patient. The help that is required is not available in prison. The Dóchas has medical staff who are trained to deal with mental health patients. The Prison Officers who supervise such prisoners are not trained to deal with mental health patients.[48]

Despite the Government's commitment to addressing mental healthcare in prisons and diverting individuals with severe mental health issues from the prison system, no concrete actions have been implemented to date.[49] Research illustrates how these are all key criminogenic factors which contribute to reoffending and they have not been adequately addressed in the community. The Chaplaincy Report in 2020 describes how a patient was transferred from a psychiatric facility:

> [A] prisoner was remanded to the Dóchas Centre after having spent over a year in a psychiatric facility. The prisoner was clearly unwell and confused to the extent that after a few days in custody the prisoner wanted to know what hospital she was in. From as soon as she arrived in the Dóchas Centre the prisoner remained in bed all day. Prison was obviously not the place for that prisoner, yet the prisoner had been charged, arraigned in court and remanded to prison. After considerable intervention by the Governor and Health Care Staff, the prisoner was removed back to the psychiatric facility that she had come from.[50]

In addition to a lack of health care facilities, the lack of low-security prisons for women sentenced to custody in Ireland also presents a significant challenge. Without these designated facilities, women serving STPS will be housed alongside inmates serving longer sentences. This cohabitation can potentially foster harmful associations or alliances during their time in custody, especially for younger women. Notably, 82% of the women committed in 2021 were under the age of 45.[51]

---

[46] Prison Reform Trust (2016), p. 6.

[47] (2010).

[48] Chaplaincy Service (2020).

[49] Irish Penal Reform Trust (2021), p. 9. On 23rd December 2021, there were 23 people in prison on the waiting list for transfer to the Central Mental Hospital (CMH) with a yearly average of 21 people on the waiting list for transfer to the CMH in 2021 (Information obtained from the National Forensic Mental Health Service on 23rd December 2021). For offenders who have substance abuse problems: In 2021, there were 43 people diverted from prison to supports in the community by the Prison In-reach and Court Liaison Service (PICLS) and 14 people diverted from prison to the CMH by PICLS.

[50] Chaplaincy Service (2020), p. 7.

[51] Irish Penal Reform Trust (2013b), p. 5.

Irish Prison Service data for 2017 illustrated how 95% of women who were incarcerated received sentences for crimes such as shoplifting or handling stolen goods.[52] That year, nearly all women served sentences less than a year long, with three-quarters of women imprisoned for less than 3 months. With no step-down facility available, women leaving prison may be offered emergency accommodation of one night in a hostel, but 'after that, they are fending for themselves.'[53]

Offenders may have direct and/or indirect criminogenic needs including financial instability, emotional problems, or substance use issues. Studies show how distinct patterns emerge regarding the initiation of substance use among women. For some women, substance use may begin during their teenage years. This may be influenced by family members or the broader community and it can be a response to 'difficulties, tensions, or abuse at home.'[54] For others, substance use can start after experiencing violence or abuse in a relationship, frequently beginning with the misuse of medication.[55] The access and availability of substances plays a significant role in shaping substance use patterns and in many cases, a partner or someone in the immediate environment supplies or facilitates access to these substances. Findings from the UK Ministry of Justice illustrate that almost 48% of female offenders committed their offences to support someone else's drug use, compared with 22% of male prisoners.[56]

Research has identified a link between substance abuse and abusive relationships. In one Irish study in 2023 which involved fourteen women, three had interactions with the criminal justice system: two due to their substance use and one related to behaviours associated with an abusive relationship.[57] This highlights the interconnectedness of STPS with various negative outcomes such as addiction, poor health, vulnerability to violence, and poverty. Substance abuse can also lead to loss of familial relationships, which has proven to be.

3.3.4 *Loss of Familial Relationships*

Both male and female offenders can be impacted by loss of relationships. For Irish women offenders, various factors can disrupt familial and interpersonal relationships. Given that there are only two detention facilities for women in Ireland, a woman under the STPS may be incarcerated far from her home. This geographical distance can hinder her ability to maintain regular contact with her family, thereby straining inter-personal relationships. Additionally, some women might choose not

---

[52] Irish Prison Service.

[53] Irish Penal Reform Trust (2021), p. 44.

[54] Morton et al. (2023), p. 9.

[55] Ibid, p. 9.

[56] UK Ministry of Justice.

[57] Morton et al. (2023).

to have their children visit them in prison, preferring to shield them from the experience. This absence can lead to a deterioration in the mother-child relationship, particularly if the mother loses legal guardianship and the children are placed with another family. Such circumstances can lead to feelings of loneliness and serve as a significant barrier to desistance.[58]

Community Service Programmes in Ireland are not specifically designed for women because the majority of participants are male.[59] The male-dominated community centres, which cater to both men and women diverted away from STPS, can feel unwelcoming and potentially threatening for women who come from backgrounds of abuse or trauma.[60] In female-only programmes, some women describe positive experiences upon their first contact with the group, highlighting the safety of the environment, the building, and the fact that it is a women-only programme.[61] Women-focused provision is increasing with the introduction of holistic women's centres in the United Kingdom, and monitoring and evaluation of these centres are beginning to address the gap in evidence on women-focused interventions.[62]

Pollack contends that community support initiatives for women offenders should be tailored to their specific needs, facilitating connections to essential resources, training, counselling, and other supportive services.[63] Women participating in these programmes often report feeling safer and more empowered within group settings, enabling them to better face the challenges associated with desistance. They have expressed that these environments allow them to 'go beyond their comfort zones'[64] fostering a sense of strength and reduced marginalisation.

A qualitative study by Carmody and McEvoy, conducted in 1996, aimed to "design and build a new female prison."[65] To achieve this, they undertook a study to "gain more knowledge about their background, their health, their psychiatric history and drug and alcohol use."[66] This research was pioneering in its effort to gather comprehensive information about female prisoners in Irish prisons. It revealed that "women prisoners are a very vulnerable group in our community with very special needs."[67] The study found that women who offend are "more likely to be from poor social backgrounds, have an average of 2 or 3 children, are less likely to be in a relationship and tend to have had prior psychiatric treatment."[68]

---

[58] Duignan (2023).

[59] The Probation Service.

[60] Gelsthorpe et al. (2007), p. 28.

[61] Woods (2020), p. 198.

[62] Convery (2009), p. 42.

[63] Pollack (2008).

[64] Woods (2020), p. 202.

[65] Carmody and McEvoy (1996), p. 1.

[66] Ibid, p. 2.

[67] Ibid, p. 24.

[68] Ibid, p. 24.

Despite these valuable insights, no comprehensive large-scale follow-up study has been conducted to examine the criminogenic needs of women offenders within prisons, like the Corston Report in the United Kingdom. This highlights a significant gap in our understanding of the specific needs and challenges faced by women offenders and the limitations in addressing those needs within the Irish prison system.

3.4 Engagement with Support and Interventions

Research has identified several factors that prompt women to seek support or intervention: the needs of her children, her health issues or perhaps her involvement with the criminal justice system.[69] The needs of a woman's children can sometimes lead to the child being taken into State care due to her substance abuse issues. This event can serve as a wake-up call, prompting the woman to seek help or support. Health concerns caused by new issues or the complications of a chronic issue, perhaps aggravated by substance abuse may also compel her to seek help.[70] Finally if an offender is arrested for committing an offence, they be subject to an intervention upon arrest. Interaction with the criminal justice system has limited supports for offenders. If they have substance abuse issues the Irish Prison Service provides comprehensive drug rehabilitation programs for prisoners, including medical and rehabilitative services such as methadone substitution treatment,[71] psychosocial services for any trauma suffered, and there are also various work and training options which prisoners can attend whilst in custody.[72]

3.5 Recidivism

Carmody and McEvoy's study highlighted that many women in Irish prisons had previous convictions and were likely to reoffend.[73] The study concluded that this was possibly due to the use of early release:

[69] Morton et al. (2023), p. 15.

[70] Duignan (2023).

[71] Upon entry, prisoners with a history of opiate use who test positive for opioids are offered a medically assisted detoxification. Healthcare staff discuss additional treatment options, including methadone maintenance for those who wish to continue this treatment during incarceration and upon release. Prisoners who are already engaged in methadone substitution programs in the community will generally opt to continue their treatment while in prison. (Irish Prison Service.ie / Prisoner Services/ Drug Treatment Services).

[72] Irish Prison Service.

[73] Carmody and McEvoy (1996).

> If a woman knows, from past experience, that she will be released from prison before her sentence is completed, she will be more likely to offend again. More space is needed to accommodate all the women prisoners. The prisoners could then settle into prison, finish their sentences, become involved in the educational, medical and psychiatric facilities.[74]

The study also found that the successful completion of drug treatment programs may reduce the likelihood of reoffending. The study noted there was also a need for expanded medical facilities to cater for the higher number of AIDS patients and drug abusers, as well as designated private and confidential rooms for counselling and care.[75] The researchers expressed optimism that the prison system could offer a suitable environment where these women could initiate the process of addressing their problems and working towards self-improvement.[76]

According to the Irish Prison Service, women ex-prisoners are at high risk of reoffending. In a recidivism study in 2013, the recidivism rate among female offenders was 57% within 3 years of release.[77] The majority of these women reoffended within 6 months post-release.[78] However, recent statistics published by the Central Statistics Office indicate that this proportion has increased, with 70% of females released from prison in 2016 reoffending within 3 years of release.[79] When an offender continues to reoffend, the cumulative impact of punishment can be significant. Frase and Roberts outlined two justifications for why a sentencer might impose imprisonment on persistent offenders. The first rationale is based on the belief that repeat offenders should receive harsher punishment due to their increased culpability, as demonstrated by their failure to respond to previous sanctions. The second rationale is that harsher sentences are intended to address the elevated risk of future reoffending associated with repeat offenders. These perspectives highlight the aim of using more severe measures to deter and address the ongoing criminal behaviour of persistent offenders.[80]

STPS are less effective in terms of reducing recidivism than custodial alternatives.[81] They are also much more expensive to administer.[82] Mills recognises that short sentences for low-level offences, which otherwise lie beneath the custodial threshold, are characteristic of criminal justice systems where prison is used as the 'backstop for the perceived failure of other criminal justice measures' to address persistent offending.[83] One of the main criticisms of the use of the STPS includes the 'cumulative' cycle of repeat short sentences that lack any rehabilitative element.

---

[74] Ibid, p. 23.

[75] Ibid.

[76] Ibid, p. 24.

[77] (2013).

[78] Irish Penal Reform Trust (2013b), p. 11.

[79] CSO (2016).

[80] Frase and Roberts (2019), Chapter 1, p. 2.

[81] Irish Penal Reform Trust (2021), p. 6.

[82] O'Donnell (2020), p. 11.

[83] Mills (2019), p. 11.

Prior to the construction of the Dóchas Centre in Ireland, the study by Carmody and McEvoy indicates that there was an intention to cater to the diverse needs of women entering the criminal justice system because the specific "needs" of Irish women offenders were sought to be captured by the study. However, the problem of under-resourcing and overcrowding appeared to leave the new women's prison promising more than it could deliver.[84]

The STPS can exert a disproportionately harsh impact on female offenders, thereby undermining the sanction's initial intent. Sentencing outcomes may diverge from the fundamental aim of delivering a fair and proportionate response, inadvertently causing an excessively punitive result. A comprehensive analysis of sentencing practices in the Irish lower courts, along with an examination of how these sentences intersect with the unique characteristics of female offences and offenders, provides deeper insight into this issue.

3.6 Conclusion

In formulating the penal policy, the Irish government examined gender-aggregated data to create a framework aimed at diverting the gender neutral 'STPS recipient.' However, the category of STPS recipients includes both males and females, whose unique characteristics and pathways into offending necessitates differentiated approaches.[85] A singular policy is inadequate for addressing the needs of both genders effectively. Furthermore, the government is unable to legislate control over the issuance of STPS in the lower courts. The constitutional prohibition against infringing upon judicial discretion in sentencing decisions prevents any regulatory measures from dictating who receives an STPS and who does not.

Liebling addresses the prison paradox by examining the 'emotional climate' of custody.[86] This work aims to measure the emotional climate of sentenced women who are diverted into the community. The stigma associated with an STPS can be particularly harmful to female recipients, as the measures that divert them from prison custody into the community are often not tailored to their specific needs. Instead, these measures are primarily designed with the male recipient in mind, who constitutes 90% of the recipients.

Scholarship acknowledges how women's pathways into and out of offending are different from those for men, and generic interventions designed to address male criminogenic needs are often inadequate and inappropriate for women offenders. The importance of re-conceptualising women's needs to take account of their life experiences and acknowledge their position in the wider socio-economic context is emphasised in this chapter.

---

[84] Irish Prison Service (2007–2017), p. 43.

[85] Duignan (2023).

[86] Liebling and Arnold (2005).

Whilst this model of identifying characteristics was somewhat useful to identify the priority of needs and the content of treatment programmes, this framework does not identify a specific 'hierarchy' of needs and may even create barriers to desistance for women. Even though gender variations in the processes of desistance have been identified in other jurisdictions,[87] there has been a lack of wide scale research in this jurisdiction focusing on women's desistance from crime.

Desistance from offending among women is associated with several themes that extend beyond factors directly related to their criminal behaviour. These themes encompass aspects of their social and personal lives that contribute to a sense of agency and empowerment, which may not be adequately recognised by treatment programmes designed for both men and women. The specific themes vary depending on the individual experiences and circumstances of women. They include factors such as social support, personal growth, building agency and autonomy, responding to gender-specific needs, and understanding the unique challenges and experiences faced by women, such as motherhood, childcare responsibilities, gender-based violence, empowerment, and self-esteem.

To promote successful desistance among women offenders, various strategies can be employed, including mentoring, positive reinforcement, and the creation of opportunities for personal achievements. It is essential to acknowledge and address the impact of societal barriers and structural inequalities, such as limited access to employment, education, and housing, which significantly influence desistance outcomes. By reducing these barriers, women are more likely to reintegrate successfully into society and maintain a crime-free lifestyle. Incorporating these considerations into the design and implementation of interventions, treatment programmes, and support services can lead to the development of a more comprehensive and gender-responsive approach, ultimately fostering desistance among women offenders.

Law

United Nations Rules for the Treatment of Women Prisoners and Non-custodial Measures for Women Offenders: Vienna: UNODC (2011)
Guidelines on Drug Prevention and Treatment for Girls and Women (2016)
Criminal Justice (Community Service) (Amendment) Act (2011)
Fines (Payment and Recovery) Act (2014)

[87] McIvor et al. (2004); Rumgay (2004).

Online Resource

Women and Men in Ireland 2019 EU at Risk of Poverty Rates 2019
CSO, *Prison Recidivsm Statistics* (Central Statistics Office 2016)
Irish Prison Service, *Prisoner Services*
Irish Prison Service, *Sentenced Committals Classified by Sentence Length & Gender from Years 2007 to 2020 - Irish Prison Service/ Home/ Information Centre/ Statistics & Information Yearly Statistics* (Irish Prison Service)
Irish Prison Service, *Persons Committed to Prison by Age and Gender* (Irish Prison Service Information Centre 2007–2017)
The Probation Service, *Community Based Organisations*
UK Ministry of Justice, *Women in the Criminal Justice System (CJS)*
World Prison Brief, *World Prison Brief Data: Republic of Ireland.*

References

Journal Article

Byrne CF, Trew KJ (2008) Pathways through crime: the development of crime and desistance in the accounts of men and women offenders. Howard J Crim Just 47:238
Carlen P (1994) Why study Women's imprisonment? Or anyone else's? "An Indefinite Article". Br J Criminol 34:131
Convery U (2009) Addressing offending by women: a literature review. Northern Ireland Statistics and Research Agency
Dallaire DH (2007) Incarcerated mothers and fathers: a comparison of risks for children and families. Fam Relat 56:440
Dallaire DH, Wilson LC (2010) The relation of exposure to parental criminal activity, arrest, and sentencing to children's maladjustment. J Child Fam Stud 19:404
Gelsthorpe L, Sharpe G, Roberts J (2007) Provision for women offenders in the community. Fawcett Society, London
Hedderman C (2004) The "Criminogenic" needs of women offenders. In: McIvor G (ed) Women who offend. Jessica Kingsley, London, pp 227–244
Liebling A, Arnold H (2005) Prisons and their moral performance: a study of values, quality, and prison life. Clarendon Press, Oxford
Melinda Tasca NR, Zatz MS (2011) Family and residential instability in the context of paternal and maternal incarceration. Crim Justice Behav 38(3):231
Mills H (2019) Stopping short? Sentencing reform and short prison sentences. UK Justice Policy Review Focus
Morton S, Gallagher B, McLoughlin E (2023) 'You can't fix this in six months': understanding the intersectionality of women's substance use in the Irish context. University College Dublin/ Merchants Quay Ireland, Dublin, Ireland
O'Neill J (2011) The inspire Women's project: managing women offenders within the community. Irish Probat J 8:93
O'Reilly A (2016) Matricentric feminism: theory, activism. Practice
Pollack S (2008) Locked In, Locked Out: imprisoning women in the shrinking and punitive welfare state. 4 Retrieved April 2008

Roberson B, Radford E (2006) The reintegration needs of women prisoners in Northern Ireland. Irish Probat J 3:110
Rumgay J (2004) Scripts for safer survival: pathways out of female crime. Howard J Crim Just 43: 405
Seymour M, Costello L (2005) A study of the number, profile and progression routes of homeless persons before the court and in custody. Centre for Social and Educational Research 10
Woods M (2020) 'Helping others and helping myself': wounded healers as peer workers. Irish Probat J 17:191–211

Book

Andrews DA, Bonta J (1998) The psychology of criminal conduct. Routledge
Carlen P (1983) Women's imprisonment: a study in social control. Routledge & Kegan Paul London
Carlen P (2002) Women and punishment: the struggle for justice. Willan
Frase RS, Roberts JV (2019) Paying for the past: the case against prior record sentence enhancements. Oxford University Press
McIvor G, Malloch M, Gelsthorpe L (2004) Women who offend, vol 44. Jessica Kingsley Publishers
Walsh DP, Sexton P (2000) An empirical study of community service orders in Ireland. Stationery Office

Media

Gataveckaite G and others (2019) Almost All Women in Irish Prisons are there for Committing Petty Crime. The Journal (23 April 2019) https://www.thejournal.ie/women-prison-ireland-petty-crime-4596708-Apr2019/
Lyon J (2007) Our social dustbins. The Guardian (14th March 2007) https://www.theguardian.com/commentisfree/2007/mar/14/comment.gender

Report

Barry M, McIvor G (2008) Chaotic lives: a profile of women in the criminal justice system in Lothian and Borders. Lothian & Borders Commnuity Justice Authority
Carmody P, McEvoy M (1996) A study of Irish female prisoners, Dublin
Chaplaincy Service (2020) Dochas Chaplaincy Annual Report
Dochas Centre Visiting Committee Annual Report (2010) Dublin
Inspector of Prisons (2011) Standards for the Inspections of Prisons in Ireland-Women Prisoners' Supplement
Irish Penal Reform Trust (2013a) Position Paper 10- Women in the Criminal Justice System: Towards a non-custodial approach
Irish Penal Reform Trust (2013b) Women in the Criminal Justice System: Towards a Non-Custodial Approach. Dublin

Irish Penal Reform Trust (2021) Progress in the Penal System (PIPS)- The Need for Transparency. Dublin
Irish Prison Service (2019) Strategic Plan 2019–2022
Irish Prison Service Recidivism Study (2013)
Jean Corston B (2007) The Corston Report: A report of a review of women with particular vulnerabilities in the criminal justice system. London
Minson S (2014) Mitigating Motherhood: A Study of the Impact of Motherhood on Sentencing Decisions in England and Wales: a Report for the Howard League for Penal Reform
O'Donnell I (2020) An evidence review of recidivism and policy responses. Department of Justice & Equality, Dublin
O'Mahony P (1997) Mountjoy prisoners: a sociological and criminological profile. Stationery Office, Dublin
Prison Reform Trust (2016) Transforming Lives: Reducing Women's Imprisonment

Thesis

Duignan S (2023) Evaluation of the effect of Irish penal policy on female short-term prison sentence recipients: the need for gender-specific policy. University of Galway

Chapter 4
The Sentencing of Women and the Impact of Policies

4.1 Introduction

From 2011-2020, the number of STPS recipients decreased and so it could be said that the government's policy of diverting STPS recipients away from prison was successful overall. However, closer examination of data reveals that this policy was less effective for the female recipients in this group. When analysed, gender-disaggregated data indicates an increasing number of female STPS recipients from 2011 to 2016. Due to the aggregation of published data, this growing number of women remained invisible until 2014.[1] The statistics for female STPS these recipients were not published as a distinct category, rendering this cohort invisible to legislators and policymakers.

A significant concern for minority groups within the Irish judicial system is the inconsistency in sentencing. This inconsistency arises due to the absence of comprehensive sentencing guidelines and the broad use of judicial discretion. Judges in Ireland are expected to follow general sentencing principles established by superior courts. However, the absence of formal constraints and detailed guidance often leads to inconsistent sentencing practices, especially in lower courts where many judges rely on their personal judgment instead of a standardised approach.[2] Judicial discretion is mainly governed by the statutory maximum sentence for each offence and is further limited in lower courts by jurisdictional limits and the principle of proportionality. Although there is a growing number of guideline judgments from the Court of Appeal and Supreme Court, these mainly address higher-level offences, leaving a gap in guidance for more common cases. Many STPS are handed down in the lower

[1] Duignan (2023).

[2] Maguire (2010), p. 30.

S. Duignan, *Transforming Justice for Women*, Gender, Justice and Legal Feminism 3, https://doi.org/10.1007/978-3-031-82455-5_4

courts without any rationale given[3] and even when judges do speak of rationales they tend to demonstrate little coherent policy.[4]

This chapter delves into the dynamics of the Irish sentencing system, particularly focusing on its lack of structured guidelines in the lower courts and the stated reliance on proportionality and judicial discretion. It questions why this approach has caused a significant decrease in the number of STPS for the male cohort, while paradoxically leading to an increase in the number of female recipients, who were also intended to benefit from diversion strategies. The chapter explores the underlying reasons for this disparity, examining how the absence of clear guidelines and the subjective nature of judicial discretion have impacted sentencing outcomes differently based on gender.

4.2 Impact of Reforms

In 1960s and 1970s Ireland, the rate of female incarceration in Ireland was relatively low.[5] Research from that period reveals a type of gender bias in judicial sentencing, where women were often treated more leniently compared to men. This meant that they were less likely to be incarcerated[6] and factors such as marriage, family, and motherhood were considered as mitigating circumstances.[7] However, despite this 'leniency' shown to women, the number of female prisoners still began to increase significantly during the 1980s. While there were only a few women in prison at any given time in 1979, by 1980, the capacity for female prisoners had reached its maximum of twenty, leading to the installation of bunk beds in 1981 to accommodate the growing number of committals. It is possible that the upward trend in female prison committals in the late 1990s was attributable to the shift in offences from public order to drug-related crimes.[8]

When the Irish government implemented its diversion policy, the STPS cohort was identified as the largest and 'safest' group to be redirected from prison custody into the community, primarily because their offences were of a less severe nature. In Ireland, probation practices developed as a pragmatic alternative to imprisonment, and the CSO was promoted as a direct substitute to incarceration.[9] Non-custodial sanctions in Ireland have not yet evolved to incorporate newer measures found in

[3] Hamilton (2005).

[4] Ibid, p. 9 Researchers in 2003 observed judges committing offenders to prison for alternate purposes of incapacitation ('can't let you roam the streets') and deterrence ('you need to be taught a lesson').

[5] O'Sullivan and O'Donnell (2003).

[6] O'Mahony (2002), p. 45.

[7] Ibid.

[8] Carmody and McEvoy (1996).

[9] Criminal Justice (Community Service) (Amendment) Act (2011), s3.

other jurisdictions, such as more diverse types of community service, electronic monitoring, or victim-offender mediation. Although men and women who were diverted were being treated as a single cohort in policy terms, the female STPS recipients exhibit varied pathways into offending and punishment outcomes, and this led to different prison experiences for women.[10]

The rate of female incarceration surged during the 2000s, with the number of women committed to prison more than doubling between 2001 and 2011, whilst the number of male inmates grew by one-third.[11] In 2024, women comprise 15% of the total prison population and over the past decade, the average daily count of female prisoners has escalated by 31%.[12] In 2012, approximately 2000 women were committed to prison under a sentence (of any length), a dramatic increase compared to about 150 in 1990.[13]

Approximately one quarter of the female prison population has been sentenced to STPS, as compared to just over ten percent of the male prison population.[14] Most offences leading to STPS for women are non-violent, predominantly involving public order and other social code violations.[15] Irish Prison Service data illustrates that just over one quarter of women remanded to custody had their most serious charge categorised as 'theft and related offences', compared to 13% for men.[16]

These figures highlight that, despite the government's diversion policy aimed at reducing prison committals, women are increasingly incarcerated. Notably, these imprisonments are for non-serious offences, often resulting in short-term sentences. This recurring pattern of recidivist offending indicates that women have become trapped in a cycle of reoffending. The lack of tiered security facilities in the female prison system fails to differentiate between the severity of offences and offenders, potentially exacerbating their criminal behaviours.

4.3 Sentencing Guidelines and Reforms

In 1988, the Supreme Court declined to establish sentencing guidelines for rape due to several factors. In the case of the *DPP v Tiernan*[17] the court was invited to consider writing a 'guideline judgment' which would offer guidance to the judiciary when sentencing as this style of judgment had become popular in the Court of

[10] Geiran (2011).

[11] Irish Prison Service.

[12] The average daily count of female prisoners has escalated from 124 in 2008 to over 160 2024 (Irish Prison Service).

[13] Mary Rogan (Dec 2013) Dec 2013.

[14] Irish Penal Reform Trust (2021), p. 44.

[15] Ibid.

[16] Data provided by Irish Prison Service to IRPT 13th August 2020 ibid, p44 Footnote 161.

[17] *DPP v Tiernan* IR 1988 250.

Appeal in England and Wales at the time.[18] At this stage, the Irish courts rejected this approach for two reasons. The first reason was 'the absence of reliable sentencing statistics or information concerning any general pattern of sentences.'[19] The second reason was the court's concern that standardising tariffs for (lesser) offences, where a variety of aggravating or mitigating factors might be present, would overly restrict the judge's ability to individualise sentences.

Over the next 25 years, while sentencing principles were discussed by the Court of Criminal Appeal and occasionally the Supreme Court, no comprehensive guidelines were established. This has been described as an 'Aristotelian'[20] approach, where appropriate sentences have been left to trial judges who are considered to possess sufficient practical wisdom and expertise in making such decisions. Then, if the sentence does significantly deviate from the established norm or standard, it can always be modified on appeal. Of course, proportionality has remained a fundamental distributive principle throughout this period as well.[21]

There was a shift in 2008, when Justice Charlton in the High Court delivered a decision in the case of *DPP v D(W)*,[22] which reflected a more structured approach to sentencing.[23] This case indicated a step towards promoting greater structure and coherence in sentencing decisions.[24] The judgment appeared to mark a departure from the Supreme Court's position in the *Tiernan* case by providing sentencing guidance in a case involving sexual assault. This was a notable development as it provided a level of consistency and predictability in sentencing outcomes, addressing concerns related to disparity and arbitrariness in the sentencing process. The sentencing guidance offered by Justice Charlton aimed to guide judges in weighing the various factors and considerations specific to sexual assault cases. It provided a framework for assessing the gravity of the offences, the level of harm inflicted on the victim, the culpability of the offender, and other relevant circumstances.[25] In doing so, the court demonstrated a willingness to address the need for guidance and consistency in this area of the law, acknowledging the importance of balancing the rights of victims with the principles of proportionality and fairness in sentencing.

Four years later, in the case of *DPP v Molloy*,[26] the court considered it good practice to set out a headline sentence for the offence. This sentence would reflect the severity of the offence, with any discounts for mitigation applied afterward. The court noted how 'an accused is entitled to have the reasoning process, by means of

---

[18] O'Donnell (2005).

[19] Scott (2017).

[20] O'Malley (2023).

[21] O'Malley (2019), p. 3.

[22] *DPP v D(W)* IR 2008 308.

[23] Ibid.

[24] Ibid (CCA).

[25] Ibid.

[26] *DPP v Molloy* IECA 2018 (IECA) 37.

which a sentencing court has arrived at the sentence which it has imposed upon him or her, rationally and adequately explained'.[27]

In March 2014, the Court of Criminal Appeal delivered two guideline judgments without any prior announcement. The first case, *DPP v Ryan*,[28] addressed possession of firearms in suspicious circumstances, while the second case, *DPP v Fitzgibbon*,[29] focused on causing serious harm. The Court emphasised the importance of maintaining sentencing consistency and providing guidance for sentencing exercises. Whilst acknowledging the previous doubts about setting standardisation of tariff or penalty, the Court asserted that it could offer 'a broad level of guidance' on appropriate sentence ranges for various offences.[30] However, the Court of Appeal stopped short of requiring a 'crude arithmetic' approach in all cases.[31]

This may have led to more guideline judgments but, in late 2014, the Court of Criminal Appeal was replaced by the current Court of Appeal. The new court faced a backlog of cases and new appeals upon its establishment and as a result the Court of Appeal was slow to provide guideline judgments. Eventually, however, it issued its first guideline in 2018 in the case of *DPP v Casey*,[32] a case which dealt with residential burglary. Like its predecessor court, the Court of Appeal provided sentence ranges as guidance.[33] For the past four decades, controlling and structuring judicial discretion in sentencing has been a prominent focus of sentencing reform and academic research worldwide. However, O'Malley cautions 'it would be premature to assert that we live in an era of sentencing guidelines'[34] like the United States or the Commonwealth jurisdictions.

Guideline judgments have gained acceptance and form an integral part of the legal framework. The Judicial Council Act 2019[35] paves the way for the implementation of formal sentencing guidelines. This legislation creates the Sentencing Guidelines and Information Committee (SGIC) within the framework of the Judicial Council. The Judicial Council is responsible for upholding standards of conduct among judges and providing ongoing education. The inclusion of provisions establishing the SGIC in the legislation came as a surprise during the late stages of its passage.[36]

Section 23 (2) of the 2019 Act gives the SGIC powers to prepare and submit to the Council draft sentencing guidelines and make any amendments to those guidelines. The SGIC then monitors the operation of the guidelines and collects

---

[27] Ibid, p. 37 para 17.

[28] *DPP v Ryan* ILRM 2014 98.

[29] *DPP v Fitzgibbon* ILRM 2014 116.

[30] *DPP v Ryan.*

[31] *DPP v Fitzgibbon.*

[32] *DPP v Casey* IECA 2018 121.

[33] The Court of Appeal Act (2014).

[34] O'Malley (2019).

[35] Judicial Council Act (2019).

[36] O'Malley (2019), p. 10.

information on sentences imposed by the courts.[37] This information is then disseminated to members of the judiciary and 'persons other than judges'.[38] Where a court departs from the sentencing guidelines, the reasons for departure must be stated in its decision. Section 92 of the legislation states:

> A court shall, in imposing a sentence, have regard to sentencing guidelines relevant to the proceedings before it, unless the court is satisfied that to do so would be contrary to the interests of justice and the reasons it is so satisfied shall be stated by the court in its decision.[39]

The Sentencing Guidelines of the Judicial Council outline the provision of guidance in court judgments, which can be categorised as either 'formal' or 'informal'.[40] The court must explicitly state its intention to offer guidance and provide advance notice in such cases. The court reviews sentencing for an entire offence or a class of offences and allows parties to submit their arguments on aspects of sentencing beyond the facts of the case. These formal guideline judgments may incorporate multiple appeals to gather a wider range of views. While individual decisions are still made, the judgment in one of the cases serves to provide guidance for the future. Formal guidance tends to be descriptive, synthesising previous decisions and suggesting indicative ranges for assessing gravity and considering aggravating or mitigating circumstances. On the other hand, informal guidance is less structured. It may not involve advance notice or submissions beyond the case at hand. It may only address specific aspects of the offence rather than the entire offence and may not be comprehensive in identifying relevant factors. Informal guidance is even more 'bottom-up' in its approach, relying on patterns observed in previous cases.[41]

4.3.1 Consistency

The Judicial Council Act 2019 acknowledges that the diversity in sentencing practices is not solely due to the absence of structured guidelines. The Act emphasises the importance of education and establishes a Judicial Studies Committee[42] responsible for facilitating ongoing education and training. The legislation demonstrates prescience by assigning the Committee regulatory responsibilities, including the possibility of investigating complaints in the judicial realm.[43] The legislation aims to provide a greater standard of uniformity to District Court sentencing, whilst

---

[37] It remains to be seen how effective this will be though as the lower courts would be very difficult to monitor in an exhaustive or comprehensive way.

[38] Judicial Council Act (2019).

[39] Ibid, s92.

[40] The Judicial Council (2021), p. 8.

[41] *DPP v. O'Sullivan* IECA 2020 331 (Edwards J).

[42] The Judicial Council (2021), p. 8.

[43] Ibid.

maintaining the independence of the judiciary. Section 23(2) of the 2019 legislation gives a Sentencing Committee the power to draft sentencing guidelines and to 'conduct research on sentences imposed by the courts'.[44] However, a fundamental lack of communication between courts in urban and rural jurisdictions has been cited as a fundamental source of sentencing inconsistency and diversity.[45]

It is difficult to determine the sentencing approach used in lower courts without having an accurate understanding of the decision-making procedures in these courts. Tonry suggests that sentencing reforms should be customised to suit the specific requirements of each jurisdiction and that they should consider the punishment context for which they are developed.[46] In examining the policy which redirects individuals from imprisonment, the decision-making processes of STPS sentencing is examined.

In the 1990s, the Law Reform Commission carried out a detailed study and evaluation of the sentencing system in Ireland.[47] The Commission referred to a Canadian study carried out by Palys and Divorski,[48] in which different judges were asked to pass sentence in the same cases and to comment on the reasons for their conclusions. Considerable differences were found in the approach of individual judges when sentencing the same case, and the Law Reform Commission concluded that:

> We have every reason to believe that in Ireland, *a fortiori*, considering the similarities in sentencing structure, similar inconsistencies would be displayed here. Intuitively, the existence of inconsistency here is a certainty.[49]

The principle of consistency traditionally dictates that similar cases should be treated similarly, while different cases should be treated differently. Conversely, inconsistency occurs when similar cases receive different treatments and different cases are handled in the same manner. Consistency refers to consistency of approach rather than consistency of outcomes. The Halliday Report observed that consistency is viewed as like cases resulting in like outcomes.[50] The current definition is inadequate as it does not account for the diversity of circumstances in criminal cases, potentially leading to similar outcomes being prioritised, regardless of the specific circumstances. A more effective approach is to seek consistent application of explicit principles and standards, acknowledging that these may result in justifiably disparate outcomes.[51] One commentator argues that:

[44] Judicial Council Act (2019).

[45] *DPP v. O'Sullivan* (Edwards J).

[46] Judicial Council Act (2019).

[47] Law Reform Commission (1993); Law Reform Commission (1996).

[48] Palys and Divorski (1986).

[49] Law Reform Commission (1993), s2.32.

[50] Home Office (2001).

[51] Ibid, para 2.21.

> Consistency is undoubtedly an important value. But what I want to argue…is that sentencing reform, whether through guidelines or any other strategy, is of little value unless it produces a sentencing system that is moderate, proportionate and constructive, as well as consistent.[52]

The need for a consistent outcome becomes obvious when one considers the numerous factors which may influence sentencers.[53] Since the 1990s, small-scale empirical studies have focused on specific aspects of sentencing in the lower courts. A 2008 study centred on specific questions using structured interviews and vignettes to discover whether sentencing had become more punitive. The researcher examined whether judges used a tariff 'which might interfere with the discretionary nature of sentencing'.[54] They were then encouraged to explain how sentencing occurs in the absence of any tariff system.[55] The study concluded that sentencing inconsistencies were related to

> the seriousness of the case, differences in the weight judges attached to aggravating and mitigating factors and, at least in relation to District Court judges, to differences in judicial views regarding the efficacy and appropriateness of various penalties.[56]

The study found that judges rarely referred to proportionality or sentencing guidelines when determining sentences. The results also highlighted how deeply judges have internalised any philosophy of individualised sentencing.[57] It appeared that, while judges may not necessarily devalue consistency, they appeared to prioritise the 'just' sentence. Although not explicitly stated, the judiciary's own descriptions of sentencing seem to align with the 'instinctive synthesis' method used by the Australian judiciary.[58] This method, where judges rely on their experience to determine sentences within a framework of proportionality. This involves a holistic assessment of the case, drawing on judicial intuition and expertise to achieve a fair and appropriate outcome.[59]

In relation to monitoring sentencing in the lower courts, the Irish state continues to rely on studies that are conducted on a small scale. Despite its small scope, Judge David Riordan's research also provides valuable insights into the sentencing practices of lower courts. As a member of the judiciary himself, and therefore with access to a qualitatively elite group of fellow judges, he was in a unique position to ask his colleague judges to give sentencing examples from their own experience.[60] His

---

[52] O'Malley (2023).

[53] O'Malley (2006), p. 46.

[54] Maguire (2008), p. 115.

[55] Ibid, p. 114.

[56] Ibid, p. 34.

[57] Ibid, p. 50.

[58] Ibid, p. 34. The instinctual synthesis approach to sentencing involves judges considering all the pertinent factors of a case, including the nature of the offence and the offender's circumstances, and then arriving at a decision on the suitable sentence without specifying the exact importance given to particular factors or sets of factors.

[59] Traynor and Potas (2002).

[60] Riordan (2009).

study concluded that the purpose for which imprisonment or CSOs are deployed 'find their meaning essentially in the practices of the judges themselves as opposed to any statutory or theoretical claims upon their use or purpose.' This suggests that judges tend to rely on their own judgment and experience to guide the sentences they impose, finding this approach sufficient without needing to adhere strictly to legal statutes or theoretical guidelines.[61] These two small studies both highlight a certain inconsistency in sentencing methods that guidelines could help to standardise. However, the implementation of such guidelines in Ireland is more complex than it might initially seem.

Whilst this legislation appears to have been welcomed across the political and legal spectrum in the hope that it will reduce sentence disparity,[62] sentencing guidelines must have as their foundation robust sentencing information. The availability of sentencing information for the District and Circuit Court remains 'undesirably sparse'.[63] However, there has now been 'a welcome increase in the availability of data... in respect of some offences'.[64] However, this information is not as transparent or exhaustive as it is required to be for the purposes of sentencing guidance.[65]

The only large-scale qualitative data collection of sentencing information was the Irish Sentencing Information System Pilot in 2007.[66] However, there were significant limitations to this pilot. The data collected was still a small, unrepresentative sample of sentences imposed in the jurisdiction. Just under 1000 sentences were collected from three locations (the urban areas of Dublin, Cork, and Limerick). The

[61] Ibid, Abstract (iv) The sentencing 'practices of the judge's themselves', adequately guided the sanctions imposed, as opposed to 'any statutory or theoretical claims upon their use or purpose'., p. 6.

[62] *DPP v Mahon* 2 ILRM 2019 where the court adopted a four-fold categorisation of assault manslaughter. This approach was like the English Sentencing Council's Definitive Guideline on Manslaughter, which became effective on 1 November 2018, where a similar four-fold classification for unlawful act manslaughter was adopted.

[63] The Judicial Council (2021), p. 4.

[64] Ibid, p. 4.

[65] Ibid.

[66] Conroy and Gunning (2009): This was a pilot project designed to provide a generalised image of how sentencing is conducted in the lower courts throughout the country. Chief Justice Susan Denham Researchers undertook an initial data collection phase between 2007 and 2009 and a second in 2013. Researchers would attend sentencing hearings on a regular basis and gather information on sentences. The pilot began in Dublin and was extended to Cork, two of the busiest court districts in Ireland. They collected data by attending the District and the Circuit Courts in selected areas, using a template to record information on the sentences imposed. The result was a database which was 'entirely descriptive in nature' and this was intended to be used as a searchable reference tool for members of the judiciary. It was hoped that this database might be of use to judges 'in forming a preliminary view on a sentence 'where in the past no such assistance might have been available' or to assist with consistency in sentencing across different courts: 'to gather comprehensive information on the various sentences that have been imposed in the past in respect of a particular offence, with the objective of locating future offences somewhere on the spectrum of sentences previously imposed'.

collected sentences still only represented a snapshot of how a limited number of judges sentenced a certain number of offences over a short period and thus provides 'no insight into the issue of inconsistency in sentencing'.[67] It was by no means a true and comprehensive reflection of sentencing throughout Ireland because of the small sample size and because of the variation in judicial commentary collected by the researchers.[68] However, despite its limitations with regard to this being a prescriptive or generalisable tool, it was still a valuable step in increasing the understanding of sentencing. One commentator noted how if 'the Central Statistics Office are involved in either the development of the system or the collection of sentencing information in the future. It could be developed into an excellent tool for understanding what influences sentencing'.[69]

A decade later, in 2017, the state media provider, RTÉ, conducted sentencing research in the country's 24 District Courts with the aim of assessing the consistency of sentencing within the criminal justice system.[70] The research monitored the percentage of prison sentences, CSOs, and fines imposed in each of the 24 areas. The findings revealed significant variations in sentencing practices among different districts. The researchers found these disparities in sentencing outcomes striking. For instance, the percentage of prison sentences ranged from 1.4% to 9.1%, indicating a substantial difference in the use of imprisonment as a punitive measure. Similarly, the proportion of CSOs varied between 0.4% and 2.1% of all orders made in certain court districts. Furthermore, the distribution of fines also exhibited significant inconsistency, representing only 13.9% of orders in one district but accounting for 35.6% in another.

At the time of writing, the government has still not conducted a large-scale study in the courts to comprehensively assess the extent of sentencing disparity. The variations identified in the RTE research underscores the need for greater structure and guidance in the sentencing process. These findings highlight the importance of addressing the issue of sentencing disparity and promoting consistency in sentencing across the Irish courts. It emphasises the significance of developing sentencing guidelines or frameworks that can provide judges with clear guidance on appropriate sentencing outcomes. Such guidelines have the potential to enhance transparency, fairness, and public confidence in the criminal justice system by promoting more consistent and predictable sentencing decisions.[71]

In 2013, the Law Reform Commission once again noted evidence of inconsistency in Irish sentencing practices.[72] This report concluded that 'the degree of inconsistency in sentencing outcomes varied according to the seriousness of the

[67] Eoin and Marder (2021), p. 107.

[68] Ibid, p. 107.

[69] Rogan (2012), p. 24.

[70] RTE (2017).

[71] Law Reform Commission (June 2013), 1.103.

[72] Ibid, 1.103; Maguire (2010), p. 31; Hamilton (2005).

offence'.[73] It noted how sentencing outcomes were most consistent for the most serious cases, whereas they were least consistent for the least serious cases. In less serious cases, judges may consider a range of alternative sentencing options, such as diversion programs, community service, or fines, in addition to imprisonment. These alternative options allow for greater flexibility but also introduce more subjectivity into the sentencing process, potentially leading to variations in outcomes.

4.3.2 *Proportionality*

Although traditionally unstructured by guidelines, the Irish system does have judicially developed principles, and a trial judge's failure to apply these principles can be considered an appealable error.[74] Despite this, the broad judicial discretion available has led some commentators to describe the sentencing system as a random 'lottery.'[75] However, this judicial discretion offers the advantage of increased flexibility, particularly in minor offence cases, allowing judges to fine-tune sentences. The principle of proportionality ensures individual fairness of outcome, allowing that the personal circumstances of the offender must be taken into consideration by the court.[76] However, the subjective nature of this 'fine-tuning' by judges (in the lower courts at least) has left the system open to criticism.[77] Some critics of the proportionality principle argue that this can lead to inconsistency of approach, not just inconsistency of outcome.[78]

When sentencing, the courts are encouraged to adopt a two-step approach. Initially, a court must assess the seriousness of the offence to establish an appropriate 'starting point'. Then the court should make any necessary reductions to account for any mitigating factors related to the offender's circumstances, such as a guilty plea. The higher courts have emphasised that any mitigation should be applied to the initially determined proportionate sentence rather than the maximum sentence. An offence may have a maximum sentence, and the court might determine that the offence is of moderate seriousness, suggesting a starting point of mid-way. However, considering mitigating factors, the final sentence might be reduced to somewhere below the half-way point.

While consistency in sentencing outcomes is always desirable, the consistency of approach can vary due to judicial discretion, which is essential for delivering

[73] Law Reform Commission (June 2013), 1.106;Maguire (2010), p. 31.

[74] Padfield et al. (2010), O'Malley, Chapter 10, p. 238.

[75] RTE (2004).

[76] *DPP v M [1994] 3 IR 306.*

[77] This is particularly evident in the lower courts, where decisions are made verbally and ex parte. In contrast, higher courts tend to exhibit less subjectivity due to the necessity for more detailed reasoning.

[78] Maguire (2010); Hamilton (2005); O'Hara and Rogan (2015); O'Nolan (2013).

individualised justice. Each case is unique and requires careful consideration of its specific circumstances and the offender's background. Striking the right balance between proportionality and individualisation is a complex challenge that the criminal justice system must navigate. Some scholars argue that consistency should not seek comparisons between two (or more) 'similar' cases and instead focus upon an application of sentencing principles relevant to the determination of sentence.[79] Whereas Lydon argues that 'inconsistency cannot be explained by legitimate factors such as crime rate or offence seriousness',[80] O'Malley contends that consistency holds value and that its significance lies in fostering distributive justice, guaranteeing equitable treatment of comparable cases.[81] Furthermore, he argues that a sentencing system perceived as consistent is more likely to inspire public confidence compared to an inconsistent one. Nonetheless, the goal should extend beyond mere consistency of outcome.[82]

The sentence chosen by a judge should optimally fulfil the objectives of sentencing relevant to each case while consistently upholding the core principles of fairness and proportionality. Proportionality mandates that a sentence must correspond to the severity of the offence and the specific circumstances of the offender.[83] The former Court of Criminal Appeal regarded it as:

> the duty of the Courts to pass what are the appropriate sentences in each case having regard to the particular circumstances of that case – not only regarding the particular crime but in regard to the particular criminal.[84]

In a constitutional democracy, the criminal justice system should be guided by fundamental values such as legality, fairness, non-discrimination, rationality, and proportionality. Kahneman et al. believe that these rights and values may be inadequately protected or respected in a system where sentencing is akin to a random outcome.[85] O'Malley emphasises that the punishment imposed on an offender should not significantly differ based on the judge presiding over the case on any given day 'to any significant degree.'[86] While some variation in sentencing is inevitable, it should be minimised. O'Malley emphasises this phrase because he argues, the complete elimination of all sentencing variation through fixed penalties would create more problems than it solves. O'Malley instead follows the wisdom of Hart and sees 'discretion as a power of discernment.[87] Hart notes

[79] Harris (2022), p. 44.

[80] Ibid, Abstract 'the notion of comparing 'like' cases is rejected as simplistic, impractical, and unprincipled'.

[81] O'Malley (2023), p. 1.

[82] Ibid.

[83] O'Malley (2009), para 22.02; *Attorney General v Poyning (1972) IR 402* 1972.

[84] *Attorney General v O'Driscoll* Frewen 1972 351.

[85] Kahneman et al. (2021).

[86] O'Malley (2023), p. 6.

[87] Ibid, p. 8.

Rather, it is about the exercise of practical wisdom, which calls for rationality and objectivity in decision-making, even where several outcomes are legitimately available.[88]

4.3.3 Judicial Discretion

Judicial discretion can be a polarising concept.[89] Where one perspective argues that discretion is essential for the fair resolution of a criminal case, enabling the judge to address the specific details of the offence and the offender the opposing view contends that discretion leads to inconsistency and disorder, and therefore should be strictly regulated. There may be validity in both viewpoints. In judicial descriptions of sentencing and when asked to pass sentence, District Court judges rarely mention the principle of proportionality.[90] Maguire argues that this 'illustrates the extraordinary extent to which judges internalised the philosophy of individualised sentencing.'[91] This reflects the view of the Supreme Court expressed in *Tiernan*[92] that judges must be free to tailor sentences to the circumstances of each case according to their own process of discernment. This process may have been very consistent once, when the judiciary were a more homogenous cohort, but the judiciary are changing.[93]

Until relatively recently in Ireland, the Irish judiciary comprised a more homogenous group which was comprised of a majority of older males.[94] Despite the judicial oath to remain impartial, judges are still human and possess subjective characteristics.[95] Judicial decisions can, quite understandably, be influenced by the particular worldview of the presiding judge.[96] One commentator note how influencing factors can be divided into four categories:[97] the views that sentencers may have regarding the facts of the case, the views that sentencers may have regarding the

[88] Herbert LA Hart (2013).

[89] Harris (2022), Chapter 3, p. 44.

[90] Maguire (2008), p. 50.

[91] Ibid, p. 50.

[92] *DPP v Tiernan.*

[93] Oireachtas Library & Research Service (2019).

[94] Ibid.

[95] Barry (2022).

[96] Fischman and Law (2009).

[97] Ashworth (2010).

principles of sentencing,[98] views regarding crime and punishment[99] and the demographic features of sentencers.[100]

Despite this variability, the sentence is predominantly driven by the court's assessment of the harm and culpability in the offence as committed by the offender under the constraints of proportionality and precedence. When determining the seriousness of retributively significant case characteristics, a certain degree of variability is inevitable. For instance, Judge A might assess one case as scoring low on a scale of seriousness, warranting a sentence of two years' imprisonment, whereas Judge B might evaluate it as scoring medium, resulting in a sentence of four. It appears that such inconsistencies in the literal sense of the term is normatively acceptable.[101] Judges all have the 'human factor' and research with members of the judiciary illustrates the fact that no two judges' sentence in the same way.[102] This is bound to give rise to a degree of inconsistency or perceived impartiality in sentencing.[103]

However, the notion of judicial impartiality is not simply impartiality applied to the judicial function, with ideas of judging equally, fairly, without bias or prejudice, and without being personally involved or invested in the outcome of a case. Judges perform their function in complex and dynamic environments. There are layers of the judicial role which make the scope of judicial impartiality more complex.[104]

Despite the fact that the judges are autonomous in their decision-making, according to Article 35.2 of the Constitution, they are bound by the Reports of the Law Reform Commission and the Reports on Sentencing.[105] For example, they are required to adhere to the principle of parsimony in sentencing, provides that any custodial sentence imposed must be for the shortest period which is commensurate with the seriousness of the offence.[106]

---

[98] In the second category are the gravity of offences; the aims, effectiveness and relative severity of the available types of sentences; the general principles of sentencing; and the relative weight of aggravating and mitigating factors.

[99] In the third category are views regarding the aims of sentencing; the causes of crime; and the function of courts passing sentence.

[100] In this category, Ashworth lists age, social class, occupation, urban or rural background, race, gender, religion, and political allegiance.

[101] Harris (2022), p. 46.

[102] Maguire (2008), p. 39.

[103] Ibid, p. 39.

[104] Charles Gardner Geyh (2013) offers a theoretical framework for understanding the multi-faceted nature of judicial impartiality. He argues that judicial impartiality possesses three dimensions: (i) a procedural dimension, (ii) an ethical dimension, and (iii) a political dimension. Each dimension concerns judicial impartiality as it applies to three different audiences: the procedural dimension concerns judicial impartiality for parties to litigation, the ethical dimension is for judges themselves, and the political dimension concerns judicial impartiality for the body politic and the wider public.

[105] Law Reform Commission (1996); Law Reform Commission (June 2013).

[106] Law Reform Commission (1996), 2.52.

Judges select as their starting point a penalty from the lower end of the range of 'just' sentence and only increase this if and when another guiding principle necessitates increased severity. This theory has been criticised on the basis that it places too much trust in the hands of judges to achieve 'mercy'. Observers note how parsimony enables 'other guiding principles, such as deterrence, to increase punishment.'[107] Von Hirsch[108] and Ashworth,[109] who are advocates of the 'just deserts' sentencing theory, agree that the overall levels of sentencing severity in the Western world should be reduced. They believe that, instead of allowing other guiding principles to increase punishment, there should be reduction of statutory maxima for all offences.[110] O'Malley notes:

> One major problem with District Court sentencing is that there is no general consensus, let alone any formal guideline, on custody thresholds. Judges of that court seem to vary enormously in their assessment of the circumstances in which custodial sentences are warranted, particularly for public order, minor assault, and theft offences. Add to this the lack of any settled policy on the use of short sentences generally and the result is that, in all probability, many offenders are needlessly being sent to prison.[111]

In England and Wales, the principle of parsimony is enshrined in statute. The Sentencing Act 2020[112] is a method of providing structure to sentencing discretion. Provisions of this legislation offer structure when applying not only the principle of parsimony[113] but also when assessing offence seriousness,[114] for community order and custody thresholds.[115] Although the principle of parsimony is not enshrined in Irish statute, the judiciary are nonetheless obligated to adhere to it due to the Law Reform Commission's recommendations.[116] These recommendations outline the philosophy, practice, and legal framework of sentencing, providing guidelines that must be followed.

While Ireland is not a guideline jurisdiction and judges have discretion, the nature of that discretion appears to be narrower than at first glance, especially in the lower courts. However, from the mid-1970s, researchers have been exploring correlations between judges' personal and demographic characteristics and their decision-making.[117] Scholarship on judicial behaviour and decision-making is becoming increasingly broad in scope. To date, research on judicial sentencing has traditionally focused on the various factors which have the potential to influence that sentencing

---

[107] Maguire (2014), p. 67.

[108] Von Hirsch (1991).

[109] Von Hirsch and Ashworth (2005).

[110] Ibid.

[111] O'Malley (2009), para 2.21.

[112] The Sentencing Act (UK)(2020).

[113] Ibid, s231.

[114] Ibid, s63.

[115] Ibid, s204 (community order) and s230 (custody thresholds).

[116] Law Reform Commission (1996); Law Reform Commission (June 2013).

[117] Darbyshire (2011); Barry (2020).

decision: the characteristics and social background of the judge,[118] the political persuasion of the judge,[119] the sentencing methodology used[120] or the psychology behind the decision.[121] Research in 2019 carried out with the Irish judiciary unsurprisingly found that 'judges are human, and susceptible to error in the same way everyone else is.'[122] The findings are important for properly understanding the true meaning and nature of judicial impartiality. More modern research measures the degree to which specific, extraneous, non-legal factors can affect judges' behaviour and decision-making. Geyh notes that this allows an objective view of what is 'impartial enough.'[123] Judicial impartiality, he explains, is more of a principle that judges seek to achieve rather than realistically attain.[124]

4.4 Impact of Unstructured Sentencing

The lack of a uniform policy or guideline on custody thresholds for District Court sentencing has resulted in judges varying significantly in their opinions on when custodial sentences are necessary, particularly for minor offences such as public order, minor assault, and theft. The absence of a clear policy regarding the implementation of STPS leads to a potential lack of consistency in both the outcomes and approaches of such sentencing. The sentencing practices observed in lower courts encompass various unknown factors that may not be effectively addressed through gender-specific policy interventions aimed at STPS recipients. However, certain aspects of these practices are ascertainable.

When considering an STPS for a woman, several factors must be considered. Firstly, there must be a suitable programme of work available. According to the Criminal Justice (Community Service) Act 2011,[125] a court cannot impose a CSO unless it is satisfied, after reviewing the offender's circumstances and a report from the probation officer, that the offender is also suitable and able for the work. Furthermore, it is essential that the offender consents to performing the community service work. This ensures that the decision is both appropriate for the offender's situation and agreed upon by the offender herself.

Prior to the introduction of the Fines (Payment and Recovery) Act 2014, offenders receiving an STPS for defaulting on fines typically faced a very short period in prison, often resulting in no actual time spent in custody. Following the

[118] Danziger et al. (2011); Gibson (1978).

[119] Schanzenbach and Tiller (2008).

[120] Traynor and Potas (2002).

[121] Lovegrove (1999).

[122] Barry (2022), p. 43.

[123] Geyh (2013), p. 494.

[124] Ibid, p. 493.

[125] Criminal Justice (Community Service) (Amendment) Act (2011).

2014 Act, default of fine has been replaced by a CSO. This could be discharged in a matter of hours but might also impose a more burdensome sanction, especially if it requires a substantial number of hours of work and travel each day.

4.5 Sentencing Guidance and Guidelines in England and Wales

Irish legislation has been significantly influenced by neighbouring jurisdictions, particularly England and Wales, which share many structural similarities in their criminal justice systems. While each jurisdiction operates within its own distinct legal framework, evaluating the performance of neighbouring systems often provides valuable comparative insights. Although domestic policy initiatives in the field of justice are no longer coordinated with Westminster, they frequently draw inspiration from successful practices and policies implemented there. England and Wales are especially pertinent for comparison due to their geographic proximity and the historical influence of Westminster laws, which Ireland inherited upon gaining independence in 1922.

Until the early 1980s, the sentencing systems in England and Wales were like that of Ireland, with courts exercising discretion in determining sentences based on statutory maximums. Guidance on sentencing was primarily derived from common law principles and court judgments. However, the two systems began to diverge in the 1980s as England and Wales adopted a more structured approach to sentencing. The recent history of sentencing guidance in England and Wales can be divided into four distinct eras: the guideline judgment era, the Sentencing Advisory Panel era, the Sentencing Guidelines Council era, and the Sentencing Council era.

In the mid-1970's, there was some 'judicial experimentation'[126] with guideline judgments when the Court of Appeal moved beyond the offences before it and proposed sentence levels for different varieties of the offences.[127] The first cases involved a sentence appeal for sexual offences. Although future courts also went on to deliver guideline judgments for drug offences and causing death by dangerous driving, the Lord Chief Justice lacked staff to assist in the preparation of these judgments. This resulted in a relatively infrequent issuance of guideline judgments during the 1980s and 1990s.[128]

The next era of sentencing guidance in England and Wales commenced with the establishment of the Sentencing Advisory Panel under the Crime and Disorder Act 1998.[129] This Panel, consisting of fourteen members appointed by the Lord Chancellor, provided advice and research to the Court of Appeal when framing or revising

[126] Ashworth and Roberts (2013), p. 3.

[127] *R v Willis* Cr App R 1974 146; *R v Taylor, Roberts and Simons* 64 Cr App R 182 1977.

[128] Ashworth and Roberts (2013).

[129] The Crime and Disorder Act (1998), s81.

sentencing guidelines.[130] The Court of Appeal was required to seek advice from the Panel before developing guidelines, and the Panel could also propose the formulation of guidelines for specific categories of offences.[131]

The establishment of the Sentencing Guidelines Council (SGC) under the Criminal Justice Act 2003[132] marked the beginning of the third era of modern English sentencing. Prior to this, the Sentencing Advisory Panel provided its advice directly to the Court of Appeal. The creation of the SGC was a response to the Halliday Report,[133] which recommended the development of comprehensive sentencing guidance. The SGC consisted of the Lord Chief Justice, seven judicial members, and four non-judicial members. The establishment of the SGC under the 2003 legislation marked a significant turning point in English sentencing law, as the creation of sentencing guidelines was assigned to a body other than a court.[134] Additionally, the 2003 Act required every court to have regard to any relevant guidelines when sentencing an offender or exercising any other sentencing function. English courts are now usually required to follow sentencing guidelines.

The Criminal Justice Act 2003[135] introduced a duty for courts to consider the sentencing guidelines produced by the SGC. Subsequently, the Coroners and Justice Act 2009[136] required courts to follow Sentencing Council guidelines unless it would be contrary to the interests of justice to do so. Following the guidelines means that if an offence-specific guideline exists, the court must impose a sentence within the specified offence range. In cases where guidelines have different categories, the court must determine which category best matches the case to establish the appropriate starting point and range. However, the Act clarifies that there is no separate duty to impose a sentence within the category range. Thus, if the court has followed the required steps outlined in the guideline, it has fulfilled its statutory duty by imposing a sentence within the broader offence range, rather than a specific category range. This provision was intended to address initial judicial resistance to the imposition of a strict 'duty to follow' the guidelines.

The Coroners and Justice Act 2009 introduced various obligations for the Council in addition to its primary role of developing sentencing guidelines.[137] The Sentencing Council was tasked with not only monitoring but also assessing the implementation and impact of its guidelines. This included examining the factors that influenced court sentencing decisions, evaluating the effect of the guidelines on

[130] Ashworth and Roberts (2013), Chapter 2.

[131] Over the next few years, the Panel shaped Court of Appeal guidelines on various offences, including domestic burglary, causing death by dangerous driving, rape, child pornography, possession of offensive weapons, and environmental offences, among others.

[132] Criminal Justice Act (England and Wales) (2003).

[133] Home Office (2001).

[134] O'Malley (2019), p. 8.

[135] Criminal Justice Act (England and Wales) (2003), s172.

[136] The Coroners and Justice Act (2009), s125.

[137] Ibid.

promoting consistency in sentencing, and assessing their impact on public confidence in the criminal justice system. These additional responsibilities aimed to ensure that the Council plays a comprehensive role in shaping and evaluating sentencing practices, ultimately promoting transparency, consistency, and public trust in the criminal justice system.[138] However, consulting with the public can be one 'notable weakness'[139] in this system. In addition, the guidelines system has become complex with its piecemeal approach of dealing with individual offence groups and occasionally categories in isolation.[140]

When developing guidelines, the Sentencing Council is required to consider several key factors. These include the sentences handed down by courts in England and Wales for similar offences, with the aim of promoting consistency in sentencing. The Council also considers the impact of sentencing decisions on victims, recognising the need to address their concerns and provide appropriate measures of justice. Another important consideration is the promotion of public confidence in the criminal justice system, ensuring that sentencing is perceived as fair and proportionate.

4.6 Sentencing Reform and Inconsistencies

There was little sentencing reform in Ireland until the 1990s, which was later than in many other countries.[141] The Law Reform Commission made some recommendations but they were largely not implemented.[142] For the most part, the legislature has pursued a policy of non-intervention in the formulation of sentencing policy, resulting in a perception of judicial ownership of sentencing.[143] As a result, the system of sentencing in Ireland has remained largely unchanged until the late 2010s, with the exception of some mandatory minimum sentences for drug and organised crime offences.[144]

A mandatory minimum sentence that had been imposed for five years for a second firearms offence was struck down in the Supreme Court in the case of *Ellis v Minister for Justice and Equality*[145] and was subsequently repealed with the Criminal Justice (Amendment) Act in 2021.[146] The court found that it is not

[138] Hough and Jacobson (2008).

[139] Ibid, p. 11.

[140] Ibid, p. 11.

[141] Maguire and Carr (2017).

[142] Law Reform Commission (1993).

[143] O'Malley (2013).

[144] Bacik (2001); Maguire (2016) Mandatory minimum sentences for repeat firearms offences were ruled unconstitutional in the case of Ellis v Minister for Justice [2019] IESC 30.

[145] *Ellis v Minister for Justice and Equality* IESC 2019 30.

[146] Criminal Justice (Amendment) Act (2021).

constitutionally permissible for the Oireachtas to specify a mandatory minimum sentence that only applies to a limited class of persons, namely, those who have committed a second or subsequent offence for one or more listed offences. The court held that the application of a mandatory minimum sentence to a distinct category of persons in such cases amounted to the administration of justice and, under Article 34 of the Constitution, justice may only be administered by the courts, not by the Oireachtas.[147]

The 1996 Law Reform Commission Report stressed that judges must think very carefully if deciding on a lighter punishment because they think the person will do well when they go back to society.[148] The report noted how more lenient punishments can be potentially contrary to the 'just deserts' system of fairness as it is contrary to proportionality, which is supposed to punish based on the gravity of the offence as committed by the offender, not how well they will do if they are given a chance.

> [I]f the likelihood of successful re-integration into society is seen to be a good reason for allowing mitigation of sentence then deserts are replaced at the mitigation stage by rehabilitative principles and the whole point of having a deserts sentencing system is overturned.[149]

The Law Reform Commission identifies deterrence, punishment, reformation and rehabilitation, reparation, and incapacitation as the justifying aims and principles of punishment distribution in the context of criminal justice sentencing.[150] Punishment can take various forms, including fines, community service, probation, imprisonment, and rehabilitation programs. The justifying aims and principles play an important role in determining the appropriate types and severity of punishments for different offences committed by diverse offenders.

Sentencing courts give priority to one or more of the aims of criminal sanctions, depending on the circumstances of each individual case. Thus, for instance, the aims of deterrence, punishment, and incapacitation will typically feature in cases involving more serious offences which attract more severe sanctions such as a term of imprisonment. The aims of reform, rehabilitation, and reparation are more appropriate for non-custodial alternatives as these attract less severe sanctions.[151]

It is difficult to gain knowledge about how judges sentence offenders in the lower courts as District Court judgments are usually unwritten and ex tempore. As such, the aims and principles of sentencing which the sentencer applies in each case in the lower courts can be unclear. The entire process lacks the clarity which guides sentencing in the higher courts. This is particularly disconcerting for STPS recipients, as the decision-making process behind such sentences is often not transparent

---

[147] (2021); the Ellis judgment only deals with mandatory minimum sentences for second or subsequent offences. This does not affect provisions in statute which provide for presumptive minimum sentences where there is judicial discretion.

[148] Law Reform Commission (1996), 3.14.

[149] Ibid, 3.14.

[150] Law Reform Commission (June 2013), p. ix.

[151] Ibid.

or documented in court records. When government policy aims to divert individuals away from custody, it can contribute to confusion and uncertainty surrounding the sentencing process.

Where an STPS is handed down in the lower courts, the sentencer appears to be guided by the sentencing aims of deterrence, punishment, and incapacitation.[152] Sentencing in the lower courts has been criticised as being 'ad hoc' and lacking in one consistent 'single, unifying sentencing aim.'[153] The Law Reform Commission in its Consultation Paper on Sentencing in 1993 was critical of the failure to prioritise sentencing aims in Ireland:

> Since one consideration may lead to a sentence dramatically different to that which another may lead to, like cases may be treated differently, and justifiably so, but there is nothing to determine which consideration is the correct one and which one should prevail. The result is inconsistency in sentencing in the way in which the criminal justice system deals with offenders, exhibiting what may be perceived as disparity, and undermining confidence in the criminal justice system.[154]

Sentencing for summary offences often takes place in either a bustling District Court or Circuit Court, where the proceedings are characterised by a fast-paced environment. In these settings, sentences are delivered as part of hastily prepared documentation and may be communicated by the presiding judge in a courtroom filled with noise and distractions. The nature of the court environment, with its limited time and high caseload, can contribute to a sense of urgency and potential challenges in ensuring clear and comprehensive communication of sentencing decisions.[155] It is not, as media scenes often depict, in a grand courtroom with a booming judicial voice clearly declaring the term of imprisonment and finalising the sentence with a gavel to signify the end of the case.[156]

The offender may be uncertain of the outcome until they are informed later, outside the courtroom by legal counsel or a social worker involved in their case. Furthermore, the range of possible disposals for summary offences can vary significantly. It is not limited to imprisonment alone but includes a wide spectrum of

---

[152] Hamilton (2005) 'When judges did speak of rationales, however, they demonstrated no coherent policy. Researchers observed judges in the Bridewell committing offenders to prison for the purposes of incapacitation ('can't let you roam the streets'); deterrence ('you need to be taught a lesson'); rehabilitation and retribution.'

[153] Maguire (2010), p. 19.

[154] Law Reform Commission (1993), p. 61.

[155] Prior to the Fines (Payment and Recovery) Act 2014, imprisonment was automatic for non-payment of fines. The number of STPS made decreased significantly after this legislation commenced in 2016.

[156] In the Republic of Ireland or the Commonwealth, gavels have never been used by judges despite many American-influenced media depictions.

sentencing options.[157] Maguire describes that a presiding judicial 'rule of thumb' relating to the offence committed usually prevails.[158] She observed how:

> The District Court in Ireland is known as the workhorse of the criminal justice system as it deals with most criminal cases proceeded against. Judges in the District Court may therefore be more likely than judges in other courts to develop 'rules of thumb' which amount to presumptions in favour of penalties for particular types of cases.[159]

The lack of a clear and consistent framework for sentencing decisions in the lower courts has resulted in significant inconsistency. A report by Carr and Maguire notes that "as a result of the legislature maintaining a 'hands-off' approach to sentencing reform, Ireland does not have a clear statutory framework of sentencing that sets out how custody and community sanctions should be used."[160] The absence of a robust framework contributes to the challenges and variations observed in sentencing decisions within the lower courts.[161]

The reliance on different factors and considerations by judges during the sentencing process can result in similar cases being sentenced in different ways, leading to a perception of disparity that undermines public trust in the criminal justice system. The absence of a clear and definitive framework for determining which considerations should take precedence can make the sentencing process appear subjective and arbitrary.

4.7 Conclusion

The lower courts, where most STPS are issued, are largely characterised by unstructured decisions, inconsistent approaches, and broad judicial discretion. However, judicially developed principles of proportionality, parsimony, and precedence guide the exercise of discretion in sentencing, ensuring that decisions are not made in a vacuum. In addition, each of the three branches of government plays a role in the sentencing process. The legislature decides upon the range of sentencing options that are available to the courts. The judiciary is responsible for the selection of sentence, when there is a selection to be made, and the executive is responsible for implementing sentences imposed by the courts.

---

[157] Disqualification; Probation Act Orders; Dismiss Probation Act; Fine; Imprisonment – Suspended; Community Service Order; Strike Out; Community Service Order – Consecutive; Imprisonment - Consecutive & Part Suspended; Imprisonment - Part Suspended; Imprisonment - Consecutive; Remand on Continuing Bail. Central Statistics Office 'Custodial/ Non-Custodial Outcomes'.

[158] Riordan (2009).

[159] Maguire (2010), p. 30.

[160] Ibid.

[161] Ibid.

This environment has been the backdrop for the introduction of the government's penal policies, which have also obscured the lack of diversion options for female STPS recipients. Although, in practice, expediency often leads to influence from the individual practices of each trial judge. In District Court cases involving low-level offenders with personal characteristics that could mitigate their offences, the Law Reform Commission allows consideration as an exception to the 'just deserts' principle. However, the rapid pace of proceedings might prevent judges from considering these factors. For minority groups, such exceptions are desirable for showing mercy in certain circumstances.

Under the new diversion policies, where a female STPS recipient falls within the custodial ambit but qualifies for CSO substitution, several conditions must be met.[162] Firstly, there must be suitable worksites available. Additionally, the woman herself must be considered suitable for work. Certain characteristics, such as childcare responsibilities or physical or psychological issues, may lead to her being seen as unable to participate in work. For this reason, diversion may be unsuccessful and can result in a STPS.

The Final Report of The Expert Group on the Probation and Welfare Service noted a decline in the number of CSOs issued by the courts in the mid-1990s, attributing this trend to the "perceived lack of suitability of community service for offenders with addictions".[163] This decline highlights the complexities and challenges faced in implementing community service as an alternative to custodial sentences, particularly for female offenders with specific needs and responsibilities.

Law

The Sentencing Act (UK) (2020)
The Crime and Disorder Act (1998)
Criminal Justice Act (England and Wales) (2003)
The Coroners and Justice Act (2009)
Criminal Justice (Community Service) (Amendment) Act (2011)
The Court of Appeal Act (2014)
Judicial Council Act (2019)
Criminal Justice (Amendment) Act (2021)

[162]Criminal Justice (Community Service) (Amendment) Act (2011), s3.
[163]Bacik (2000), p. 362 in O'Mahony (2002).

Online Resource

Seanad Éireann Debate -Wednesday, 3 Nov 2021 Vol. 279 No. 11 2021
Irish Prison Service, *Daily Prisoner Population*
Irish Prison Service, *Sentenced Committals Classified by Sentence Length & Gender from Years 2007 to 2020 - Irish Prison Service/ Home/ Information Centre/ Statistics & Information/ Yearly Statistics* (Irish Prison Service)
Oireachtas Library & Research Service, *Women and the Law* (2019)

Case Law

DPP v M [1994] 3 IR 306 171
Attorney General v O'Driscoll 1972Frewen179 (1)
Attorney General v Poyning (1972) IR 402 1972178
R v Willis 1974Cr App R180 (60)
R v Taylor, Roberts and Simons 197764 Cr App R 1821764
DPP v Tiernan 1988IR192 (1988)
DPP v D(W) 2008IR199 (1)
DPP v Fitzgibbon 2014ILRM212 (2)
DPP v Ryan 2014ILRM211 (2)
DPP v Casey 2018IECA217
DPP v Molloy 2018IECA IECA216
DPP v Mahon 20192 ILRM1751
Ellis v Minister for Justice and Equality 2019IESC218
DPP v. O'Sullivan 2020IECA224

References

Book

Ashworth A (2010) Sentencing and criminal justice. Cambridge University Press
Ashworth A, Roberts JV (2013) Sentencing guidelines: exploring the English model. OUP, Oxford
Barry BM (2020) How judges judge: empirical insights into judicial decision-making. Informa Law from Routledge
Darbyshire P (2011) Sitting in judgment: the working lives of judges. Hart Publishing
Harris L (2022) Achieving consistency in sentencing. Oxford University Press
Kahneman D, Sibony O, Sunstein CR (2021) Noise: a flaw in human judgment. Hachette UK
Maguire N (2016) Sentencing. The Routledge handbook of Irish criminology, Routledge
O'Mahony P (2002) Criminal justice in Ireland. Institute of Public Administration
O'Malley T (2006) Sentencing law and practice, 2nd edn. Thomson Round Hall
O'Malley T (2009) The criminal process, 1st edn. Roundhall

O'Malley T (2013) Living without guidelines. In: Andrew Ashworth JVR (ed) Sentencing guidelines. Oxford University Press
O'Nolan C (2013) The Irish district court: a social portrait. Cork University Press
Padfield N, Smit DVZ, Dünkel F (2010) Release from prison: European policy and practice. Taylor & Francis
Von Hirsch A, Ashworth A (2005) Proportionate sentencing: exploring the principles. Oxford Monographs on Criminal Law and Justice, Oxford University Press

Journal Article

Bacik I (2000) The practice of sentencing in the Irish courts. In: Criminal justice in Ireland. Institute of Public Administration, p 348
Barry BM (2022) Judicial impartiality in the Judicial Council Act 2019: challenges and opportunities
Conroy B, Gunning P (2009) The Irish sentencing information system (ISIS): a practical guide to a practical tool. Judicial Stud Inst J 1:38
Danziger S, Levav J, Avnaim-Pesso L (2011) Extraneous factors in judicial decisions. Proc Natl Acad Sci 108:6889
Eoin G, Marder ID (2021) Using data to design and monitor sentencing guidelines: the case of Ireland. Common Law World Rev 50:103
Fischman JB, Law DS (2009) What is judicial ideology, and how should we measure it. Wash Univ J Law Policy 29:133
Geiran V (2011) Defining what we do: the meaning of 'supervision' in probation. Irish Probat J, 8
Geyh CG (2013) The dimensions of judicial impartiality. Fla Law Rev 65:493
Gibson JL (1978) Judges' role orientations, attitudes, and decisions: an interactive model. Am Polit Sci Rev 72:911
Hamilton C (2005) Sentencing in the District Court: Here be dragons. Irish Crim Law J 15:9
Hart HL (2013) Discretion. Harv Law Rev 127:652
Hirsch AV (1991) Proportionality in the philosophy of punishment: From why punish to how much. Isr Law Rev 25:549
Lovegrove A (1999) Theoretical and methodological issues in the psychological study of judicial sentencing. Psychol Crime Law 5:217
Maguire N (2010) Consistency in sentencing. Judicial Stud Inst J 2:14
Maguire N (2014) When is prison a last resort? Definitional problems and judicial interpretations. Irish Crim Law J 24:62
O'Donnell I (2005) Putting prison in its place. Judicial Stud Inst J 5:54
O'Hara K, Rogan M (2015) Examining the use of community service orders as alternatives to short prison sentences in Ireland. Irish Probat J 12:22
O'Sullivan E, O'Donnell I (2003) Imprisonment and the crime rate in Ireland. Econ Soc Rev 34
Palys TS, Divorski S (1986) Explaining sentence disparity. Canadian J Criminol 28:347
Rogan M (2012) Rehabilitation, research, and reform: prison policy in Ireland. Irish Probat J 9:6
Schanzenbach MM, Tiller EH (2008) Reviewing the sentencing guidelines: judicial politics, empirical evidence, and reform. Univ Chicago Law Rev 75:715
Scott L (2017) Developments in Irish sentencing. Irish Judicial Stud J 1:1
Traynor S, Potas I (2002) Sentencing methodology: two-tiered or instinctive synthesis. Sentencing trends and issues 25

Report

Carmody P, McEvoy M (1996) A study of Irish female prisoners. Dublin

Home Office (2001) The Halliday report: making punishments work: review of the sentencing framework for England and wales
Hough M, Jacobson J (2008) Creating a sentencing commission for England and wales: an opportunity to address the prisons crisis
Irish Penal Reform Trust (2021) Progress in the penal system (PIPS)- the need for transparency. Dublin
Law Reform Commission (1993) Consultation paper on sentencing. Dublin
Law Reform Commission (1996) Report on sentencing. .Dublin
Law Reform Commission (June 2013) Report on Mandatory Sentences (LRC 108-2013). Dublin
Maguire N, Carr N (2017) Individualising justice: pre-sentence reports in the Irish Criminal Justice System
RTE (2004) Prime time investigates the district court. Prime Time. RTE 1
RTE (2017) Law & disorder: Court orders. Law & Disorder: Court Orders
The Judicial Council (2021) Sentencing guidelines and information committee – sentencing judgments

Conference Paper

Bacik I (2001) Crime and punishment- retribution or rehabilitation. The Bar Council of Ireland
O'Malley T (2019) Sentencing guidance and guidelines. Annual National Prosecutors' Conference
O'Malley T (2023) From practical wisdom to guidelines: the future of sentencing and regulation. Annual Distinguished Lecture
Rogan M (2013) Women in the criminal justice system in Ireland. Irish Penal Reform Trust, Seminar on Women in the Criminal Justice System

Thesis

Duignan S (2023) Evaluation of the effect of Irish penal policy on female short-term prison sentence recipients: the need for gender-specific policy. University of Galway
Maguire N (2008) Sentencing in Ireland: an exploration of the views, rationales, and sentencing practices of district and circuit court judges, Trinity College Dublin
Riordan D (2009) The role of the community service order and the suspended sentence in Ireland: a judicial perspective, (Ph.D). University College Cork

Chapter 5
Penal Policies and the Interaction with Women's Needs in the Justice System

5.1 Introduction

There were over sixteen thousand female STPS recipients from 2011–2020. The majority (85%) fell into the group that were sentenced to between 0–3 months custody. Only 9% of all recipients were sentenced to 3–6 months while 7% were sentenced to 6–12 months imprisonment.[1] This was not the cohort envisaged by s3 of the 2011 Act which purports to divert the 12 months or less STPS recipients away from custody.

> (1) (a) Where a court, by or before which an offender stands convicted, is of opinion that the appropriate sentence in respect of the offence of which the offender is convicted would, but for this Act, be one of imprisonment for a period of 12 months or less, the court shall, as an alternative to that sentence, consider whether to make an order (in this Act referred to as a 'community service order') in respect of the offender and the court may, if satisfied, in relation to the offender, that the provisions of section 4 have been complied with, make a community service order in accordance with this section.[2]

This chapter explores the effects of penal policy reforms on female STPS recipients, with a detailed examination of each principal reform strand. It focuses particularly on the Irish government's policies and their impact on female STPS recipients, underscoring the unsuccessful outcomes and the unnoticed rise in their numbers from 2011 to 2020. When focusing on the impact on female STPS recipients, this chapter draws on in-depth interviews with research on five Irish women who have engaged with the criminal justice system during this period and were diverted away from custody after being convicted of low-level offending.[3]

---

[1] Irish Prison Service.

[2] Criminal Justice (Community Service) (Amendment) Act (2011), s3.

[3] Duignan (2023).

S. Duignan, *Transforming Justice for Women*, Gender, Justice and Legal Feminism 3, https://doi.org/10.1007/978-3-031-82455-5_5

5.2 Impact of Irish Penal Policy Reforms on STPS Offenders

Despite a significant proportion of sentences imposed in Ireland being STPS, there remains a limited understanding of the circumstances surrounding their imposition or predictability.[4] Research shows that these sentences have punitive outcomes which offer little or no opportunity for rehabilitation,[5] and according to Central Statistics Office figures, they can often lead to re-offending.[6]

The STPS recipient will not remain in prison custody long enough to address addiction, homelessness or mental health issues that may be a part of their offending lifestyle.[7] It is not feasible for STPS recipients to engage with any health, education, or training facilities during a brief custodial stay, even where such facilities are available.[8] The brevity of their incarceration means there is insufficient time for the prison authorities to devise an adequate programme for integrated release back into the community.[9] STPS are primarily as a retributive measure to impose a significant punishment on convicted individuals and due to their limited duration, they are not appropriate method of rehabilitation or addressing the underlying factors that contribute to criminal behaviour.[10] Retributivism requires that an offence be met with a disposal proportionate to the seriousness of the offending, to punish the offender and to illustrate society's disapprobation. Another aim of imposing a STPS might be deterrence. This situation can be particularly detrimental for more vulnerable individuals who have complex needs and face various challenges, such as a history of trauma, substance abuse, and socio-economic disadvantage.[11]

A lack of sufficient support and resources during or after any incarceration period, however short, can further compound these challenges, leading to an increased likelihood of re-offending upon their release.[12] This situation can promote disparity where two similar cases receive different sentences because the sentencing judges opt for conflicting purposes of sentencing. One judge might focus on retribution and deterrence, handing down a STPS, while another might prioritise the purpose of

---

[4] Department of Justice (2022).

[5] Ibid.

[6] Central Statistics Office (2022).

[7] Prison Reform Trust (2011), p. 9.

[8] Ibid. p. 9.

[9] Irish Prison Service (ISM) Under ISM, 'a newly committed prisoner with a sentence of *one year or greater* is assessed by an ISM coordinator. A personal plan for the prisoner to complete during his/her time in prison is then drawn up. The plan is reviewed regularly between the ISM coordinator and the prisoner, with written reports feeding in from the relevant services and agencies.' (Irish Prison Service/ Home/ Prisoner Services/ Integrated Sentence Management).

[10] O'Malley (2010), p. 3.

[11] Carlen (1994); Seymour and Costello (2005); Irish Penal Reform Trust (2013).

[12] Irish Penal Reform Trust (2020).

rehabilitation, opting for a CSO. There is no judicial guidance on how to address such discrepancies.

The Central Statistics Office Prison Reoffending Statistics acknowledges that 60% of individuals who committed public order offences in 2019 reoffended after being released from prison.[13] Almost half of individuals who received a fine sentence in 2019 reoffended within one year.[14] Seventy percent of women released from prison in 2016 reoffended within three years, compared to only 62% of men.[15] Maguire notes that 'during the sentencing vignettes, several District Court judges explained that they usually send repeat offenders straight to prison, especially if the offender is unlikely to change his or her ways.'[16] In her study, she found that judges were less willing to extend chances to those with previous records. This was particularly evidenced during the sentencing vignettes, with few judges prepared to extend chances to those with numerous convictions. Persistence is perhaps a reason why District Court judges continue to impose custodial sentences on offenders who commit relatively minor and non-violent offences.[17]

One sentencer in Maguire's research cohort explained how a minor who persistently offends may be deemed to be unsuitable for a suspended sentence because if they 'received a number of chances in the past from the courts in the form of lenient penalties, he may come to believe that in effect he will never be sanctioned.'[18] This indicates a judge's perspective that an offender has a finite number of 'chances' before reaching the threshold for custody. As noted by Riordan in his research the following year, the point at which custody is considered a last resort may vary between different judges.[19]

Consequently, while the STPS aims to serve as a serious punishment, it may fail to adequately address the root cause of the individual's behaviour and even exacerbate this behaviour, thereby potentially resulting in more negative consequences because of the way the sentence is delivered in the District Court. While legal factors are significant, research indicates that judicial interpretations of an offender's character, attitude, and certain aspects of their personal and social circumstances, such as employment and relationship status, play a crucial role in determining whether to impose a custodial or non-custodial penalty. These subjective perceptions and considerations can have a substantial impact on sentencing decisions.[20]

Considering the lack of sentencing guidance available to Irish judges in the lower courts and, given the constitutionally mandated requirement for sentences to be proportionate to both the crime and the personal circumstances of the individual, a

---

[13] Central Statistics Office (2019).

[14] Ibid, Table 6 illustrates how 23.2% of women are still imprisoned for fine default.

[15] Ibid.

[16] Maguire (2014), p. 13.

[17] Ibid.

[18] Ibid, p. 15.

[19] Riordan (2009).

[20] Tombs and Jagger (2006); Millie et al. (2007); Maguire (2008).

key question surrounds the extent to which judges rely upon pre-sentence reports as a form of guidance when sentencing.

5.3 Pre-Sentence Reports

A Pre-Sentence Report (PSR) is a document prepared by a probation officer or court official that provides the judge with information about the offender's background, criminal history, and other relevant information to assist in determining an appropriate sentence. It will include details about the offender's family history, education, employment, or potentially any substance abuse history. A PSR is typically prepared after a guilty plea or conviction and is used to help the judge determine a sentence that is appropriate for the offence committed. When asked about what guidance they rely on when sentencing, some judges replied that they used probation reports and confirmed that this offer guidance which helps to inform their sentencing.[21]

Ireland occupies a distinctive position when it comes to the context of PSRs. As the Irish sentencing system is characterised by a lack of structure and limited guidance, there is an awareness that judges have considerable discretion when determining the appropriate sentences for individual cases.[22] However, the contribution that probation officers make to sentencing, through the provision of PSRs, is relatively unexplored.[23] Traditionally, the role of the probation officer in the criminal justice system was considered to be more welfare than control oriented. As a result of this, probation officers would be expected to recommend the use of non-custodial over custodial sanctions.[24] In many ways, because of the Probation Service ethos to 'advise, assist and befriend', practitioners would expect PSRs to focus on the social aspects of the defendant's situation and contain information which would assist consideration of the appropriateness of a community-based sanction.[25] However, it is an important to indicate that PSR evaluation for offenders is not always straightforward, and the process of evaluation can be quite confusing for some.[26] When a group of Irish women diverted into a Community-Based Organisation (CBO) were asked whether they had been evaluated by a Probation Officer for a report, only three women understood that the questions posed by the officer were for the purpose of a PSR.[27]

[21] Maguire (2010).

[22] Ibid.

[23] Carr and Maguire (2017).

[24] McNally (2009).

[25] Healy et al. (2015).

[26] Duignan (2023).

[27] Ibid, p. 243.

The Probation Service's internal PSR guidance manual states that courts are 'encouraged to seek a PSR before making a supervised community sanction',[28] although it is not known how widely shared this expectation is. Carr et al. caution that 'the potential for PSRs to play a large role in promoting greater use of community supervision over the use of imprisonment should not be overplayed.'[29] Notwithstanding this caution, a small-scale in-depth study in 2017,[30] commissioned by the Irish Probation Service, focuses on understanding the process of communication of probation officers and judges. This illustrates some interesting findings regarding PSRs as they can 'provide a professional opinion on a person's willingness and capacity to engage with a community sentence.'[31]

The study found that probation officers utilise both clinical judgment and interpretative frameworks provided by risk assessment tools in constructing pre-sentence reports. While this construction process is influenced by what is known as the 'risk-need-responsivity'[32] model, it is also shaped by broader social constructs like class and gender. The research found how the interaction between the probation officer and the client during interviews plays a role in constructing the report, allowing for an evaluation of the client's credibility and motivations. It also found that PSRs serve as a means of communication with the court, and the degree to which probation officers consider the court's expectations in their work.[33]

PSRs are becoming increasingly common in the criminal justice system, particularly when a court is considering imposing a CSO or custodial sentence. The court will typically request a PSR before imposing a CSO or custodial sentence, unless it deems it unnecessary. For example, where legislation mandates a specific presumptive custodial sentence.[34] Whilst Carr and Maguire's study gives a unique insight into how PSRs are read and interpreted by judges in Ireland, the qualitative research is limited to nine PSRs and is only a snapshot picture.[35] A longitudinal research study, conducted over a number of years would record the intermittent attitudinal

---

[28] Carr and Maguire (2017), p. 54.

[29] Ibid, p. 55.

[30] Ibid.

[31] Ibid, p. 68 This research examines the PSRs of nine cases in the District Court (n = 5) and Circuit Court (n = 4) with a range of penalties from a €750 fine, supervision & CSO to 3 year suspended custodial sentences.

[32] HM Inspectorate of Probation.

[33] Carr and Maguire (2017).

[34] There were mandatory sentences under the firearms and drugs offences: possession of a firearm while taking a vehicle without authority (s.57, Criminal Justice Act 2006); 5 years; use of a firearm to assist or aid an escape (10 years; s. 58 Criminal Justice Act 2006); possession of a firearm or ammunition in suspicious circumstances (5 years; s.59, Criminal Justice Act 2006); carrying a firearm with criminal intent (5 years; s.60 Criminal Justice Act 2006); shortening the barrel of a shotgun or rifle (5 years; s.65 Criminal Justice Act 2006) These have since been repealed under the Criminal Justice (Amendment) Act 2021.

[35] Carr and Maguire (2017), p. 54.

and ideological 'bursts' that previous research has aimed to capture in other jurisdictions.[36]

Research undertaken in 2003 on the interpretation of Scottish PSRs (called Social Enquiry Reports 'SERs') to gain deeper insight into the judicial interpretation of PSRs and to highlight the judiciary's autonomy in sentencing decisions. This study which examines how PSRs are used and interpreted, noted that, like any other provider in a marketplace, the service seeks to 'condition sentencer opinion'.[37] It sought to illustrate how, even with high-quality report writing, community penalties cannot be 'sold' to sentencers.[38] Twenty-six sheriffs (sentencers) took part in the research and the study used a combination of interviews, focus groups and moot sentencing exercises to produce a picture of how they use SERs and the significance of the reports in the sentencing process. The consensus among lawyers, sheriffs, and report writers is that the identity of the sentencer plays a crucial role in determining the sentencing outcome of a case. There was a widely held perception amongst report writers of sentencing disparity among sheriffs, whether in terms of a generally more punitive or lenient approach across cases or within specific case types.

> It was very widely believed by lawyers, sheriffs, and report writers that an important factor determining the sentencing outcome of a given case was who the sentencer is.[39]

Report writers typically were unable to predict which sheriff would read their report and furthermore they were ambivalent, even in cases where they could anticipate which sheriff would review their report.[40] Even if there was no sentencing disparity, report writers face significant challenges in determining the typical or 'normal' sentencing outcomes for different types of cases. Scotland lacks an extensive set of sentencing guidelines, and report writers do not have access to a sentencing database containing previous decisions to aid them in this regard. Consequently, the sources available to report writers for establishing the customary 'going rate' for various case types are extremely limited.

For the sentencer reading the report, 'the sections of the report which seemed to matter most to sentencers (i.e. those dealing with offending) were also the least credible.'[41] Sheriffs felt that social workers faced limitations in their access to police reports and witness statements, resulting in their reliance on offenders' accounts when discussing the offence to be sentenced. When additional information available to the sentencer contradicted the presented version of events, it diminished social workers' credibility in the eyes of sheriffs. Moreover, scepticism regarding risk assessment further diminished the significance of social workers' statements regarding potential future offending. Tata et al. note how 'this fundamental vulnerability

---

[36] Tata et al. (2007).

[37] Tata et al. (2008).

[38] Ibid, p. 835.

[39] Tata et al. (2007), p. 11.

[40] Ibid.

[41] Ibid, p. 15.

renders the influence of social enquiry fragile.'[42] The research found that a combination of 'technical improvements in SERs (through fixed quality standards or improved training) or judicial familiarity with particular social workers in small courts'[43] provided some satisfaction for judges and enhanced the report writers' credibility somewhat. However, the research showed that under 'the dominant discourse of judicial ownership of sentencing, there can be no single conception of an exemplary report in any given case.'[44]

5.4 Diversion into the Community

The 2011 legislation is directed at low-level STPS recipients of those sentenced to offences meriting 12 months or less in prison. However, the STPS category is not just one homogenous category but rather can be seen as a spectrum made of tiers of levels of 0–3 months, 3–6 months, and 6–12 months. Research which gender disaggregates the small cohort of female STPS from men in highlights the fact that from 2011–202, 85% of all female STPS recipients from 2011 to 2020 are those in the 0–3 months tier.[45] The primary focus of the 2011 Act is on addressing higher-tier offenders serving STPS as the CSO is a direct substitute for 12 months custody. Thus, the legislation is unsuitable for 85% of women.[46]

If the primary objective of government policy was to reduce STPS for women, it was unsuccessful, as the number of female STPS recipients initially increased.[47] The second objective was to promote the use of the Community Service Order (CSO). To evaluate the success of promoting alternatives to custody for women, it is necessary to assess all alternatives to custody that were promoted under the government's diversion policy.

The Criminal Justice (Community Service) (Amendment) Act 2011 states:

> (b) Where a court… is of opinion that the appropriate sentence in respect of the offence of which the offender is convicted would… be one of imprisonment for a period of more than 12 months… the court may make a community service order in accordance with this section.[48]

---

[42] Ibid.

[43] Ibid.

[44] Ibid.

[45] The total number of female STPS recipients from 2011–2020 is 16,072: (0–3 months) 13,589; (3–6 months) 1431; (6–12 months) 1052.

[46] Duignan (2023).

[47] Maguire (2010); Duignan (2023).

[48] Criminal Justice (Community Service) Act (1983) s1 A court shall not make a community service order unless the following conditions have been complied with: (a) the court is satisfied, after considering the offender's circumstances and a report about him by a probation and welfare officer (including, if the court thinks it necessary, hearing evidence from such an officer), that the offender

In this context, the judge is tasked with determining whether the offender's offence falls within the custodial range of twelve months. If a court concludes that the offence meets this custodial threshold, they can then utilise the provisions of the legislation to consider substituting a CSO in lieu of a STPS for the offender in question.[49]

5.5 CSO Promotion

The intention behind the 2011 Act is to discourage the use of STPS and encourage the use of CSOs. Although the 2011 Act requires the court to 'consider' making a CSO as a direct alternative to custodial sentences of twelve months or less,[50] the judge must still come to a concrete decision about the offender in relation to whether they deserve a custodial or non-custodial sentence. The judge is still completely autonomous in sentence selection and thus may decline to give any consideration to the substitution suggested in the 2011 Act, without giving any reasons whatsoever—this remains judicial prerogative.[51] However, the earlier 1983 Act remains an important part of the STPS diversion process.

Section 3(1) of the 1983 Act simply lists a CSO as an option open to the court instead of dealing with the offender in any other way.[52] When the 2011 Act was introduced, it was anticipated that the number of CSOs would increase and the number of STPS recipients in custody would decrease.[53] However, this was not the case, and the CSO remains under-used.[54] In Riordan's 2008 study, he notes that when the 1983 Act created the CSO as a direct alternative to custody, some judges indicated that they did not completely trust the Probation Service's competence in implementing sanctions.[55] Some members of judiciary appeared reluctant to have complete faith in the supervisory ability of the Probation Service.[56]

There also remains a certain level of judicial confusion with the older CSO legislation. Riordan explains this with reference to the court's discretion in dealing

is a suitable person to perform work under such an order and that arrangements can be made for him to perform such work, and (b) the offender has consented.

[49] If the offender is not considered to fall within this level of seriousness, then an alternative sanction will be imposed such as a fine, a dismissal under the Probation Act, a caution, an order to keep the peace, a curfew or another non-custodial disposal.

[50] Criminal Justice (Community Service) (Amendment) Act (2011), s3.

[51] Criminal Justice (Community Service) Act (1983), s 4.1 (a).

[52] Ibid, s3.1.

[53] Walsh and Sexton (2000).

[54] O'Hara and Rogan (2015).

[55] Riordan (2009).

[56] Ibid, p. 85.

with offenders who breach the CSO.[57] The confusion lies with a lack of clarity around legislation which was imported almost wholesale from the English system. The original legislation, inter alia, gives a very broad discretion when dealing with offenders who have breached the terms of the CSO.[58] It has never been clarified in the Irish jurisdiction whether the court should consider individual factors in a case where an offender is deemed unsuitable for a CSO.

The discretion, which vests in the courts under Sections 7, 8, and 11 of the Criminal Justice Act 1983,[59] is disconnected from the original requirement that a custodial sentence must be warranted before the CSO is first imposed. Riordan traced the broad discretion back to the original English statute which introduced community service in England. Section 17(3) of the Criminal Justice Act 1972 provided for the same discretion in almost the exact same formula of words. In that section, a fine not exceeding £50 could be imposed for breach of community service requirements or the court could revoke the order

> and deal with the offender, for the offence in respect of which the order was made, in any manner in which he could have been dealt with for that offence by the court which made the order if the order had not been made.[60]

Under the 1983 legislation, the person convicted must be over the age of sixteen and give their consent to the CSO.[61] The court must be satisfied based on an assessment report prepared by a probation officer, that the convicted person is a 'suitable person' under Section 4(1)(a).[62] An evaluation of a 'suitable person' might be interpreted in different ways. The legislation itself does not clarify whether the convicted person should be capable of simply attending the work stipulated or completing the entire order. This evaluative responsibility shifts to the Probation Service with the complementary document 'The Management of the Community Service Order.'[63]

After the 1983 Act was signed into law, the Probation and Welfare Service was given responsibility for the management and operation of the CSO. The Probation Service's own document, 'The Management of the CSO,'[64] which explains the practical operation of the sanction, provided guidance to probation officers in the performance of their duties under the legislation. It also establishes the correct procedure to be used in assessing the suitability of an offender candidate for a CSO sanction.

---

[57] Ibid.

[58] Criminal Justice Act (1972).

[59] Criminal Justice (Community Service) Act 1983.

[60] Criminal Justice Act (1972), s17(3).

[61] Criminal Justice (Community Service) Act 1983, s2.

[62] Ibid, s4(1)(a).

[63] Probation and Welfare Service (1984).

[64] Ibid.

Originally, the role of the probation officer under the Probation of Offenders Act 1907 was to 'advise, assist and befriend'.[65] Riordan suggests that the 1983 legislation altered this role, and the role of the probation officer became 'largely... the management of a punitive measure, permeated with certain discretionary practices by the probation officer, to ensure compliance with the order.'[66] He argues that the implementation of the 1983 legislation led to a transformation in the role of probation officers, shifting from an 'advisory' role to a more 'managerial' one.

Under this new framework, probation officers were primarily focused on ensuring the offender's compliance with the conditions of the CSO. His study highlights the perception among some judges that the CSO represented a relinquishment of direct supervision, placing greater reliance on the Probation Service to oversee the offender's progress and adherence to the sanction.[67] The structured approach outlined in the legislation may provide reassurance to members of the judiciary, fostering greater confidence that this method will ensure more consistent opinions in probation reports.[68]

When an offender is assessed by a Probation Officer, a dichotomous relationship may emerge. On one hand, the Probation Officer may develop a rapport with the offender through regular meetings, fostering a desire to see the individual succeed. On the other hand, the officer is obligated to provide an accurate and truthful account to the court, thereby enhancing the trust and confidence between the judiciary and the Probation Service.

5.6 Unchanged Core Elements of the CSO

In 1998, the government first commissioned a study on 'an evaluation of the operation of the Criminal Justice (Community Service) Act, 1983.'[69] The purpose of this was, inter alia, 'to assess the manner in which a CSO sanction is implemented and supervised.'[70] In order to gather information about the functioning of CSOs that could not be obtained from files or court surveys, interviews were conducted with a group of probation and welfare officers across different regions in the country. These interviews aimed to access valuable insights and first-hand experiences related to the practical implementation and operation of CSOs.[71]

For example, the report detailed how a Community Service Report should evaluate the offender's suitability for work under a CSO and determine if suitable

[65] Probation of Offenders Act (1907), s4(d).

[66] Riordan (2009), p. 208.

[67] Riordan (2000).

[68] Riordan (2009).

[69] Walsh and Sexton (2000).

[70] Ibid, p. 7.

[71] Ibid, p. 11.

arrangements can be made for the assigned work. This grants probation officers significant discretion in deciding the level of detail to include in the report. If necessary, a concise report may be supplemented with oral evidence provided by the officer. Additionally, there is no restriction on submitting a probation report on the offender, which can be supplemented with oral evidence as needed to evaluate the offender's suitability and identify an appropriate work project.[72]

However, the evaluation indicated that the demographic profile of the offender who partakes in the CSO is an unemployed, young, single man, poorly educated and living in the parental home.[73] In addition, in the sample used by Walsh and Sexton's empirical study, over half of the offenders had previous criminal records and a high proportion had previously been imprisoned. The report suggested a certain typology of user, indicating that the CSO might not be suitable for the low-level first-time offender.

To promote the use of the revitalised CSO, a further review was carried out in 2009 by the Value for Money Review Group (VFM).[74] The report noted that there was a lack of uptake in the CSO.[75] The review highlighted the limited adoption of CSOs and identified the need for increased promotion and uptake of this alternative sentencing option. In response, a dedicated team, led by a senior manager, was established to implement the recommendations outlined in the report. The VFM Review Group consulted with stakeholders and considered the contents of the report before developing a new model for community service. Their aim was to reverse the declining trend in CSO usage and actively promote its effective implementation as an alternative to traditional custodial sentences.[76]

The VFM group concluded that, in certain parts of rural Ireland, courts were reluctant to use the CSO because they saw it as a 'letting go' of the punishment function.[77] The report emphasised the need for research and development of the CSO, particularly in rural court areas, to promote its effective implementation. It identified several key issues, including the lack of confidence among some judges regarding the ability of CSOs to serve as a genuine alternative to imprisonment, provide punishment, rehabilitation, and benefit the community. The report also highlighted a lack of communication between the probation service and the judiciary.

To address these concerns, the report put forward eleven recommendations. These recommendations aimed to improve the operation of CSOs, conduct empirical research on their impact, coordinate an information campaign within the Probation

[72] Ibid, p. 18.

[73] Ibid.

[74] The Probation Service (2009).

[75] Ibid, p. 4.

[76] Ibid.

[77] Riordan (2009).

Service, and enhance the dissemination of information about CSOs and their effects to the judiciary through the Court Service.[78]

In January 2010, a pilot programme was initiated in the Dublin area to introduce a new model for community service as a precursor to its nationwide implementation. This involved the establishment of a dedicated community service unit with improved administrative support and streamlined processes. The aim was to enhance judges' confidence in this sanction and its effectiveness. To ensure successful implementation, efforts were made to communicate the details of the new model to the judiciary. Prior to the launch of the pilot scheme, specific communication was conducted with judges in the Dublin area.

Additionally, the director of operations at the Probation Service disseminated information about the new community service model to judges attending the Judicial Studies Institute Conference in 2010. These proactive measures aimed to increase awareness and understanding of the revised approach to community service among judges, fostering greater acceptance and utilisation of this alternative sentencing option.[79] The Probation Service reported numerous benefits arising from the pilot scheme such as more timely and efficient assessments, prompt starting of court orders, improved attendance at worksites and an increase in the number of orders being made during the period of the pilot scheme.[80]

In 2011, the Probation Service initiated the expansion of the new community service model to various parts of the country. Same-day assessments were permanently implemented in Dublin, followed by their introduction in the children's court and subsequently at other court sittings nationwide. This expansion occurred in areas with enough referrals and where facilities were available for probation officers to complete same-day assessment reports.

Despite efforts to revitalise the CSO, the core elements of the Irish CSO remained unchanged. By understanding aspects of the CSO framework, it becomes possible to assess the extent to which the government diversion policy addresses the root causes of offending for women. This clarifies whether the policy truly provides an effective and tailored approach for female STPS recipients. The unchanged core elements of the Irish CSO identify areas for improvement and advocate for a more comprehensive and impactful diversion policy that caters to the specific needs of women in the criminal justice system.

Since the CSO was first introduced in Ireland, the core elements of the sanction have remained the same. The Irish CSO is notably different from those in neighbouring jurisdictions such as Scotland or Northern Ireland. In these jurisdictions, the CSO has undergone fundamental changes, allowing community service to

[78] The Probation Service (2009), p. 74.

[79] The Probation Service (2011), p. 18.

[80] Ibid, p. 9 8 out of 10 CSOs successful starts within 10 days of induction; 7 out of 10 were completed within six months and the number of new CSO's imposed in the pilot area rose by one third.

be combined with a wide range of welfare packages.[81] The Irish CSO does not operate in the same manner and risks being overstated and open to criticism, where it is expected 'to achieve more than it is designed to achieve.'[82]

Walsh and Sexton's seminal study in 1999 on Community Service Orders suggests that the demographic profile of the offender who partakes in the CSO is an unemployed, young, single man, poorly educated and living in the parental home.[83] Typically, this cohort is overrepresented in the offending population, making the use of CSOs varied and inconsistent, with no clear guidelines on which categories of crimes or offenders they should target. The research recommended that to determine the effectiveness of CSOs in reducing recidivism, further study should be conducted on their sample group after three years to evaluate whether the order was beneficial and served as a viable alternative to incarceration. However, no subsequent study has been carried out on offenders who have received CSOs in Ireland. The absence of such research hampers our understanding of the long-term impact and efficacy of CSOs in reducing recidivism and providing effective alternatives to imprisonment.

It is still possible to gain certain insight into the contemporary perception of 'work in the community' by considering a 2014 joint study conducted by the Irish Prison Service and the Probation Service. This research focused on the Community Return Programme.[84] Distinct from the CSO, this programme enables eligible prisoners to be released early from custodial sentences ranging from one to eight years, with the requirement of completing unpaid community work as a condition of their reviewable temporary release. While the CSO serves as a substitute for a term of imprisonment, the Community Return Programme operates as a separate initiative. Examining this study provides a comparative lens through which to explore attitudes and perspectives towards community-based work in more recent times. However, there are similarities in core objectives. The 2014 study holds significance as it serves as a valuable indicator of participants' perceptions regarding the fairness of work in the community and the extent to which unpaid community work fosters receptiveness to its restorative and re-integrative dimensions. By examining the findings and insights from this study, it is possible to gain insights into the participants' perspectives on the nature of community-based work and its potential to contribute to the restoration and reintegration of individuals involved in the criminal justice system. This makes the 2014 study a useful indicator of participants' receptiveness to its restorative and re-integrative dimensions.[85]

When examining release and recall to prison, which can be viewed as 'backdoor' sentencing, both the legal framework and its practical application are crucial. Although focus is predominantly on the regulations for imposing imprisonment

[81] Barry and McIvor (2008).

[82] Guilfoyle (2019), p. 201.

[83] Walsh and Sexton (2000).

[84] Irish Prison Service and The Probation Service (2014).

[85] Rex (1999).

rather than those governing release from prison, comparison of both aspects is equally important. Comparative research of sentencing law also tends to concentrate more on the theoretical aspects, rather than its practical implementation and for this reason, large-scale practical research is scarce.

Engaging in work within the community as part of a CSO offers several advantages for participants. It provides a structured routine, facilitating reintegration and fostering a work ethic and enhanced self-esteem. Participants also benefit from improved community standing, as their contribution demonstrates accountability and commitment to societal reintegration. Moreover, the work experience acquired through a CSO equips individuals with transferable skills, enhancing their employability. From a broader perspective, the utilisation of CSOs presents cost-saving benefits by offering an alternative to incarceration, optimising resource allocation within the criminal justice system.[86]

Although the difficulties and advantages are not divided across gendered groups, challenges listed include the strictness and frequency of the signing-on conditions, difficulties accessing entitlements and income maintenance payments, costs associated with travelling to the worksite and the actual distance to some work sites (particularly in rural areas). This could foreseeably have more of an impact on women with children in their care. A study in the UK in 2012 highlights how unpaid work should not be used as a penalty for women, primarily due to their unique childcare responsibilities.[87] Overall, this study found that 'women may be punished more harshly than men for similar offences, due to lack of other punitive community alternatives.'[88] Due to its multiple objectives, the Community Service Order (CSO) has a greater potential for unfairness compared to incarceration. While the primary objective of incarceration is incapacitation, the main objectives of a CSO are to serve as an alternative to incarceration, make reparation for offending, and facilitate reintegration into the community.

5.6.1 As an Alternative to Incarceration

Research has shown that sentencing women to unpaid work can prevent unnecessary imprisonment, thereby allowing them to make reparation for their offences.[89] However, Patel et al. highlighted that, in the UK in 2008, unpaid work was used more frequently with men than with women.[90] Gelsthorpe et al. agreed, noting that placements had mainly been designed for men, and that new placements need to

[86] Irish Prison Service and The Probation Service (2014).

[87] Marougka (2012).

[88] Ibid.

[89] Dickie (1995).

[90] Patel and Stanley (2008).

be designed to be accessible and responsive to women's particular circumstances and needs.[91]

In Ireland, Seymour acknowledged the uniqueness of probation and notes what differentiates it from other sentences.[92] However, her research questions how homeless offenders could be effectively 'engaged' within the community given their high level of need and the lack of corresponding resources to meet those needs.[93] After the publication of the Corston Report,[94] it was discovered that 'women are often remanded to prison for their own safety.'[95] While many women within the criminal justice system may not have severe mental illnesses warranting hospitalisation, it is acknowledged that they may have other emotional and well-being requirements that could be better addressed within a healthcare setting. By attending to these needs, unnecessary remand periods can be avoided, promoting more appropriate outcomes for women involved in the criminal justice system.[96]

In the author's research involving five women required to attend a CBO as part of their sentence, the emphasis was on their participation in education classes, therapeutic engagement, and appointments with probation or welfare officers. Rather than focusing on their past offences, the CBO aimed to prioritise helping the women understand how to stop offending and identifying their individual barriers to desistance.

One of the participants likened her offending cycle to a 'train' and the CBO was akin to a new direction:

> It's not easy getting off the train you're on and admit that it's going in the wrong direction… You can't stand around, you know at the new station? You have to get on a new train and go somewhere new.[97]

5.6.2 *To Make Reparation for Offending*

A central concept of community service work is that it comprises tasks which would otherwise be left undone and that it also benefits or provides reparation to the community.[98] These core objectives have not changed in Ireland, even though other jurisdictions have made substantial changes to the sanction itself.[99] The Irish

---

[91] Gelsthorpe and McIvor (2007).

[92] Seymour (2004).

[93] Ibid, p. 10.

[94] Loucks et al. (2006).

[95] Ibid, p. 21.

[96] Ibid.

[97] Duignan (2023), p. 240 'Emma'.

[98] Walsh and Sexton (2000).

[99] Like the Scottish Community Payback Order.

jurisdiction has not been motivated by the need to fundamentally change the nature of the CSO, possibly due to the associated costs of fine-tuning the order itself.

However, it could be argued that making fundamental changes to the CSO in the short term would have long-term benefits. The CSO should mean much more than the old notion of 'penal servitude' or mindless work tasks. Pease, a leading authority on CSOs in England and Wales, argues that the idea of work by the wrongdoer or the enemy of the community as a means of punishment or restitution is outdated. Pease viewed other work-based penal sanctions such as slavery, transportation, penal servitude, houses of correction, and impressment as community service's 'less reputable forebears.'[100]

As discussed in Chap. 1, although Ireland has a less than salubrious history of non-prison places of incarceration, Kilcommins argues that the focus should not be on the distant past of community service. Instead, the specific sanction of community service is based on a particular set of penal, social, cultural, political, and economic practices. Thus, while community service may have a 'long past' in that sanctions have embodied work since ancient times, it has a 'short history' in that it is driven by a particular and specific complex of penal strategies, agencies, representations, and techniques which render anachronistic any unqualified collations between it and past penal work practices.[101]

Kilcommins invites modern-day thinkers to re-imagine the CSO in terms of work in the community today rather than making unhelpful associations with the old work practices that have been engaged in historically. The Probation Service today recognises that offenders under their supervision often have 'complex problems such as alcohol or drug dependencies - or may have poor literacy and social skills. These offenders require a wide range of support and assistance in the community.'[102] While the responsibility for providing therapeutic services cannot be solely placed on the Probation Service, Kilcommins acknowledges the intricate interaction of strategies and techniques that the Service must consider and be aware of in addressing the needs of these individuals.

Unfortunately, most of the CBOs are centralised in the capital cities.[103] For low-level female offenders in rural areas, suitable work programmes may be unavailable or difficult to access due to transportation or childcare issues. Additionally, judicial awareness of these programmes may be lacking, as women-only programmes are not established on a statutory basis in Ireland. These women may be assigned to unsuitable programmes, increasing the likelihood of breaching their CSO. In some cases, an STPS may be seen as preferable due to the perceived safety, comfort, and camaraderie it offers. For instance, a female STPS recipient described the comfort she experienced while in prison, noting that she was allowed to stay an

[100] Pease (1980).

[101] Kilcommins (2002).

[102] Worrall and Gelsthorpe (2009).

[103] 'The Probation Service' https://www.probation.ie.

additional week before returning home. Ironically, she highlighted how she behaved as a model prisoner specifically because she did not want to leave.

> They gave me another week after that and then they said I have to go. Obviously, they didn't have the room but they looked at me to be the person who wasn't really a trouble- maker in there.[104]

5.6.3 *To Facilitate Reintegration into the Community*

Offenders will face certain obstacles when recovering from a criminal lifestyle, and work in the community may assist in this process. There are various opinions about this. In one study, when probed about specific reasons for abstaining from crime, 'free will' to break with the past was among the most common self-reported explanations, followed by having a good marriage and a desire to pursue a career.[105] Others argue that subjective changes in mindset or cognition are of little importance to change, in comparison with structural and social factors.

Despite the unchanged elements of the Irish CSO, research recognises that a distinct approach should be adopted for women:

> Women have been marginalised within a system largely designed by men for men for far too long and there is a need for a "champion" to ensure that their needs are properly recognised and met.[106]

Research studies in England and Wales illustrate the inadequate nature of community alternatives and prison facilities which are not gender-specific.[107] This emphasises how 'equal treatment of men and women does not result in equal outcomes.'[108] Marginalisation occurs where women are housed in geographically dispersed prisons which 'have for the most part been designed for men.'[109] Because of the small number of women's prisons and their location, women tend to be located further from their homes than male prisoners, to the detriment of maintaining family ties, receiving visits, and resettlement back into the community.[110] In addition to this, community alternatives may be unsuitable where services are male-dominated[111] or childcare facilities unavailable.[112]

---

[104] Duignan (2023), p. 242 'Anna'.

[105] Mischkowitz (1994).

[106] Jean Corston (2007), p. 2.

[107] Ibid; Gelsthorpe et al. (2007).

[108] Jean Corston (2007), p. 3.

[109] Ibid, p. 3.

[110] Ibid, p. 3.

[111] Gelsthorpe et al. (2007), p. 31.

[112] Ibid, p. 32.

In the author's research study, five women spoken to in the CBO had all lost contact with family members at some point as a direct or indirect consequence of their offending.[113] Anna, despite facing various indirect criminogenic needs, such as feelings of loneliness due to family estrangement, recognises that these factors still contribute to her substance abuse.[114] Nevertheless, she reports that attending the CBO provides her with a sense of belonging and familial support and describes the CBO 'like a family to me because I don't have a family. This support network aids her in abstaining from drug use and criminal activities, while also facilitating her stabilisation and eventual cessation of methadone use.

Despite legislative encouragement to replace more STPS with CSOs, the legislation does not take gender into account. Core elements of the CSO have remained largely unchanged and are expected to apply equally to both male and female offenders trying to desist from offending. However, without addressing the root causes of offending, the CSO may be more punitive for those for whom it is unsuitable, potentially leading to breaches and even more severe sentences.

5.7 Fines Legislation

Whilst there was a substantial reduction in the overall use of STPS for fine default from 2010–2020, the proportion of female offenders receiving these sentences increased.[115] The number of female STPS recipients for other offences follows this trend, increasing from 2010 to 2015 before decreasing in 2020. Despite the overall decline in STPS recipients, the percentage of women among those receiving STPS for fine default steadily rises, starting at 15.80% in 2010 and reaching 23.20% in 2020, reaching a peak of 27% in 2015.[116]

The government's diversion policy was implemented with a dual legislative approach, aiming to promote the CSO as a direct alternative to imprisonment[117] and to reduce STPS for non-payment of fines.[118] However, despite efforts to encourage the use of the CSO through the 2011 legislation, there was no significant increase in its implementation. Furthermore, an examination of gender-disaggregated statistics reveals that the use of STPS for women did not decrease as intended.

The introduction of the Fines (Payment and Recovery) Act 2014 ('the 2014 Act') had a notable impact on the imprisonment of women, particularly in cases of

[113] Three were a direct result because of offending, custodial stays and self-admitted behavioural issues, one was because of parental neglect, and one spoke of children being taken into care.

[114] Duignan (2023).

[115] Ibid, p. 137.

[116] Ibid, p. 137.

[117] Criminal Justice (Community Service) (Amendment) Act (2011), s3.

[118] Fines (Payment and Recovery) Act (2014).

non-payment of fines. Enacted in April 2014, its provisions were not commenced until January 11, 2016. The Act introduced several new features relevant to STPS recipients, including the ability to pay a fine by instalment over 12 months,[119] the substitution of fine default for community service,[120] and the appointment of receivers. The Act's overarching objectives are to support the administration of justice when fines are imposed by the courts, ensure the collection of fines, and 'reduce to the minimum possible the number of people committed to prison each year for the non-payment of a fine.'[121]

Prior to the Fines legislation, when a court imposed a fine, the sentencing process included specifying the amount and deadline for payment and determining a concurrent sentence of imprisonment in the event of default. For fines imposed summarily, the length of the custodial sentence for default could vary from 5 to 90 days. This practice meant that individuals who failed to pay their fines on time faced the risk of immediate imprisonment.[122]

If a fine was imposed on indictment, a custodial sentence of up to twelve months might be imposed upon default. Following the commencement of the 2014 Act in January 2016, fine default no longer led to the automatic application of the STPS stipulated. Section 19 of the 2014 Act enables the judge to revisit the fine punishment upon default and consider imposing a CSO as an alternative to imprisonment.

The instalment option under the 2014 Act is only available for fines exceeding €100.[123] For individuals who default on fines below the €100 limit, the option to pay in instalments is not applicable. In such cases, the default triggers the application of alternative measures to custody, as outlined in the 2014 diversion legislation. These alternatives provide consequences for fine defaulters that do not involve STPS.

Section 3 of the 2011 legislation provides that between 40 and 240 h of unpaid work may be substituted as a direct alternative to a STPS.[124] Therefore, the 2011 legislation benchmarks a maximum of 240 h of community service against a maximum of 12 months imprisonment. However, under the 2014 Act, if a fine is imposed summarily, the court can order that, in the event of default, a maximum of only 30 days imprisonment be served or an alternative CSO of a maximum of 100 h work be completed.

Thus, the 2014 Act benchmarks a maximum of 100 h of unpaid work against a maximum of 30 days imprisonment. CSO substitution is therefore a more onerous sentence for offenders sentenced under the 2014 Act than those under the 2011 Act, who might face an alternative maximum of 12 months in prison, whereas the latter would face an alternative maximum of 30 days in prison. As the Central Statistics

[119] Ibid, s 6(1)(a)(ii).

[120] Ibid, s 7(1)(c).

[121] Courts Service (2019).

[122] Ibid.

[123] Fines (Payment and Recovery) Act (2014), s 5(a)(ii).

[124] Criminal Justice (Community Service) Act, s3.

Office found, 94% of fine defaulters in 2019 served less than one day in custody, if any.[125]

Although the fines legislation led to an overall decline in STPS for fine default among women, when fine default STPS are removed from the statistics, the number of female STPS recipients remains unchanged.[126] When introducing the legislation, the then Minister for Justice, Frances Fitzgerald, spoke optimistically about the Act's implementation, expecting it would 'lead to a reduction in the number of committals to prison on short sentences.'[127] However, the number of female STPS made each year continued to increase despite the 2011 legislation. Probation Service statistics also show relatively little change in the number of CSOs made for women from 2011 to 2020. When the fines legislation was introduced in 2016, the number of female STPS, excluding fine defaults, remained relatively unchanged throughout the government's policy of diversion.[128]

Under the 2014 Act, an offender who defaults on a fine will no longer automatically face a short custodial term. Instead, they will be evaluated for alternative, non-custodial punishments.[129] For smaller fines, this could mean probation supervision or another form of community-based sanction. Rather than imposing a brief prison sentence, the offender is now returned to the community. However, the increased supervision and additional requirements of these alternative sanctions can make desistance from offending more challenging—especially in the absence of adequate support.

In the author's research study one participant mentioned that she received a STPS for not paying fines for other offences.[130] 'Kelly' was aware of the fact that if she did not pay the fines, any STPS handed down would be for a matter of hours and said 'I didn't pay the fines because I knew I wouldn't make it past [*prison*] reception, I knew that it'd be thrown out.'[131] Recognising the nominal nature of the STPS, she quipped 'The judge'll give you custody for a week for talking in court and then he makes you go back up at the end and apologise. Well, actually, you just get a free lunch.'[132]

With the Fines Act substituting a STPS for fine default with a CSO, future consequences could become more severe, as this change would place low-level offenders like Kelly within the custodial ambit. While serving a CSO, an offender like Kelly would then be on the penal continuum, which directly leads to STPS if she breaches or defaults.[133]

---

[125] Guilfoyle (2017).

[126] Duignan (2023).

[127] Fitzgerald (2014), p. 1.

[128] Ibid.

[129] Fines (Payment and Recovery) Act (2014).

[130] Duignan (2023), p. 248 'Kelly'.

[131] Ibid, p. 248.

[132] Ibid, p. 248.

[133] Criminal Justice (Community Service) (Amendment) Act (2011), s3.

5.8 Community-Return and Reintegration Programmes

As part of the government's policy of diversion from custody, the Community Return Programme has been an early release scheme implemented in Ireland since October 2011, jointly managed by the Irish Prison Service and the Probation Service. The primary objective of the Community Return Programme is to provide an incentivised early release scheme for prisoners who are serving sentences ranging from 1 to 8 years and who are actively committed to desisting from reoffending. It aims to identify and support individuals who demonstrate genuine efforts to rehabilitate themselves and reintegrate into the community. However, while STPS recipients are ineligible for the Community Return Programme, they may be considered for release under the Community Support Scheme, which is aimed at the recipient of sentences from 3 months to 364 days.[134]

These programmes also provide an opportunity for eligible individuals to reintegrate into society while also ensuring they adhere to conditions of their release such as engagement in rehabilitation programs and ongoing supervision by the Probation Service. In the Corston Report, it was noted these conditions could be problematic for women. Women in rural areas can experience difficulties in accessing probation programmes and can then often find themselves in a small minority on programmes primarily designed for men. These women can also have more difficulty in accessing services from agencies designed to tackle issues linked to their offending, such as substance misuse.[135]

The Irish Prison Service developed the Integrated Sentence Management System to facilitate structured release or reintegration programmes for sentenced prisoners.[136] The Integrated Sentence Management (ISM) approach involves the collaboration of twenty-four ISM Coordinators who are spread across the prison estate. These coordinators work with prison management and a multi-disciplinary team within the prison setting. The team consists of various services, including the Psychology Service, Education Service, Work Training Service, Chaplaincy Service, Probation Service, Resettlement Service, Addiction Service, and the Prison Healthcare team. These groups work together to assess and address the needs of individuals in custody, focusing on their personal development, rehabilitation, and successful reintegration into society. By engaging with the different services available, prisoners are provided with opportunities for re-integration. Scholarship recognises the importance of successful reintegration into the community for offenders as it has been shown to reduce the likelihood of reoffending.

Community engagement and involvement play a vital role in the successful reintegration of prisoners. According to the Mandela Rules, the period of imprisonment must in so far as possible support "the reintegration of such persons into society

[134] Review Group for Penal Policy (2014).

[135] Jean Corston (2007).

[136] Irish Prison Service.

upon release so that they can lead a law-abiding and self-supporting life."[137] The aim of this is to ensure that individuals who have been incarcerated are not excluded from society because of their imprisonment.

One of the Irish Penal Reform Trust's standards for the penal system, reviewed in its 2021 report, includes "community engagement and involvement."[138] The report notes how maintaining connections with the community significantly enhances the chances of a successful resettlement after release from custody. There is typically a high prevalence of criminogenic needs amongst STPS recipients and because they are unlikely to have had a 'stay' in prison for a long period of time, STPS recipients typically require access to welfare services or treatment rather than any re-adaptation to living in the community.[139] Marginalisation experienced by STPS recipients may stem from their involvement in criminal activities rather than their residing in custody.

The Corston Report in the United Kingdom recommended that the accessibility of a comprehensive range of services could be enhanced through a multi-agency 'one-stop shop.'[140] This approach could mitigate the likelihood of re-engagement in criminal activities through the effective evaluation and subsequent addressing of the criminogenic needs of women who are released after sentencing in treatment programmes. While the Community Support Scheme cannot be said to be part of the government's diversion policy as it deals with offenders who have already been sentenced to STPS, it shares similar objectives to the policy in that its goals are to decrease STPS levels. Although it is also conducted in the community, rather than in prison, it aims to improve reintegration and reduce recidivism for minor offenders, and it thus shares the same diversion policy objectives. This is potentially an important aspect of diversion policy as reduction of STPS diverts individuals into the community, but as yet, it has remained under-developed. There have not been any large-scale developments or evaluations carried out on this scheme since its inception. In the United Kingdom, outcome evaluations of community-based projects have yielded important findings. These evaluations provide insights into the efficacy of such initiatives, offering valuable information on what works and what can be improved in community-based interventions for female offenders.

---

[137] Standard Minimum Rules for Non-Custodial Measures A/RES/45/110 (1990) 68th Plenary meeting.

[138] Irish Penal Reform Trust (2021), Standard 20, p. 80.

[139] Larkin (2015).

[140] Jean Corston (2007), p. 66.

5.9 Conclusion

A persistent gender disparity in the sentencing process underscores the need for a more nuanced and gender-sensitive approach that addresses the distinct circumstances and challenges faced by female offenders. Female offenders often have unique needs and pathways into crime, which are not adequately addressed by a one-size-fits-all policy that simply encourages 'more' alternatives to imprisonment. These alternatives should be carefully identified and assessed to prevent reoffending.

Research indicates that providing access to essential support services such as counselling, childcare, and educational opportunities, along with rehabilitation programs tailored to the specific challenges faced by female offenders, can significantly promote desistance. This approach can reduce the number of women entering the custodial system and, consequently, decrease the prevalence of STPS in the criminal justice system.

Large-scale qualitative research is crucial for understanding the underlying reasons behind the increase in female STPS recipients being diverted into the community. By gaining a deeper understanding of the factors contributing to this trend, policymakers can design pragmatic interventions that more effectively target the root causes of female offending and ensure better outcomes.

Law

Criminal Justice (Community Service) Act (1983)
Standard Minimum Rules for Non-Custodial Measures A/RES/45/110 (1990)
Probation of Offenders Act (1907)
Criminal Justice Act (1972)
Criminal Justice (Community Service) (Amendment) Act (2011)
Fines (Payment and Recovery) Act (2014)

References

Book

Gelsthorpe L, McIvor G (2007) Dealing with difference and diversity. In: Gelsthorpe L, Morgan R (eds) Handbook of probation. Willan Publishing, Cullompton

Healy D et al (2015) The Routledge handbook of Irish criminology. Taylor & Francis Group

Kilcommins S (2002) The introduction of community service orders: an historical interpretation. Barry Rose Law Publishers

Loucks N et al (2006) Evaluation of the 218 Centre. Scottish Executive Justice Department

Patel S, Stanley S (2008) The use of the community order and the suspended sentence order for women. Centre for Crime and Justice Studies, London

Pease K (1980) A brief history of community service. In: Pease K, McWilliams W (eds) . Scottish Academic Press, Community service by order

Walsh DP, Sexton P (2000) An empirical study of community service orders in Ireland. Stationery Office

Journal Article

Carlen P (1994) Why study women's imprisonment? Or anyone else's? An indefinite article. Br J Criminol 34:131

Carr N, Maguire N (2017) Pre-sentence reports and individualised justice: consistency, temporality and contingency. Irish Probat J 14:52

Dickie D (1995) Women offenders and social enquiry reports: a study of women and social work practice in Lothian. Unpublished MSc thesis, Department of Applied Social Science, University of Stirling

Gelsthorpe L, Sharpe G, Roberts J (2007) Provision for women offenders in the community. Fawcett Society, London

Guilfoyle E (2017) An exploration of the potential negative effects of using Community Service Orders as an alternative to imprisonment for fine defaulters. Irish Crim Law J 26:94

Maguire N (2010) Consistency in sentencing. Judicial Stud Inst J 2:14

Maguire N (2014) When is prison a last resort? Definitional problems and judicial interpretations. Irish Crim Law J 24:62

McNally G (2009) Probation in Ireland, Part 2: the modern age, 1960s to 2000. Irish Probat J 6:187

Millie A, Tombs J, Hough M (2007) Borderline sentencing: a comparison of sentencers' decision making in England and Wales, and Scotland. Criminol Crim Justice 7:243

Mischkowitz R (1994) Desistance from a deliquent way of life? Cross-national longitudinal research on human development and criminal behavior 303

O'Hara K, Rogan M (2015) Examining the use of community service orders as alternatives to short prison sentences in Ireland. Irish Probat J 12:22

O'Malley T (2010) Time served: the impact of sentencing and parole decisions on the prison population. Paper delivered to the Irish Penal Reform Trust, Morrison Hotel Dublin, vol 28

Rex S (1999) Desistance from offending: experiences of probation. Howard J Crim Justice 38:366

Seymour M (2004) Homeless offenders in the community: the issues and challenges for probation supervision. Irish Probat J 1:3

Seymour M, Costello L (2005) A study of the number, profile and progression routes of homeless persons before the court and in custody. Centre for Social and Educational Research, p 10

Tata C et al (2008) Assisting and advising the sentencing decision process: the pursuit of 'quality' in pre-sentence reports. Br J Criminol 48:835

Tombs J, Jagger E (2006) Denying responsibility: sentencers' accounts of their decisions to imprison. Br J Criminol 46:803

Worrall A, Gelsthorpe L (2009) 'What works' with women offenders: the past 30 years. Probat J 56: 329

Media

Larkin L (2015) Prisoners 'Prefer Jail To Having To Live On Streets,' Says Mayor. Irish Independent. Independent.ie 3 May 2015. <https://www.independent.ie/regionals/herald/news/prisoners-prefer-jail-to-having-to-live-on-streets-says-mayor-31192408.html>

Report

Barry M, McIvor G (2008) Chaotic lives: a profile of women in the criminal justice system in Lothian and Borders. Lothian & Borders Commnuity Justice Authority

Department of Justice (2022) Criminal Justice Policy Review of Policy Options for Prison and Penal Reform 2022-2024. gov.ie/en/collection/

Irish Penal Reform Trust (2013) Position Paper 10- Women in the Criminal Justice System: Towards a non-custodial approach

Irish Penal Reform Trust (2021) Progress in the Penal System (PIPS)- The Need for Transparency. Dublin

Jean Corston B (2007) The Corston Report: a report of a review of women with particular vulnerabilities in the criminal justice system. London

Marougka M (2012) Sentencing women: considering the factors that influence decision-making. Interviews with sentencers and probation officers

Prison Reform Trust (2011) Report of the Woman's Justice Taskforce- Reforming Women's Justice

Probation and Welfare Service (1984) The Management of the Community Service Order

Review Group for Penal Policy (2014) Strategic review of penal policy- Final report. Dublin

The Probation Service (2009) Value for Money and Policy Review of the Community Service Scheme. Department of Justice, Equality and Law Reform

The Probation Service (2011) Community Return Programme

Conference Paper

Tata C et al (2007) 'To Inform and Advise'? The interpretation and use of pre-sentence reports in the sentencing process. Reform of the Criminal Law 2007: 20th Anniversary Conference

Thesis

Duignan S (2023) Evaluation of the effect of Irish Penal Policy on female short-term prison sentence recipients: the need for gender-specific policy. University of Galway

Guilfoyle E (2019) An examination of the community service order in Ireland: recommendations for change. University of Limerick

Maguire N (2008) Sentencing in Ireland: an exploration of the views, rationales, and sentencing practices of district and circuit court judges. Trinity College, Dublin

Riordan D (2000) Diversion to treatment: a study of drug-related cases in the Dublin Metropolitan District Court. Trinity College, Dublin

Riordan D (2009) The role of the community service order and the suspended sentence in Ireland: a judicial perspective. (Ph.D)University College Cork

Online Resource

Central Statistics Office (2019) Prison Re-Offending Table: Custodial Period Served by Individuals who Received Fine Sentences

Central Statistics Office (2022) Prison Re-Offending Statistics 2011-2018. CSO

Department of Justice Speech by the Minister for Justice and Equality, Frances Fitzgerald TD at the publication of the Final Report of the Penal Policy Review Group 2014

Fines (Payment and Recovery) Act 2014 Information Document 2019

HM Inspectorate of Probation, The Risk-Need-Responsivity Model

Irish Penal Reform Trust, Scotland: Impact of Presumption Against Short Sentences (2020)

Irish Prison Service, Sentenced Committals Classified by Sentence Length & Gender from Years 2007 to 2020 - Irish Prison Service/ Home/ Information Centre/ Statistics & Information/ Yearly Statistics (Irish Prison Service)

Irish Prison Service and The Probation Service (2014) Community return: a unique opportunity- a descriptive evaluation of the first twenty-six months. Irish Prison Service/ Irish Probation Service

Irish Prison Service, Integrated Sentence Management

Irish Prison Service, Prisoner Services, Resettlement and Reintegration

Work in the Community, 'The Probation Service'. <https://www.probation.ie> accessed

Chapter 6
Effective Practices: Approaches and Models for Addressing Deficiencies

6.1 Introduction

Comparative analysis of legal frameworks in other jurisdictions offers essential insights which deepens our understanding of the operations and highlights potential deficiencies in criminal justice systems. Each jurisdiction maintains its unique criminal justice structure, making comprehensive evaluations often reliant on comparisons with systems in other nations. Ireland's legislative environment, for instance, has been significantly shaped by its neighbouring jurisdictions which exhibit many structural similarities with the Irish system.

Although Ireland's domestic policy initiatives in justice are no longer directly aligned with Westminster, they are frequently influenced by strategies and policies that have been effectively implemented in these neighbouring countries. The geographical proximity and the historical influence of Westminster laws, which Ireland inherited upon its independence in 1922, make England and Wales pertinent comparators.

This chapter explores elements of government policy that have been ineffective for women diverted from prison custody. The 2011 Amendment Act encourages courts to replace short prison sentences for minor offences with community service. While this initially appears to reduce the number of STPS recipients, in fact the small number of female STPS recipients within this group increases. Five years later, the Fines Act aims to achieve similar results with STPS for fine default. Although the overall number of STPS recipients declines significantly, the number of female STPS recipients begins to rise again following its implementation.[1] In the absence of a large-scale empirical review of Irish female STPS recipients, it is useful to compare the experience of England and Wales when examining the use of custodial alternatives under the 2011 Act.

[1] Duignan (2023).

S. Duignan, *Transforming Justice for Women*, Gender, Justice and Legal Feminism 3, https://doi.org/10.1007/978-3-031-82455-5_6

6.2 The Use of Custodial Alternatives in England & Wales

The Criminal Justice Act 2003[2] in England and Wales shares similarities with the Irish Criminal Justice (Community Service) (Amendment) Act 2011, as the focus of both pieces of legislation is to encourage the use of custodial alternatives available to the courts. The 2003 Act sought to promote alternatives to imprisonment while fostering the rehabilitation and reintegration of offenders. Both pieces of legislation acknowledge the potential of community service as an effective form of punishment that address the underlying causes of offending while minimising the use of STPS. By prioritising community-based interventions, these laws align with a broader shift towards addressing offenders' needs within their communities.[3] The 2003 legislation established a sentencing framework outlining key principles for determining custodial sentences, stating that custody should be 'targeted at serious dangerous and violent offenders.'[4]

Section 152(2) of the 2003 Act states:

> The court must not pass a custodial sentence unless it is of the opinion that the offence, or the combination of the offence and one or more offences associated with it, was so serious that neither a fine alone nor a community sentence can be justified for the offence.[5]

The 2003 Act aimed to increase the 'credibility' of community sentences and make them more appealing to magistrates and judges. It replaced the previous orders with a single non-custodial sanction called the Community Order (CO). The credibility of community sentences was aimed to be enhanced by making the new sanction more punitive and demanding, while also simplifying and rationalising the previously disorganised array of community penalties.[6]

The new CO allowed sentencers to select from a wide range of requirements when sentencing an offender, addressing the underlying issues contributing to offending. Depending on the nature of the offence, the need for punishment, and the issues that need to be addressed to prevent re-offending, the CO can be tailored to the individual offender.[7]

However, this reform increased the workload of the Probation Service, necessitating a more 'managerial' approach and reducing the emphasis on interpersonal relationships and social work methodologies. This shift resulted in a decrease in flexibility in case management and an increase in recalls to prison for released supervisees. A representative of the National Association of Probation Officers

---

[2] Criminal Justice Act (England and Wales) (2003).

[3] Ibid.

[4] Commons Select Committee (2007–2008), 9.

[5] Criminal Justice Act (England and Wales) (2003), s152.2.

[6] Mair (2011).

[7] The Criminal Justice Act also introduced the Suspended Sentence Order (SSO), a non-custodial punishment of custodial level punitiveness, as it requires the offence to be considered 'custodial' initially but served in the community if adhered to.

attributed the rise in recalls to the introduction of strict enforcement rules by the Home Office since 1999, stating that 'Probation staff have been obliged to follow strict national standards on enforcement. Previously, there was greater professional discretion.'[8] Initially, it was thought that the increasing number of recalls resulted from changes in offenders' behaviour. However, Reitz explains that this rise in recalls cannot be solely attributed to such behavioural changes. He argues that failure rates on post-release supervision do not directly reflect the actual behaviour of those released from prison.[9]

Reitz further elucidates that the number and rate of revocations in any jurisdiction are influenced not only by parolees' behaviour but also by the supervision system's responsiveness and sensitivity to violations. Sensitivity involves several factors, including the formal definitions of violations, the level of surveillance conducted by parole officers, the institutional culture within different field services, and the severity of sanctions imposed for violations. These elements collectively shape the system's effectiveness in detecting and addressing violations. Varying sensitivity levels across jurisdictions can lead to differences in revocation rates, with some systems being more proactive and responsive in managing violations, while others adopt a more lenient or reactive approach.[10]

The prison population in Britain for individuals serving sentences longer than 12 months was 32,000 in 1995.[11] The 2003 legislation aimed to reserve custodial punishment for serious and violent offenders who posed a risk to the public and to promote robust community sentences for most non-violent offenders. However, the changes made under the 2003 Act did not achieve their intended goals. By 2005, the number of prisoners serving sentences over 12 months had increased to 54,000, representing a 70% rise.[12] The government acknowledged this trend, noting that

> sentencing has become tougher over the last decade, with offenders more likely to get a prison sentence and [...] the sentence is likely to be longer. The total number of offenders sentenced to immediate custody for indictable offences increased by 26% from 1995 to 2005.[13]

It was reported by the Lord Chancellor and Secretary of State for Justice that the average sentence length had risen from 14.7 months in 1995 to 16.8 months in 2005. The Chief Inspector of Probation recognised that this 'up-tariffing' had occurred as a direct result of the 2003 Act's changes.[14] Elsewhere, commentators observed how sentences became substantially more severe, with community penalties displacing

[8] Fletcher (2003), p. 1.

[9] Reitz (2004).

[10] Ibid, p. 215.

[11] Commons Select Committee (2007–2008).

[12] Ibid, 13.

[13] Ibid.

[14] Ibid, 13.

financial penalties and immediate custody displacing community penalties and suspended sentences.[15]

6.3 The Carter Report

In December 2003 Lord Carter's Report, titled 'Managing Offenders, Reducing Crime: A New Approach,' was published.[16] It received positive feedback from ministers and led to the establishment of the National Offender Management Service (NOMS).[17] Expectations for NOMS were high, with the belief that it would help reduce the demand for prison places by assisting offenders in transitioning between custody and the community.

The Carter recommendations, along with the new sentencing provisions in the Criminal Justice Act 2003, were expected to keep the prison population below 80,000 by 2009. However, it became evident that these expectations would not be met, as prison numbers continued to increase.[18] In response to the ongoing rise in prison numbers, Lord Carter was once again called upon for assistance.

Lord Carter's review of prisons, titled 'Securing the Future: Proposals for the Efficient and Sustainable Use of Custody in England and Wales,' was published in December 2007.[19] In this report, he was asked to consider options for improving the balance between the supply of, and demand for, prison places.[20] The Review proposed the establishment of a permanent Sentencing Council in England and Wales. In January 2008, the British government announced its decision to create a

[15] Ibid, Professor Rod Morgan Change in Trends in the Prison Population 14.

[16] Patrick Carter (2003).

[17] NOMS was established in 2004. Created because of the government's response to the Carter Review, which recommended a unified management structure for prisons and probation services, it was responsible for the management and coordination of the prison and probation services in England and Wales. Its primary objectives were to improve public protection, reduce reoffending, and ensure the safe and secure custody of offenders. NOMS aimed to achieve these goals through collaboration between prisons and probation services, ensuring seamless transitions for offenders between custody and community supervision. The agency was dissolved in 2014, and its functions were transferred to Her Majesty's Prison and Probation Service (HMPPS).

[18] This was due to the imposition of indeterminate sentences for public protection (IPPs) governed by the Criminal Justice Act 2003 (and abolished under the Legal Aid, Sentencing and Punishment of Offenders Act 2012). IPPs were introduced as a response to public concern about dangerous offenders and aimed to protect the public by keeping such individuals in prison until they were deemed no longer a risk. IPPs allowed for an initial minimum term to be set, but the actual release was determined by the Parole Board based on an assessment of the individual's risk. However, the implementation of IPPs resulted in challenges related to the availability of suitable programs and resources for rehabilitation, as well as delays in the Parole Board's decision-making process. As a result, many individuals with IPPs ended up serving longer sentences than initially anticipated, contributing to the overall increase in the prison population.

[19] Patrick Carter (2007).

[20] Ibid.

sentencing commission under Lord Justice Gage to examine the advantages, disadvantages, and feasibility of a structured sentencing framework and a permanent sentencing commission.[21]

The creation of a Council was seen as a means of enhancing the transparency, predictability, and consistency of sentencing, thereby bringing the demand for imprisonment and the supply of prison places into closer alignment. The Criminal Justice Act 2003 had introduced indeterminate sentences for public protection (IPPs) as a response to public concern about dangerous offenders. These sentences aimed to protect the public by keeping such individuals in prison until they were deemed no longer a risk. IPPs allowed for an initial minimum term to be set, but actual release was determined by the Parole Board based on an assessment of the individual's risk. However, the implementation of IPPs led to challenges related to the availability of suitable programs and resources for rehabilitation, as well as delays in the Parole Board's decision-making process. Consequently, many individuals with IPPs ended up serving longer sentences than initially anticipated, contributing to the overall increase in the prison population.

6.4 Comparison with Judicial Council Act 2019

The Irish Judicial Council Act 2019 does not specifically mention offence categories. However, it provides a broad framework for the framing of guidelines like those produced by the English Sentencing Council. When drafting guidelines and amendments, the Sentencing Guidelines and Information Committee must consider numerous factors, including sentences imposed by the courts, promoting consistency in sentencing, the impact on victims, public confidence in the justice system, financial costs, and the effectiveness of diverse types of sentences in preventing re-offending.[22]

Section 92 of the Judicial Council Act 2019 mandates criminal courts to consider relevant guidelines when imposing sentences. Courts must adhere to these guidelines unless doing so would contravene the interests of justice, with an obligation to state their reasons for any such decision. This provision amalgamates aspects of Section 172 of the English Criminal Justice Act 2003, which necessitated courts to consider guidelines, and Section 125 of the Coroners and Justice Act 2009, which requires adherence to guidelines unless contrary to the interests of justice.

The English guidelines have successfully balanced consistency and individualisation, accommodating the competing values intrinsic to sentencing. The criteria which are utilised to assess offence seriousness, alongside the factors deemed aggravating or mitigating in specific offences, may be valuable when the Sentencing Guidelines and Information Committee come to develop guidelines in

[21] Sentencing Commission Working Group and Great Britain (2008), p. 9.

[22] O'Malley (2019).

Ireland. However, there are quite significant differences in the prison release systems of England and Wales and Ireland. For instance, in England and Wales, prisoners are typically conditionally released after serving half of their sentence, whereas in Ireland, release is only considered after three-quarters of the sentence has been served, contingent upon good behaviour.[23]

6.5 Transforming Rehabilitation

Despite the implementation of sentencing guidelines in England and Wales, committals to custody continued to rise, necessitating further reforms due to the persistently high reoffending rates among individuals serving short sentences. Transforming Rehabilitation (TR) reforms were initiated in 2013.[24] This series of reforms, outlined in a consultation document by the Ministry of Justice, were incorporated into the Rehabilitation of Offenders Act 2014.[25] A central feature of this policy was the establishment of 'Community Rehabilitation Companies' (CRCs), private and third sector organisations operating under a 'payment-by-results' contract. This was designed to incentivise innovation and decentralise practice.[26] Before the TR reforms, individuals serving sentences of less than 12 months were released unconditionally at the halfway point of their sentence, without any post-release involvement from statutory services such as the Probation Service. After the TR reforms, CRCs were compensated for monitoring released prisoners in the community.

However, the so-called 'rehabilitation revolution', which was aimed at improving probation services, in fact left them underfunded, fragile, and lacking credibility in the eyes of the courts. Although initially welcomed as an opportunity to provide support for a neglected cohort,[27] the reliance on CRCs to deliver probation services based on performance outcomes placed additional financial strain on these organisations, raising doubts about the effectiveness of the reform. As a result of the mounting pressure on services, recalls to prison increased,[28] further highlighting the reality of the 'revolving door' of imprisonment.[29]

---

[23] Ibid, p. 14.

[24] Ministry of Justice (2014).

[25] Ministry of Justice (2013).

[26] Ibid, para 12.

[27] Burke (2016).

[28] Padfield (2016).

[29] Cracknell (2023), p. 223.

6.6 Declining Use of Alternatives to Custody

The number of COs imposed annually in England and Wales decreased by 46% between 2009 to 2019.[30] One reason which has been highlighted for the reduction in the use of COs is a possible lack of magistrates' confidence in the sanction. In a 2022 survey by the England and Welsh Sentencing Council on public confidence in sentencing and the criminal justice system, over a third of magistrates (37%) were not confident that community sentences are an effective alternative to custody. Additionally, two-thirds (65%) were not confident that community sentences reduced crime, and just under half (45%) were not confident that community sentences effectively rehabilitate offenders.[31] These findings suggest that some magistrates had reservations about the efficacy and impact of community sentences compared to custodial sentences, contributing to their decreased use and a preference for other sentencing options.

In Ireland, it appears that the 2011 Amendment Act primarily focuses on promoting the CSO for offenders who would otherwise receive twelve months in prison, rather than emphasising a reduction in STPS imprisonment.[32] This direct substitution targets offenders at the higher end of the STPS cohort, resulting in little reduction for women, who rarely meet this threshold.[33] Despite the evidence from England and Wales, in Ireland there was an overall increase in the number of CSOs.[34] Thus, contrary to small-scale research on the subject, it appears that, in general, the Irish judiciary did not share the same lack of confidence in community service as a sentencing option.[35] However, this had little impact on the cohort of women, where offending rarely meets the criteria for up to twelve months' imprisonment at the higher end of the STPS cohort.[36]

The introduction of the Fines legislation in Ireland in 2016, which specifically targets offenders at the lower end of the STPS cohort, led to a notable decrease in the number of female STPS recipients. The Scottish experience indicates that offering judges a wider range of alternatives to custody does not necessarily result in a decrease in STPS. Instead, it can lead to an increase in the number of individuals placed under the control of the criminal justice system. This suggests that without careful planning and implementation, expanding the range of alternatives may inadvertently broaden the net of punitive measures, thereby increasing the overall reach of the criminal justice system rather than reducing reliance on incarceration.

[30] Ministry of Justice UK (2009–2019).

[31] Sentencing Council (2022), key findings published 12th December 2022.

[32] Criminal Justice (Community Service) (Amendment) Act (2011), s3.

[33] Irish Prison Service.

[34] O'Hara and Rogan (2015).

[35] Riordan (2009) some participant judges in this study indicated that they were uncomfortable with placing their complete faith in the CSO.

[36] Irish Prison Service.

6.7 Scotland: Solution or Warning?

The Scottish model, which prioritises community-based alternatives over STPS, offers valuable insights and potential solutions for addressing the needs of diverted female offenders. By emphasising diversion programs and community interventions over custodial sentences, this approach aims to provide effective support and rehabilitation, addressing the underlying issues contributing to criminal behaviour and promoting successful reintegration into society.

6.7.1 *The Commission on Women Offenders*

The Scottish Government recognised the need to develop more effective processes and practices to address female offending. In response, the Angiolini Commission on Women Offenders[37] was established to assess conditions within Corton Vale, the women's prison, and propose improvements to enhance outcomes for women in the criminal justice system. In 2008 the prison system was in crisis as the number of prisoners in Scotland exceeded 8000, which brought the number of inmates to over 156 per 100,000 inhabitants.[38] In addition to this, the number of female prisoners doubled.[39]

The report of the Commission noted that acute over-crowding in prisons was undermining rehabilitation efforts, decreasing living standards, and presenting daily challenges for prison staff.[40] The complexity of female imprisonment is compounded by the diverse needs of female offenders, many of whom have a history of sexual and physical abuse and struggle with severe mental health and substance abuse issues.[41] Additionally, a considerable number of these women had received short sentences for minor offences often connected to their addictions.[42] Women generally pose a lower risk to public safety, raising questions about the necessity of incarcerating them at the current rate.[43] Addressing these issues was a central concern for the Commission.

The Angiolini Commission's report highlights the characteristics and specific challenges faced by women who receive STPS. These women are described as 'frequent reoffenders with complex needs that relate to their social circumstances, previous histories of abuse, and mental health and addiction problems.'[44] The report

[37] Scottish Government (2019a, b).

[38] Aebi and Delagrande (2013), p. 39.

[39] (2012), p. 14.

[40] Ibid, p. 5.

[41] Ibid, p. 3.

[42] Scottish Government (2019a, b), p. 3.

[43] Ibid, p. 4.

[44] Angiolini (2012), p. 3.

emphasises that STPS have limited impact on reducing reoffending among this group. In fact, it notes that a significant proportion (70%) of women offenders who received a prison sentence of three months or less were reconvicted within two years. This suggests that alternative approaches are needed to address the underlying issues and support rehabilitation more effectively.[45]

The report underscores the cost disparity between prison sentences and community disposals and emphasises that prison is a more expensive option compared to community-based alternatives. The average cost of a CSO is approximately half the cost of a three-month prison sentence. This cost difference highlights the potential benefits of investing in community-based interventions that can provide tailored support and address the complex needs of women offenders in a more cost-effective manner.[46]

6.7.2 *Presumption Against Short-Term Sentences*

Scotland has implemented measures particularly relevant to diverted female offenders. The Presumption Against Short Sentences (PASS) was introduced to discourage the use of short prison sentences, specifically those of three months or less. The presumption aims to promote alternative community-based measures as more effective and appropriate responses to non-serious, low-level offending. Initially established under the Criminal Justice and Licensing (Scotland) Act 2010, PASS was expanded to include sentences of twelve months or less following the approval by the Scottish Parliament on 4 July 2019. Not an outright ban on their use, courts retain the discretion to impose short prison sentences if deemed necessary and justified based on the case's particular circumstances. However, when departing from the presumption, the court must record its reasons for choosing imprisonment over alternative community-based options.[47]

Statistical data from Scotland indicates that individuals released from short-term prison sentences are twice as likely to be reconvicted compared to those serving a CPO (Community Protection Order[48]). The Scottish Government has recently released monitoring information covering the period from July to December 2019.[49] Although it is too early to attribute changes in sentencing patterns solely to the extended PASS, there is emerging evidence indicating a reduction in the number of short custodial sentences in Scotland.[50]

---

[45] Ibid, p. 3.

[46] Ibid, Average cost of a CPO was £2400 in 2012.

[47] Section 204(3A) of the Criminal Procedure (Scotland) Act 1995, as amended by Section 17 of the Criminal Justice and Licensing (Scotland) Act 2010.

[48] Part 2 of the Criminal Justice (Scotland) Act (2016).

[49] Scottish Government (2019a, b).

[50] Criminal Justice and Licensing (Scotland) Act (2010).

The monitoring information published by the Scottish Government details the sentencing patterns observed in the courts following the implementation of the extended presumption. It covers the period from 4 July 2019 to 31 December 2019, representing the initial six months after the introduction of the extended presumption, with only a small number of offences falling under the new policy's purview being disposed of by the courts during this period.[51]

6.7.3 Community Payback Orders

CPOs were established in Scotland in 2011 as an alternative to custody.[52] They share similarities with Irish CSOs in that they involve the provision of 'suitability' reports to the judge, which provide background information about the person being sentenced. These reports may include details about previous offences, the person's risk of reoffending, their need for behavioural change, and information about their health and living situation. One key difference between CPOs and Irish CSOs is the involvement of a criminal justice social worker assigned by the local authority to supervise the requirements of the CPO. The social worker's role includes consulting with relevant parties, such as judges, police, voluntary groups, community councils, and victim support groups, as required.[53]

The CPO offers nine different requirements that can be tailored to the specific offender, with the judge determining which requirements should be included based on the nature of the offence and what measures are necessary to prevent further offences. This flexibility allows for a more individualised approach to addressing an offender's needs and reducing the likelihood of reoffending. This sanction is visible in its usage: In 2012, 11,000 CPOs were made in Scotland.[54] However, in the same year, Scotland's imprisonment rate was one of the highest in Europe at 148.8 per 100,000, well above the average of 136.3.[55]

The effectiveness of this measure is in some doubt, not only due to the impact of Covid-19 and the associated suspension of court cases in Scotland, resulting in a backlog of cases. Figures for 2020 indicate that the proportion of all disposals accounted for by custodial sentences of 12 months or less was 9.9% in January 2020, rising to 12% in December 2020. This increase may reflect an unintended consequence of the CPO where an increase has been recorded in both STPS and community sanctions. A 2008 study found that, unlike men, women tend to have a higher likelihood of breaching orders due to non-compliance rather than engaging in further criminal behaviour. Although the use of community sanctions increased in

[51] Scottish Government (2019a, b).

[52] Part 2 of the Criminal Justice (Scotland) Act (2016).

[53] IRPT (2020).

[54] Review Group for Penal Policy (2014), p. 47.

[55] Aebi and Delagrande (2013).

Scotland for women, this increase has been in higher tariff disposals of probation and community service at the expense of fines, which then decreased.[56]

The presence of increasing therapeutic options such as CPOs and the implementation of a presumption against short prison sentences (PASS) may not fully address the challenges faced by women receiving short-term prison sentences in Ireland. The underlying issue is more likely to lie in the under-resourced communities to which these women are diverted. Insufficient resources and support within the community can hinder successful rehabilitation and reintegration, leading to a cycle of reoffending.

Thus, if sufficient resources, funding, and support services were available within the community to effectively address the complex needs of these women, it could facilitate a more successful reintegration. With these provisions, a more comprehensive approach that combines appropriate diversion programs, community-based support, and tailored resources could potentially disrupt the cycle of reoffending and promote positive outcomes for women in the criminal justice system.

6.8 Net-widening

Net-widening refers to a situation where the use of alternatives to custody leads to a broader range of individuals being subjected to punitive outcomes. This means that instead of reducing the number of individuals involved in the criminal justice system, more individuals may end up being subjected to punitive measures than originally intended. The net-widening metaphor was coined by Stanley Cohen in 1979, when he wrote:

> the major results of the new movements towards 'community' and 'diversion' have been to increase rather than decrease the amount of intervention directed at many groups of deviants in the system and, probably, to increase rather than decrease the total number who get into the system in the first place. In other words: 'alternatives' become not alternatives at all but new programs which supplement the existing system or else expand it by attracting new populations.[57]

If the implementation of alternatives to custody is not well-planned, if the assessment of risk is miscalculated, or if there is a high rate of non-compliance with the alternatives, there is a possibility of 'net-widening' occurring. One potential reason why community service can be susceptible to the net-widening problem is its structure and implementation. For alternatives to be considered viable substitutes for prison, a level of punishment should be imposed on the offender that is seen as sufficiently meaningful and deterrent. Otherwise, if the costs associated with these alternatives are perceived as lower than the benefits of committing a crime, individuals may still choose to engage in criminal behaviour.

---

[56] Part 2 of the Criminal Justice (Scotland) Act (2016).

[57] Cohen (1979).

Furthermore, for any alternative sanctions imposed to be effective, they need to be viewed as legitimate by both society in general and the judges or magistrates who administer them. If there is a lack of public confidence in the effectiveness or fairness of the alternatives, or if sentencers do not consider them to be suitable punishments, there may be less inclination to utilise them as substitutes for prison sentences. This can result in a situation where, rather than reducing reliance on incarceration, the use of the alternatives instead expands the scope of the criminal justice system, and more individuals become trapped in its 'net'.[58]

In Ireland, under the government's policy of diversion, the 2011 legislation provides the CSO as a direct substitute for the STPS.[59] Under the 2014 legislation, default of fine no longer results in immediate imprisonment.[60] However, the alternatives to custody set out in both pieces of diversion legislation may still potentially result in custody where they interact with criminogenic needs. When alternatives to custody are not carefully planned, when risk assessments for these alternatives are inaccurate, or when there is a high rate of breaches, the phenomenon known as 'net-widening' can occur and the following may be evidence of this: In 2019–2020, the average proportion of females receiving STPS increased to between 12–14%. Similarly, the proportion of females receiving CSOs also rose to this same range (12–14%) during this period.[61]

The Irish Prison Reform Trust has monitored the recent expansion of the PASS in Scotland because of the similarities with Irish legislation.[62] However, there are still some notable distinctions. Under Scottish legislation, the court is explicitly prohibited from imposing custodial sentences of less than twelve months unless no other suitable method of dealing with the individual is deemed appropriate. In contrast, in Ireland, if the court determines that a sentence of less than twelve months is appropriate, they are obligated to consider a Community Service Order as an alternative to imprisonment.[63] In Scotland, when a court imposes a sentence of 12 months or less, they must provide a justification for their opinion that no other alternative is suitable. It is important to note that, despite the Penal Policy Review Group's recommendation for courts in Ireland to provide reasons for imposing custodial sentences, this legislation has not been enacted.[64] Mandating judges to justify their sentencing decisions in detail could be viewed as an infringement on

[58] Ibid.

[59] Criminal Justice (Community Service) (Amendment) Act (2011).

[60] Fines (Payment and Recovery) Act (2014).

[61] Duignan (2023).

[62] IRPT (2020).

[63] Criminal Justice (Community Service) Act 1983 as amended by the Criminal Justice (Community Service) (Amendment) Act 2011 s2.

[64] Review Group for Penal Policy (2014).

judicial independence and perceived as the legislative branch overstepping its boundaries by dictating how judges should perform their duties.[65]

6.9 Conclusion

The Irish jurisdiction seemed to centre its penal policy on a single primary goal: reducing costs by cutting STPS and promoting community-based alternatives. However, this approach led to an increase in STPS and more CSOs being made for women. Examining how other jurisdictions have tried to reduce offending through community corrections highlights the need for a broader evaluation of what works, considering the evidence on how and why people desist from crime. Consequently, a more diverse approach to measuring effectiveness is essential, and the evidence used to assess these community interventions should be varied and comprehensive.[66]

There is a risk that if a policy is overly retributive, it may result in the net-widening of the criminal justice system. Additionally, when offenders are treated as mere subjects of rehabilitative measures rather than as the primary beneficiaries, 'rehabilitation' tends to serve the perceived interests of broader society rather than the offenders themselves.[67] However, when the offender becomes the central focus of an intervention, the role of evidence enhances the effectiveness of the intervention or program. Desistance theories emphasise the importance of life events and social bonds, as well as narrative changes in the offender's self-perception.[68] and this please: It appears that if someone believes that the person involved in the criminal justice system can 'make good' and supports them, desistance can, be kept it alive, even where social circumstances preclude it.

Law

Constitution of Ireland (1937)
Criminal Justice Act (England and Wales) (2003)
Criminal Justice and Licensing (Scotland) Act (2010)
Criminal Justice (Community Service) (Amendment) Act (2011)

---

[65] Constitution of Ireland (1937) Ireland, Article 6 separation of powers in the Irish constitutional framework ensures that the judicial, legislative, and executive branches of government operate independently and without undue influence from one another.

[66] O'Hara and Rogan (2015), p. 43; McNeill et al. (2012), p. 3.

[67] Garland (2001).

[68] Maruna (2001).

Fines (Payment and Recovery) Act (2014)
Part 2 of the Criminal Justice (Scotland) Act (2016)

Online Resource

Sentencing guidelines in England and Wales: An evolutionary approach 2008
Irish Prison Service, Sentenced Committals Classified by Sentence Length & Gender from Years 2007 to 2020 - Irish Prison Service/ Home/ Information Centre/ Statistics & Information/ Yearly Statistics (Irish Prison Service)

References

Book

Burke L (2016) The Resettlement Road Map, vol 63. SAGE Publications Sage UK, London, England
Garland D (2001) The culture of control. Oxford University Press, Oxford
Maruna S (2001) Making good. American Psychological Association, Washington, DC

Journal Article

Cohen S (1979) The punitive city: notes on the dispersal of social control. Contemp Crises 3:339
Cracknell M (2023) The resettlement net: 'revolving door' imprisonment and carceral (re) circulation. Punish Soc 25:223
Fletcher H (2003) Prison licence, community order breaches and the prison population. Napo News 149:349
Mair G (2011) The community order in England and Wales: policy and practice. Probat J 58:215
McNeill F et al (2012) Reexamining evidence-based practice in community corrections: beyond "a-confined view" of what works. Justice Res Policy 14:35
O'Hara K, Rogan M (2015) Examining the use of community service orders as alternatives to short prison sentences in Ireland. Irish Probat J 12:22
Padfield N (2016) The magnitude of the offender rehabilitation and "through the gate" resettlement revolution. Crim Law Rev:99
Reitz KR (2004) Questioning the conventional wisdom of parole release authority. Future Imprisonment 199:219

Media

Ministry of Justice (2014) New law will see support extended to 50,000 more prisoners

Report

Aebi M, Delagrande N (2013) Council of Europe Annual Penal Statistics. Switzerland
Angiolini E (2012) Commission on Women Offenders: Final Report. Scottish Government, Edinburgh
Commons Select Committee (2007–2008) Select Committee on Justice- Fifth Report. Justice Committee Publications parliament.uk/ parliamentary business/ publications & records/ committee publications/ all select committee publications/ Commons Select Committees/ Justice
IRPT (2020) Scotland: Impact of Presumption Against Short Sentences
Ministry of Justice (2013) Transforming rehabilitation: a revolution in the way we manage offenders. London
Ministry of Justice UK (2009–2019) Number of Offenders Under Probation Service Supervision 31 December 2009 to 2019. Table A4.13 of the Annual Probation Tables
Patrick Carter L (2003) Managing offenders, reducing crime (A new approach, Home Office Strategy Unit, London). Ministry of Justice, London
Patrick Carter L (2007) Securing the future: proposals for the efficient and sustainable use of custody in England and Wales. Ministry of Justice, London
Review Group for Penal Policy (2014) Strategic Review of Penal Policy- Final Report. Dublin
Scottish Government (2019a) Presumption Against Short Periods of Imprisonment (Scotland) Order
Scottish Government (2019b) Extended Presumption Against Short Sentences: Monitoring Information July 2019 – December 2019
Sentencing Council (2022) Public confidence in sentencing and the criminal justice system: 2022 (Analysis & research). Research and Resources

Conference Paper

O'Malley T (2019) Sentencing Guidance and Guidelines. Annual National Prosecutors' Conference

Thesis

Duignan S (2023) Evaluation of the effect of Irish Penal Policy on female short-term prison sentence recipients: the need for gender-specific policy. University of Galway
Riordan D (2009) The role of the community service order and the suspended sentence in Ireland: a judicial perspective. (Ph.D)University College Cork

Chapter 7
Reintegration: Overcoming Challenges and Addressing the Woman's Needs

7.1 Introduction

The aim of this chapter is to illustrate how community-based alternatives have been evaluated and adapted in other jurisdictions, in the absence of any large-scale Irish review. It draws on research involving in-depth interviews with five women who have interacted with the criminal justice system in Ireland. Despite the small sample size, the impact of penal policies is evident in the participants' life stories: from the difficulties faced during childhood, through turbulent teenage years, into periods of active addiction, multiple offending, and, eventually, receiving convictions. This work challenges some of the prevailing assumptions about desistance and examines issues such as gender disparity in policymaking. It provides a practice-oriented overview of academic research on desistance and offers a comprehensive, multidisciplinary perspective on the process of achieving desistance.

7.2 Evaluating Community-Based Alternatives in Other Jurisdictions

Between 1996 and 2006, the imprisonment of women in England and Wales surged by 94 per cent, compared with a 38 per cent increase for men.[1] In response to this increase, the Labour government introduced the 'Women's Offending Reduction Programme',[2] aiming 'to reduce women's offending … by providing a better tailored and more appropriate response to the particular factors which have an impact on why women offend.'[3] The programme intended to demonstrate 'how a

[1] Ministry of Justice/ NOMS (2008).
[2] UK Home Office (2004).
[3] Ibid.

S. Duignan, *Transforming Justice for Women*, Gender, Justice and Legal Feminism 3, https://doi.org/10.1007/978-3-031-82455-5_7

multi-agency approach in the community could address women's complex needs more effectively.'[4]

Statistics revealed an increase in the use of custodial sentences by the courts, even though the nature and severity of women's offending had not worsened. The Home Office report noted, 'the evidence suggests that courts are imposing more severe sentences on women for less serious offences.'[5] The programme aimed 'to reduce… the number of women in custody.'[6] It sought not to give women offenders any 'preferential treatment but instead sought to achieve equality of treatment and access to provision.'[7] Initially, no additional resources were allocated for this purpose.[8] However, approximately £9 million was allocated to support the 'Together Women' project in five locations in the North of England for three years, commencing between late 2006 and early 2007.

The primary objective of the project was to demonstrate how a collaborative approach involving multiple agencies in the community could more effectively address the complex needs of women. It aimed to reduce reoffending among current offenders and prevent individuals deemed 'at risk' from engaging in criminal activities by demonstrating 'how a multi-agency approach in the community could address women's complex needs more effectively.'[9] It incorporated best practice lessons from longstanding schemes for women such as the Asha Centre[10] and the 218 Centre.[11] The specific ranges of support available to women included training and interventions on parenting, managing mental health, and life skills. It also served as a drop-in centre, where women could access various activities, such as reading groups and complementary therapies.[12]

After three years, the Ministry of Justice commissioned an outcome evaluation of the Together Women Project.[13] Despite being promoted as a demonstration project, little information about its effectiveness was published by the Ministry of Justice.[14] Hedderman criticised that the only evaluation undertaken was:

> [A] small number of interviews with sentencers about whether they diverted women from custody into Together Women. Otherwise, the evaluation is assessing impact by measuring reconviction rates and examining project files to measure changes in factors such as

[4]Hedderman et al. (2008).

[5]UK Home Office (2004).

[6]Ibid, p. 5.

[7]Ibid, p. 5.

[8]Hedderman et al. (2008), p. 5.

[9]UK Home Office (2004).

[10]Rumgay (2004a, b, c).

[11]Loucks et al. (2006).

[12]Ibid.

[13]Hedderman et al. (2008).

[14]Ibid.

substance misuse, mental health, and employment. The outcome evaluation will not include an up-to-date assessment of the service user's perspective.[15]

After this three-year evaluation, further developments were limited. Gelsthorpe et al. observed that a community-based support programme tailored to women's needs would not be cost-effective within the UK system: 'The level of demand in terms of sheer numbers is too small, and the complexity of women's needs is too great, to make this an area for easy or quick profits.'[16]

There were some positive developments in community programmes which addressing offending behaviour. However, these programmes have inherent problems regarding their suitability for all offenders.[17] Commentators have highlighted how offender treatment programs are primarily designed for the majority: white, male, adult offenders, with minimal adjustments for other minority groups.[18] There is evidence that men do tend to respond to interventions focusing directly on offending behaviour but evidence suggests that women who offend need more practical and emotional support for a broader range of issues during periods of crisis.[19]

A Scottish study in 2008 supported these findings, focusing on how decisions by criminal justice professionals impact the effectiveness of addressing female offenders' underlying problems.[20] The study examined the profile of women offenders in one Community Justice Authority in Scotland and gathered qualitative data from 22 professionals and an analysis of 27 criminal justice social work case files. The purpose was to 'describe and analyse those characteristics and needs' not only based on quantitative data pertaining to women involved in the criminal Justice system in Lothian and Borders during a twelve-month period, but also based on qualitative data elicited from practitioners and policy makers about the issues surrounding women offenders within the criminal justice system.[21]

Barry and McIvor argued that harsher responses to women's offending often start at the prosecutor's decision-making point.[22] National data showed that sixty-five per cent of all reports sent to the procurator fiscal in 2006/7 resulted in prosecution.[23] The study also found that sentencers, 'when sentencing women, did not always make decisions that were based on women's needs as identified in SERs.'[24] Concerns were raised that some sentencers were using probation inappropriately as a welfare option

[15] Hedderman et al. (2011).

[16] Gelsthorpe and Hedderman (2012), p. 387.

[17] Ibid, p. 375.

[18] Ogloff (2002).

[19] Barry and McIvor (2008).

[20] Ibid.

[21] Ibid, p. 6.

[22] Ibid, p. 30.

[23] Scottish Government (2008).

[24] Barry and McIvor (2008), p. 31 (SERs are the equivalent of Pre-Sentence Reports in Scotland).

for women at low risk of reoffending, rather than responding to their actual likelihood of reoffending.[25]

The study also revealed high reoffending rates following imprisonment,[26] and any gains from interventions during custody could be lost upon release, where women faced significant difficulties.[27] Women in the criminal justice system were found to have low self-esteem prior to release and required additional care and support in the community.[28]

For female STPS recipients, conviction rates did not decrease without effective diversion,[29] and reconviction rates increased without effective desistance.[30] Barry and McIvor used qualitative interviews to understand 'the characteristics and needs of women in the criminal justice system.'[31] They acknowledged evidence that men and women might have similar criminogenic needs but recognised the necessity for specific interventions for women, which were more informal, less structured, and more 'supportive.'[32] This identification was made through a qualitative examination of the woman's entire journey through the criminal justice system, revealing:

> [H]arsher attitudes towards women who offend,... [resulting in] limited opportunities to intervene effectively to address women's wider needs in the context of wider professional and structural constraints, and strict enforcement criteria which leave little room for flexibility.[33]

Qualitative research carried out for the Corston Report in both women's prisons and the community in the United Kingdom reflects a traditional male-centric criminological approach. They rely on mainstream methods to assess the effectiveness of treatment programs or predict reoffending likelihood among specific minority groups and this can lead to inaccurate predictions.[34] This methodology underscores the importance of interviewing women in trying to understand the causes of

---

[25] Ibid, p. 32.

[26] Gelsthorpe and McIvor (2007).

[27] Woods (2020).

[28] Social Exclusion Unit (2002).

[29] Central Statistics Office (2022).

[30] Ibid.

[31] Barry and McIvor (2008), p. 6. They could then see how the main issues which women presented with tended to be mental health, drugs/alcohol, traumatic childhood experiences, domestic abuse and self-harm, and financial problems.

[32] Ibid, p. 37.

[33] Ibid, p. 37.

[34] False negatives can occur when individuals or groups are predicted to have a low risk of reoffending, but they subsequently engage in criminal behaviour West and Farrington (1973) West and Farrington undertook an assessment on a group of 7-year-olds would be convicted of an offence by the age of 14 and which would still be offending at the age of 21. Despite considering the normal indicators, they only got half of their assessments right. Such failure in prediction leads to false negatives or false positives. On the other hand, false positives happen when a person or group is inaccurately identified as being at risk of reoffending. These situations are challenging to identify because individuals in these cases may have been incarcerated even though they would not

women's offending and their experiences in the criminal justice system.[35] Their stories, as Heidensohn explains, 'make the connection between private troubles and public issues.'[36] A female centric methodology is required to highlight what works best in promoting desistance and reducing reoffending.[37] The identification of needs is central to evaluating offenders and is at the core of offender treatment and assessment models, which have been associated with reductions in reoffending.[38]

7.3 Identifying Needs

The Risk-Need-Responsivity (RNR) model has emerged as the predominant framework globally for evaluating and treating offenders.[39] The core principles of RNR involve identifying risk and appropriate criminogenic needs, which then become the focus of targeted interventions. Responsivity pertains to how these interventions should be delivered. However, the RNR model has faced criticism for its emphasis on individual factors without considering the broader social context of women offenders. Specifically, the model has been critiqued for its failure to adequately address systemic disadvantages, gender-based discrimination, and social marginalisation that often contribute to women's criminal behaviour.[40]

The 'risk' principle focuses on identifying risk and matching the level of services to the individual's risk level for reoffending, with higher risk necessitating more intensive intervention. This principle comprises two elements: prediction and matching. To classify offenders and provide appropriate intervention, it is essential to assess and predict everyone's reoffending risk. The intervention's intensity must then align with this risk level. Prediction of criminality involves identifying risk factors empirically related to subsequent offending, which can be static or dynamic. Effective measurement of need is crucial for the formal assessment of criminogenic need and, hence, the risk of offending. The 'needs' principle advocates for the identification and treating changeable or dynamic risk factors directly linked to offending. Thus, only factors directly associated with reoffending require to be targeted in interventions. The 'responsivity' principle suggests that intervention programmes should be tailored to the characteristics of the person with convictions.[41]

---

have committed an offence if they had remained free: Thomas Mathiesen, Prison on Trial, 3rd English ed (2006).

[35] Hedderman et al. (2011); Heidensohn (2006); Sheehan et al. (2011), p. 14.

[36] Heidensohn and Heidensohn (1989), p. 14.

[37] Bloom and Covington (1998).

[38] Andrews and Bonta (1998).

[39] HM Inspectorate of Probation.

[40] Hollin and Palmer (2006a, b).

[41] Bonta and Wormith (2007).

RNR instruments can reliably differentiate lower-risk offenders from higher-risk ones. However, the level of risk and the seriousness of offending often do not justify custody, and the increasing number of women being sentenced to imprisonment remains a significant concern.[42] In 2017, in England and Wales:

> [A]lmost half (47%) of women sentenced to a short custodial sentence had committed shop theft. The majority (94%) of women in custody serving a short sentence of under 12 months are a low or medium public protection risk.[43]

Several explanations have been proposed for this increase. Some attribute it to a perceived shift in societal attitudes towards control and punishment, while others argue that women's offences have become more severe and persistent, justifying harsher penalties.[44] Additionally, there is the idea that women's prisons have evolved into modern-day 'social services' facilities.[45]

Overall, however, women still tend to commit less serious crimes compared to men and are less likely to persist in criminal behaviour. Thus, the justification for the increased use of custodial sentences based on offending behaviour is weak. Effective evaluations are needed to ensure that sentencing and probation services are aware of the potential for effectively working with women offenders in the community. By focusing on community-based interventions, appropriate support and resources can be provided to address the specific needs and circumstances of women offenders, promoting rehabilitation and reducing the reliance on custodial sentences.

Increasingly, research indicates that women who offend have individual needs which highlight significant differences in pathways into and out of crime compared to men.[46] In particular, this recognises that indirect factors may interact with other psychological and social factors (criminogenic needs) to increase the risk of offending.[47] This school of thought notes how adverse life events can potentially interact with each other and how, in turn, this interaction relates to offending.[48] Hannah-Moffat acknowledges that contemporary definitions of need within the criminal justice system are often intertwined with risk assessments.[49] She suggests that the 'criminogenic needs' of offenders might be reframed as dynamic risk factors, while other needs that cannot be addressed through criminal justice interventions, such as poverty or structural discrimination, are being ignored. Risk assessment, despite appearing objective and scientific, is being influenced by professional

[42] Gelsthorpe et al. (2007).

[43] Prison Reform Trust (2018).

[44] Gelsthorpe et al. (2007).

[45] Carlen (2002).

[46] Irish Penal Reform Trust (2011, 2013, 2021); Inspector of Prisons (2011).

[47] Byrne and Trew (2008).

[48] Hedderman et al. (2008), p. 8.

[49] Hannah-Moffat (2005).

subjectivity.[50] It seems that not all needs can be managed or manipulated, and the definition of needs may depend on the resources available to address them.

Consequently, correctional interventions prioritise what is pragmatic rather than what is meaningful to the offender. This approach positions individuals as potential recipients of predefined services rather than active agents in identifying their own needs. This, Hannah-Moffat argues, is why the current emphasis on evaluating criminogenic needs disadvantages women offenders.[51]

Similarly, assessment of non-criminal history items, such as drug abuse, tends to focus on past behaviours, which may not reflect an individual's current situation. Criminal history and other factors related to past behaviour are considered fixed risk factors, overlooking the possibility of positive changes in offenders. This approach has a major limitation as it does not account for the potential reduction in risk. In other words, the scales used for assessment do not consider the possibility that an individual's risk level may decrease over time. Instead, they only account for a constant or increased risk, even if an individual has made positive changes or is no longer engaged in previous risky behaviour.

If needs relate to past experiences of victimisation, for example, they may only be addressed if statistically linked to recidivism and amenable to intervention. This redefinition of needs as criminogenic risk factors can increase the perception of women offenders as 'risky' due to high needs translating into high-risk scores. Thus, 'women with a relatively short criminal record may find themselves subject to elevated levels of criminal justice system control.'[52]

Conversely, the high levels of welfare-related needs among female offenders, coupled with their lower likelihood of recidivism compared to men, may lead to their needs being overlooked or considered unsuitable for criminal justice intervention. As a result, the gender-specific requirements women might have are often inadequately addressed within the system.

Concerns about the RNR framework have led to the emergence of the 'pathways' approach, which acknowledges the needs of women offenders and those at risk of offending as more complex, interrelated, and distinctive.[53] It is unclear whether the static or dynamic items contribute most to the assessment of reoffending risk, although Gendreau et al. suggest that dynamic predictors perform at least as well as static predictors.[54] Rather than focusing on a single criminal act, the pathways perspective examines the entire life history of an individual to gain insight and understanding into why an individual may have committed an offence.

This approach helps uncover patterns of behaviour and provides insight into effective prevention methods. It incorporates a whole-life perspective in studying crime causation and is based on extensive interviews with women offenders to

---

[50] Gelsthorpe et al. (2007), p. 18.

[51] Ibid, p. 19.

[52] Ibid, p. 19.

[53] Ibid, p. 13.

[54] Healy (2010).

discover factors such as the role of violence, trauma, and substance misuse, the type of offence and reoffending patterns, and the impact of responsibilities and connections with violent and substance-abusing partners. This female-centred research indicates that the focus should not be limited to a narrow set of 'dynamic' factors. Instead, emphasis should focus on a wide range of both indirect factors[55] and direct factors,[56] all of which may be relevant to finding the pathways out of crime.[57]

Scholarship has highlighted concerns about the applicability of a distinct model for women offenders in terms of how adequately it assesses women's needs and the effectiveness of programmes targeting those needs. A report by the Northern Ireland Office in 2009 observed that 'generic risk scales have been developed for men.' The report showed that studies on the effectiveness of interventions targeting these needs are primarily based on samples of male offenders.[58]

Studies of treatment programmes including females have yielded inconsistent results[59] and concerns were raised about their methodological rigour.[60] Blanchette[61] refers to the suggestion made by some authors[62] that the focus should be on a woman's 'strengths and capabilities' rather than her criminogenic 'needs'. She concludes, however, that whatever response is adopted, the most essential element for creating effective provision for women is considering them to be 'a heterogeneous group, distinct from their male counterparts.'[63] Blanchette also recognises the need to acknowledge the diverse range among women who offend in terms of unchanging factors such as age, culture, and ethnicity. This was also recognised by Kemshall[64] and Gelsthorpe[65] who note that it may be more helpful to think of women's needs as desistance-related rather than 'criminogenic.'[66]

In the Irish jurisdiction, female STPS recipients were not only treated the same as men in terms of policy when aggregated statistically, but there is also insufficient disaggregation between the categories of STPS recipients. There is no differentiation of seriousness in the STPS recipient cohort[67] even though, according to the Irish

---

55 Issues that can affect self-identity, self-esteem, and confidence can indirectly lead to offending, like, for example abuse and histories of trauma.

56 Issues that directly affect offending might include financial difficulties or substance abuse where an offender steals to feed themselves or their addiction.

57 Gelsthorpe et al. (2007), p. 14.

58 Blanchette (2004), p. 234.

59 Ibid.

60 Hedderman (2004), p. 242.

61 Blanchette (2004), p. 234.

62 Hannah-Moffat (2005); Sheehan et al. (2011).

63 Blanchette (2004), p. 234.

64 Kemshall (2004).

65 Gelsthorpe and McIvor (2007).

66 Gelsthorpe et al. (2007).

67 STPS recipients who receive sentences of imprisonment of <3 months, 3–6 months, and 6–12 months are all published in the same category of 'STPS recipients'. Most women are in the <3 months tier.

Prison Service Annual Reports, women tend to receive sentences in the lowest category.[68] Increased transparency of data is likely to produce more detailed policy and tailored interventions. By recognising the importance of flexibility and tailored interventions to address specific women's needs, community sanctions could be designed to better support female offenders and reduce the risk of reoffending.

7.4 Risk Management in England and Wales

As noted earlier, the Probation Service in Ireland does not have as long a history as in England and Wales, but the two agencies share similar origins and outlooks. The impact of the Probation Service's 'risk management' may have influenced interventions for women. The Probation of Offenders Act 1907 ('the 1907 Act') in Britain and Ireland created a new cohort of professionals within the criminal justice system, known as probation officers. Their role was based on the work which court missionaries had previously fulfilled, however many of these professionals quickly 'aspired to a more secular, professional and 'scientific' standing.'[69] However, the two services have diverse histories and have evolved in different ways regarding the assessment of females.

In England and Wales in the 1970s and 80s, the reformative, rehabilitative model began to shift towards a 'treatment' model like that used in the United States.[70] This placed a new emphasis on risk and public safety and led to the decline of the penal welfare approach. Rehabilitation was increasingly justified not by its positive impact on offenders' lives, but by its potential to improve the safety of future victims.[71] Traditionally, probation perceived the offender as a 'sinner' capable of moral reform, but by the 1970s and 1980s, this perception shifted. Offenders were now seen as 'patients' who might be cured through treatment, and eventually as 'risk-bearing subjects' whose risks must be assessed, managed, and reduced if possible.[72] As the Probation Service became increasingly focused on 'risk' and its containment, commentators note how the service expanded its supervisory role in the community, utilising punishments such as curfews and electronic tagging, thus becoming more punitive.[73]

A new type of 'managerialism' emerged, modifying rehabilitation ideals through the increasing application of 'actuarial' or 'insurance-based' techniques to problems

[68] Duignan (2023).

[69] Garland (1985).

[70] Bottoms and McWilliams (1979).

[71] Flew (1954).

[72] Feeley and Simon (1992).

[73] Garland (2001); Cohen (1985); Hough et al. (2003).

of control. Garland argues that these new rehabilitative interventions gained legitimacy by contributing to the broader goal of risk management.[74] The aims of imprisonment and supervisory penalties shifted from purely reforming or rehabilitating offenders to managing risk. Effective rehabilitation became synonymous with effective risk management, incorporating a moral dimension to successful rehabilitation.[75]

One development in probation practice in England and Wales during the late 1990s, which undoubtedly had a knock-on effect, was the severance of probation officer training from its traditional grounding in social work education. This development, instigated by the English and Welsh Conservative government, aimed to 'toughen up' probation's image and was followed by similar efforts to increase the punitive nature of community-based penalties.[76] Offenders could only be 'treated' in drug abuse programmes, anger-management groups, and offence-reduction programmes to the extent that such treatment was deemed capable of protecting the public, reducing risk, and being more cost-effective than straightforward punishment. In this new framework, 'rehabilitation' was viewed as a means of managing risk, not a welfarist end in itself.[77]

Feeley and Simon observed that the characteristics of the old penology were more concerned with individual responses to offenders based on their moral worth.[78] They noted that the new risk paradigm focused on actuarial calculations of risk, involving techniques for identifying, classifying, and managing groups.[79] Clinical judgment and professional discretion were replaced by evidence-based risk assessments—highly structured instruments that include comprehensive assessments of client characteristics, attentive to responsivity, strengths, idiosyncratic risk factors, and their integration into case management strategies. Despite indications that interventions should embody a more holistic approach to rehabilitation,[80] some critics argued against developing individual objectives because they were not amenable to measurement.

The disconnection of rehabilitation from welfare became evident in the distinction drawn between offender 'needs'. Offender criminogenic 'needs' are those requirements directly linked to the individual's propensity to offend. Under a welfare-based approach, criminogenic needs would be addressed. Under a risk-based approach, criminogenic needs no longer merit attention or resourcing where they are not linked to risk, as addressing them would not contribute to reducing the likelihood of offending and enhancing public protection. Thus, if an offender is homeless or has mental health issues, this would not require intervention under the

[74] Garland (2004).

[75] Sparks and Simon (2012).

[76] Carr and Robinson (2021).

[77] Garland (2001).

[78] Feeley and Simon (1992).

[79] Ibid, p. 29.

[80] Sparks and Simon (2012).

risk-based paradigm. However, research has shown that the risk of reoffending is high when these factors are not addressed.[81]

7.5 Evolution of Irish Probation Policy

Ireland was akin to England and Wales in enacting legislation to provide judges with the ability to sentence offenders to perform unpaid work in the community. Throughout the 1980s and 1990s various government policy documents and reports advocated for increased resourcing and utilisation of the Probation Service.[82] There was a shift in thinking that led to significant changes in Irish probation policy and practice, requiring practitioners to adapt to a new orientation.

Some commentators suggest that a 'new punitiveness' emerged in Ireland, influenced by the adoption of a 'zero tolerance' approach to crime control.[83] There was a discernible absence of criminological debate and a notable indifference from the government towards criminological research in Ireland. Kilcommins observes a growing trend towards the 'crime control' model of justice aimed at maximising efficiency, control, and risk reduction.[84] Richardson also notes that concerns related to accountability, cost-effectiveness, and managing individuals deemed 'risky' contributed to an ideological shift in Probation from rehabilitation and welfare, leading to an increased focus on risk assessment and offender management.[85]

Despite the Whitaker Report recommending that prison should be used as a sentence of last resort and advocating for the expanded use of community-based penalties,[86] the usage of CSOs declined in the years leading up to 2007.[87] The government carried out the Value for Money and Policy Review of the Community Service Scheme, a review of the CSO which took place almost 9 years after Walsh and Sexton's report.[88] However, this was primarily an analysis of the cost-effectiveness of the community service infrastructure and resource utilisation rather than a policy analysis of the nature, scope, and effectiveness of community service from the perspectives of varying penal paradigms.[89]

This approach aligns with Garland's concept of the 'systemisation of criminal justice' as a governmental response to the challenges posed by high crime rates and the inherent limitations of traditional crime control methods employed by criminal

[81] Clear et al. (2001).

[82] Prendergast (2012), p. 117.

[83] O'Donnell and O'Sullivan (2001).

[84] Kilcommins (2005), p. 20.

[85] Richardson (2008), p. 20.

[86] Department of Justice (1985).

[87] McCarthy (2014).

[88] The Probation Service (2009) was carried out 9 years after Walsh and Sexton (2000).

[89] McCarthy (2014), p. 128.

justice agencies. In this regard, Garland maintains that it is part of a broader set of adaptive strategies aimed at implementing a level of process and information management previously lacking.[90]

The government's five-year plan for the Management of Offenders[91] recommended an expanded role for the Probation Service, which was positioned as an alternative to custody in the context of prison overcrowding. It was not until the 2000s that increased Probation involvement was realised with the introduction of five foundational pieces of legislation, heralding a multitude of developments in the criminal process and in penal policy.[92] Campbell notes that these statutory measures 'altered the topography of the Irish criminal justice system, presaging the erosion of pre-trial rights, the introduction of presumptive sentences, the use of restorative justice techniques, and the establishment of civil asset forfeiture.'[93]

Following the investigations of the Joint Committee in July 2013,[94] the government published the Strategic Review on Penal Policy in 2014.[95] This Review appeared to take new strides towards more rehabilitative principles and offered insights into the government's view on sentencing policies, alternatives to custody, custodial accommodation and regimes, reintegration and rehabilitation, and issues relating to women offenders.[96]

However, in the years since the Strategic Review's publication, there has been limited articulation on how to translate these rehabilitative principles into legislation or more detailed policies. As a result, the Probation Service and other criminal justice agencies have only received a general framework for these new rehabilitative policies. Beyens notes that penalties have found a middle ground between the two extremes of rehabilitative probation and retributive and deterrent imprisonment, undermining their substitutive nature. This may explain why CSOs have not replaced STPS, but rather, both penalties have increased.[97]

The changing public and political attitudes towards crime, coupled with economic constraints, led to a shift in Irish probation policy towards a more managerial approach focused on effectiveness and cost-efficiency. Target setting, monitoring, and efficiency became core elements of the policy. To enhance efficiency and effectiveness, various tools and measures were introduced, including risk assessment tools, national standards, templates, guidelines, and procedures, along with

---

[90] Garland (1996).

[91] Government of Ireland (1994).

[92] Children Act (2001); Sex Offenders' Act (2000); Criminal Justice Act (2006); Fines Act (2010); Criminal Justice (Community Service) (Amendment) Act (2011).

[93] Campbell (2008), p. 2.

[94] Defence and Equality Joint Committee on Justice (2013).

[95] Review Group for Penal Policy (2014).

[96] Ibid, Recommendation 26: 'The Review Group recommends that all offenders must have the opportunity to avail of any necessary services or programmes to aid their rehabilitation and reintegration.'

[97] Beyens (2010), p. 9.

supporting policy documents. These developments align with the broader international trend known as actuarial justice, which emphasises risk assessment and management. The new approach aimed to achieve better outcomes and aligned with the principles of effectiveness and value for money.[98] Hayles argues that basing punishment on risk lengthens that punishment indeterminately. In other words, 'once a risk, always a risk'.[99] She also argues that risk assessment tools 'label' for longer periods than is perhaps warranted by the type and severity of the offence.

7.6 Analysis of Approaches in the Irish Probation System

There are three main categories of risk assessment tools: clinical, actuarial, and structured clinical judgment. Clinical methods involve professional judgment based on individual information and research on risk factors. Considered subjective and impressionistic, they are often made with limited information and scientific evidence, resulting in poor predictive accuracy for future harm. Actuarial approaches, on the other hand, employ mathematical calculations to compare an individual's key factors with statistical data on similar risks within a matched sample. While they may yield higher predictive power, they lack guidelines for risk management. Evaluators may be lulled into a false sense of security in dealing with actuarial risk assessment tools, not least because of the seeming reliability of mathematical calculation and scientific sophistication.[100]

There are concerns that the 'language of risk' obscures the underlying social and personal challenges that offenders face, while also portraying victims as the primary recipients of risk assessments.[101] Research indicates that, especially in the United States, risk management has overtaken punishment as a means of exclusion and separation. While risk assessments may appear to possess scientific rigour and accuracy, their primary function often lies in providing an organisation with a veneer of credibility in addressing crime, managing staff, and mitigating liability in case of mishaps.[102]

There are inherent pitfalls associated with risk assessments, particularly the inaccuracies of 'false positives' and 'false negatives.' False negatives occur when high-risk cases are incorrectly assessed as posing no risk, while false positives arise when low-risk cases are wrongly assessed as high risk. These errors in risk assessment can have significant implications: false negatives may overlook individuals who genuinely pose a danger, whereas false positives may lead to unnecessary interventions or restrictions for those who do not pose a genuine threat. Research

[98] Feeley and Simon (1992); Kemshall and Wood (2013).

[99] Hayles (2006).

[100] Barry (2007a, b), p. 14.

[101] Horsefield (2003), p. 376.

[102] Ibid, p. 376.

into this phenomenon demonstrates that by isolating individual risk factors from their broader context—such as biography, place, and social structure—risk assessment tools focus more on managing offenders than on addressing the root causes and cessation of individual offending.[103]

In Ireland, the Level of Supervision Inventory – Revised (LSI-R) is a hybrid risk/ needs assessment tool, used to facilitate a wide range of decisions from sentencing to release. This tool was one of the first attempts to formalise the assessment of criminogenic needs and the LSI-R is the primary risk/ needs assessment instrument used by the Probation Service to determine the appropriate level of criminogenic needs.[104] It consists of a 54-item measure, completed through interview and file review, composed of 10 subscales that assess domains of criminogenic need: these subscales are criminal history, education/employment, finance, family/marital relationships, accommodation, use of leisure/recreation time, companions, alcohol/drug problems, emotional/personal issues, and attitudes/orientation. The subscales are formed from a combination of items that address both the static and dynamic dimensions of a need. For example, the emotional/personal subscale contains items concerning both previous and current treatment for mental health problems. The scoring produces ten subcomponent scores that give a total score; the total score can be translated into a risk score for likelihood of future offending.

Hollins cautions that some needs domains within the LSI-R are deceptive regarding their likelihood of change; for example, it might appear that 'criminal history' is a static need but it has a dynamic element in that it can change over time, even over the course of a prison sentence.[105] Standardised assessment tools claim to offer a less moralistic attitude to the assessment of offenders as they offer standardisation of assessment processes and outcomes and Fitzgibbon notes how, prior to the LSI-R, there was a belief in certain circles that the traditional approach to probation casework led to subjective and unreliable results.[106] Studies have suggested that the LSI-R has strong predictive utility in terms of recidivism.[107]

The Irish Probation Service moved from the more traditional approach, which relied solely on practitioner clinical judgement, to a more structured approach based on actuarial risk assessment after literature from Canada,[108] the US, England, Wales, and Scotland exhibited this shift towards 'risk management.'[109] As risk has become the primary focus for nearly all probation work, the new managerial style of supervision has affected a wide range of offenders, including those on early release, those serving alternatives in the community, and those under probation supervision post-release. The use of actuarial instruments to predict future harm for minority

[103]Webster et al. (2006), p. 18.
[104]Kelly and Bogue (2014).
[105]Hollin and Palmer (2006a, b).
[106]Fitzgibbon (2007).
[107]Gendreau et al. (2002).
[108]Bonta and Wormith (2007).
[109]Feeley and Simon (1992).

groups is particularly problematic, as minority traits may be misinterpreted and categorised as 'risk.'

Ireland adopted the instrument later than other jurisdictions and Prendergast noted how research into risk assessment/risk management in Irish probation practice was limited.[110] However, Kelly and Bogue examined gender differences between offenders on criminogenic needs as measured by the LSI-R in 2014. Although their study did not examine gender-specific needs, the findings are significant as criminogenic needs as measured by the LSI-R are distributed differently in male and female offenders. The study notes how this has implications for how resources in supervision and interventions for female offenders are best directed. Firstly, accommodation appears to be 'an extremely problematic area for female offenders.'[111] This reflects the fact that homelessness is a significant problem for them. The study also showed the importance of addressing emotional and mental needs, 'otherwise they could act as a potential barrier to addressing other criminogenic needs.'[112] They found that female offenders would benefit from training/education and employment opportunities with childcare services available for women with children. They found that women with young children may find it difficult to access employment/training due to childcare requirements, perhaps finding it more difficult to escape from reliance on social welfare.

Some women may also become involved in offending in the context of a relationship.[113] This is likely to impact a female offender's attitude to offending. An offender may even rationalise their behaviour after committing an offence, allowing them to experience less responsibility for their actions.[114] Offenders can develop anti-social attitudes based on the partners that they are with or the company that they keep. Kelly et al. remark that a programme that targets criminogenic attitudes in female offenders is unlikely to reduce recidivism without addressing the influence the women's partners and families have on their offending. The study found that there was no significant difference in the area of antisocial attitudes, although cognitive behavioural programmes designed for men may not have the same impact in reducing female offending.[115]

There is still a debate over whether these differences are better addressed in terms of 'responsivity targets'[116] which could take consideration taken for gender non-specific factors such as parental stress[117] and other factors relating to poor mental health. There is a concern that if gender-specific needs are identified as risk

[110] Prendergast (2012), p. 117; Davies (2007).

[111] Kelly and Bogue (2014).

[112] Ibid, p. 100.

[113] Holtfreter and Cupp (2007).

[114] Kelly and Egan (2012).

[115] Brown and Blanchette (2006).

[116] Kelly and Bogue (2014), p. 90.

[117] Rettinger and Andrews (2010).

factors as opposed to responsivity factors, there may be an over-classification of risk levels for female offenders, which could have negative outcomes for women.[118]

Two years after its introduction into Irish probation practice, Richardson's thesis investigated the attitudes of Probation Officers working with adult offenders in Dublin.[119] It asked whether that the LSI-R led to the prioritisation of risk over the identification of needs.[120] She found there was a 'a commitment by probation officers to retaining clinical judgement when making decisions about risk.'[121] Ultimately, the probation officers were found to be erring on the side of 'professional judgment.'[122] However, the approach adopted may be flawed as it indicated a practice of relying on self-reported information from the offender, and whether the probation officer believes the offender is a prospective risk. The making of risk decisions based on guess work is neither an objective nor consistent approach and thus may be indefensible. Monahan observes how risk assessment is, at best, good guess work and therefore gathering information from several sources is integral to making defensible decisions.[123]

The most important factor in making decisions that can hold up to public scrutiny is having defensible reasoning. Risk assessment involves investigative methods that entail sharing data among criminal justice agencies and utilising clinical interviews and actuarial predictors. Therefore, this model must be supported by criminal justice agencies by making all information available to the risk assessor. In the absence of such information, probation officers are vulnerable to public accusations of failure when risk decisions transpire to be flawed due to under or over prediction. Thus, it would appear, for want of more recent research in this area, that offenders in Ireland, are assessed using a blend of stringent LSI-R criteria and probation officer experience. Prendergast's study found that most respondents reported using the instrument to validate their own judgement or assessment and ensuring that 'important aspects did not get overlooked'. Practitioners reported that such assessments helped ensure that they did 'not take short cuts' or 'ignore things that might be important'.[124]

However, for certain diverted persons in the community who feel increased pressure of meeting high demands of supervision, like women, this may lead to increased recall. A report in England and Wales revealed that over 1700 women were recalled to prison in England and Wales during 2019.[125] That government's Female Offenders Strategy, published in June 2018, brought together empirical evidence regarding women in conflict with the criminal justice system. It

[118] Holtfreter and Cupp (2007).

[119] Richardson (2008).

[120] Ibid.

[121] Ibid, p. 37.

[122] Ibid, p. 37.

[123] Monahan (1981).

[124] Prendergast (2012).

[125] Prison Reform Trust (2018).

summarised the social circumstances they struggled with and set out a plan to improve responses to women by making them more integrated and gender specific.

Contact with the criminal justice system may cause these women to go into crisis or prevent them from coming out of it. Conviction can mean a loss of accommodation and employment, disruption to families and children and the beginning of a cycle of intergenerational offending.[126] The Corston Report noted that 'community sentences must be designed to take account of women's particular vulnerabilities.'[127] The report cautioned that the rates of reoffending among women will remain high unless there is more of a focus placed on desistance.

7.7 The Impact of Government Policies on Desistance and Rehabilitation

The concepts of desistance are crucial considerations when assessing the impact of government STPS reduction policy on women in the community, as it maintains a focus on the diverted cohort as actors, rather than passive agents in the diversion process. The orthodox risk, need, responsivity (RNR) model, where offenders are provided with interventions according to their level of risk and 'criminogenic need', focuses on changing thought patterns and attitudes addressed through cognitive behavioural programmes.[128] While the RNR model primarily employs cognitive-behavioural interventions to target specific criminogenic needs and risk factors,[129] the desistance model recognises the importance of a more holistic and individualised approach. It emphasises the need for tailored interventions that consider the unique circumstances and strengths of each individual, facilitating a positive and pro-social identity. The 'good lives' or 'strengths-based' approach provides an alternative perspective on offender rehabilitation. Unlike the RNR model, which focuses on identifying and targeting risk factors and criminogenic needs, the desistance model emphasises the personal strengths and positive aspects of offenders' lives.[130]

Maruna gained insight by contrasting the mind-sets of two types of persistent offenders by identifying a cohort within the group who view themselves as more long-term 'desisters'.[131] Using life history narratives for fifty-five men and ten

---

[126] Ministry of Justice (2019).

[127] Jean Corston (2007), p. 58.

[128] Radcliffe and Hunter (2015).

[129] Maruna (2001); Farrall (2004).

[130] Addressing criminal behaviour and reducing risk have clear budgetary implications which are beyond the scope of this thesis. Carlen (2002) talks of the 'political risk' of not being seen to do something about crime and much risk management in community care and child protection could also arguably be seen to be addressing the needs of the tabloids rather than those of the wider community.

[131] Maruna (2001).

women drawn from a targeted and snowball sampling frame, he found that 'going straight' was a complex process for ex-offenders that involved a distinct change in self-concept. Maruna found that desisters had a strong sense of control over their future, were optimistic and had high self-esteem, and were able to derive meaning from their prison experience and their criminal past. Those who were able to remain crime-free also tended to be more 'other' oriented, and often took on a helper role, advising and mentoring individuals who were once in their position. Conversely, persistent offenders revealed a fatalistic mindset wherein they felt powerless to change their situation and were almost self-sabotaging in their reckless despair and sense of being 'doomed to deviance'.[132]

In the context of Ireland, O'Donnell conducted a study to examine the relatively less researched phenomenon of primary desistance.[133] The study involved interviewing seventy-three male probationers in Dublin who were in the early stages of their transition away from criminal activity. Unlike Maruna's previous research, the narratives provided by the probationers did not establish a clear distinction between individuals who had successfully desisted from crime and those who remained actively involved in offending. The findings of the study indicate that during the initial phases of pursuing a law-abiding lifestyle, individuals did not exhibit a strong sense of personal agency. Instead, they experienced a sense of fatalism when confronted with challenges and barriers to their successful reintegration into society.

Gelsthorpe et al. highlight that the needs of women who offend or are at risk of offending are complex, interrelated, and distinct.[134] Therefore, the provision of services should consider the unique features of women's lives and needs to facilitate effectiveness. This emphasis on 'gender-informed' or 'gender-sensitive' provision aligns with Corston's call for a distinct and holistic approach that is women-centred and integrated.

Hedderman emphasises that effective service planning should be informed by a deeper understanding of factors that are specific or more relevant to women who offend, rather than solely focusing on criminogenic factors that apply to men. Convery argues that in Northern Ireland, the need for increased knowledge in this regard is particularly important due to the lack of research on women who offend, including their motivations for offending, experiences within the criminal justice system, and factors influencing desistance.[135] Additionally, limited research exists on decision-making processes within the police, prosecution, probation, and courts, as well as the practices involved in supervising women in the community. Gender-responsive programming emerged (particularly in North America) as part of a concern that women offenders' complex needs were not acknowledged by apparently gender-neutral assessment and in programmes designed to address offending

[132] Ibid.

[133] Healy and O'Donnell (2008).

[134] Gelsthorpe et al. (2007), p. 15.

[135] Convery (2009), p. 1.

behaviour.[136] Hannah-Moffat argues that there cannot be any official recognition of different factors to predict reoffending for men and women since women's health and welfare needs are converted into indicators of risk in assessment technologies.[137]

The desistance model for understanding how offenders can be effectively rehabilitated has focused on how positive changes in one's personal identity or sense of self can be achieved.[138] The desistance model acknowledges the significance of factors such as personal motivations, social connections, identity formation, and the creation of a positive future orientation. It recognises that offenders often need help in accessing and developing these positive aspects of their lives, such as employment opportunities, education, stable housing, and supportive relationships. By addressing these areas, the desistance model aims to promote resilience, self-worth, and a sense of belonging, which can contribute to sustained desistance from criminal behaviour.

Feminist sociology and criminology offer a reframing of 'success' regarding women and desistance from offending.[139] By defining 'success' as addressing individual needs or deficits, it replaces the responsibility for desistance away from the state and back on the STPS recipient. It does not contextualise issues within the social, structural, and economic issues created by the State.

In addition to this, Heidemann et al.'s study creates a new narrative on how women who have been imprisoned define 'success' post incarceration.[140] Notably, while women identify avoiding recidivism as a marker of success, participants also define success as achieving a 'normal life', accessing accommodation, reuniting with their children and families, meeting challenges, being resilient, achieving independence from surveillance by the criminal justice system and engaging in caretaking and helping others. There creates a difference between state-based narratives of what success should look like personal perceptions of success.

The desistant woman who is attending a community-based group and is abstaining from past behavioural pathways that led to offending like: using substances, remaining in abusive relationships, unemployment will often not see herself as having 'vulnerabilities. Literature suggests that some women may have a transformation or a type of theoretical 'identity shift'.[141] Those with a history of drug use and criminal justice involvement often describe how they are drawn to work with others and share their lived experiences to help others also 'exit a life of crime'.[142]

For most women, their own personal identity shift is just a stepping-stone in the desistance process. They will also need the practical support with the dynamic needs which will be aggravated with the addition of further offences. The Inspector for

---

[136] Bloom and Covington (1998); Worrall (2002).
[137] Hannah-Moffat (2008).
[138] Sampson and Laub (2003); Maruna (2001).
[139] Morash et al. (2019); Carlton and Segrave (2016).
[140] Heidemann et al. (2016).
[141] Maruna (2017).
[142] Ibid, p. 15.

Prisons noted that, whilst women prisoners tended to pose lower risk than male prisoners,[143] there remained no step-down facilities for them when they are nearing the end of their sentence.[144] Acknowledging the research showing that women prisoners have complex physical and mental criminogenic needs, he also noted how the effects of imprisonment could be more detrimental on the woman than on the man. Baroness Corston argued that where desistence has been achieved for any period of time, 'sending a woman to prison where she has established links with caring agencies in the community could rapidly unravel and undermine' any desistence.[145] International research on women in prison identifies that many women lose their homes within the first few weeks of being imprisoned and in many cases their children are more likely to be placed in care.[146] Padfield et al. explain the destabilising nature of interaction with the criminal justice system.

The system removes already vulnerable citizens from their spouses, homes and families of origin; takes away their legal means of employment (if they had any prior to incarceration) and sends a clear signal of suspicion to any future employers; puts them in an environment in which they are surrounded by others in similar circumstances; then, releases them back into the community'.[147]

The structural desistance theory emphasises the role of social bonds. Hirschi's 'control theory' emphasises the importance of these bonds as emotional ties to others and investment in relationships in accessing legitimate activities and securing better commitment to the rule of law.[148] This theory stresses that it is the strength and quality of the bond rather than merely the bond itself that is important in encouraging desistance.[149] These social control theories have been criticised for being overly structural and not including the individual agency to change.

More subjective theories of desistance focus on the age, attitude and personal characteristics of the desister. These paradigms focus on the 'maturation' of the offender, the effects of 'burn out', the deterrent effect of the criminal justice system[150] or cognitive changes in attitude or identity,[151] relational dynamics[152] or a re-evaluation of the pros and cons of living a life of offending.[153] Maruna focuses on offenders' self-identity and the use of 'redemption scripts' to enable and permit

[143] Social Exclusion Unit (2002).

[144] Inspector of Prisons (2011), p. 5, 2.5.

[145] Jean Corston (2007).

[146] Inspector of Prisons (2011), p. 5, 2.7. HM Chief Inspector of Prisons Women in Prison: A Thematic Review (1997) Penal Reform International Study showed that many women prisoners lost their home within 42 days of being imprisoned.

[147] Padfield and Maruna (2006), p. 337.

[148] Hirschi (1969).

[149] Sampson and Laub (2003).

[150] Gottfredson and Hirschi (2022).

[151] Rex (1999); Healy (2010).

[152] Weaver et al. (2012).

[153] Clarke and Cornish (1985).

ex-offenders to break with their past identities and to forge new ones, but 'acknowledges the possibility that without adequate social supports in their immediate milieu, good motives and personal determination alone will be insufficient to effect change'.[154]

The concept of 'capital investment' combines both the agency of the offender and the external structures. This has become integral to understanding the desistance process and is relevant to this study in terms of links to the availability of support networks, like CBOs, in the community to where the person is diverted.[155] This theory stipulates that CBOs are merely instrumental in motivating and encouraging individuals, where they then accumulate and invest in the capital. Such theories believe that the offender possesses the inherent capacity to create their own rehabilitation by developing their social skills to create change in their lives.[156]

This 'capital' may be elusive for several reasons. Burnett and Maruna note that even though an offender's 'narrative' for change may be strong, his or her motivation can be seriously undermined by persistent financial or accommodation problems.[157] In a study of reintegration needs of women prisoners in Northern Ireland, Roberson and Radford found that 64% of women were dependent on social security benefits prior to their committal to custody.[158] However strong the hope of 'rehabilitation', there are many practical problems faced by many ex-offenders in the community where they are diverted. Without practical support networks, all the encouragement and motivation in the world will be insufficient. On the other hand, even with practical help, Maguire notes how 'it is important also to maintain sensitivity to the mental processes involved in serious attempts to desist from crime, the problem of sustaining motivation, and the need for support in the face of setbacks.[159]

Some offenders and ex-offenders may experience negative social capital in the form of stigma and rejection.[160] In the past, many will have used 'criminally-based social capital'.[161] Farrall regards continuous positive social capital as intrinsic to the desistance process.[162] McCartan and Kemshall describe 'recovery capital' as the total of all the resources available that an individual can draw on is important to desistance.[163] This includes personal skills such as, pro-social values, beliefs and attitudes that can sustain non-offending which 'enhance social conformity and rule compliance'. Promoting and improving recovery capital is essential to enabling

---

[154] Barry (2013), p. 48.
[155] Barry (2006).
[156] Barry (2007a, b).
[157] Burnett and Maruna (2006).
[158] Roberson and Radford (2006).
[159] Maguire and Raynor (2006), p. 19.
[160] Best and Savic (2014).
[161] Ibid.
[162] McNeill (2006).
[163] McCartan and Kemshall (2020).

long-term self-risk management. Gender variations in the processes of desistance have also been identified.[164] Hedderman suggests that what emerges from the evidence is that, while men and women both have needs, there are certain needs pertaining to women which require help in relation to desistance-based programmes.[165]

Both models offer valuable insights into offender rehabilitation, and their effectiveness may vary depending on the context and the specific needs of the individual. It is important to consider a combination of approaches and continually evaluate and refine rehabilitation programmes to enhance their impact on reducing recidivism and supporting successful reintegration into the community. Those needs tend to be personal (relational), social and situational.

7.7.1 Personal Needs

In 2010, the Department of Justice, Equality and Law Reform acknowledged the significance of prevention and early intervention in stopping offending and breaking the cycle of poverty, crime, and imprisonment. It called for an increased emphasis on preventative measures and early interventions, which should form a key component of any youth justice system.[166] It involves providing support and services to children, families, and communities at an early stage. According to the National Crime Strategy of 2002, early intervention should be the fundamental principle and a key target of all crime prevention strategies.[167] The strategy found that, to be effective, early intervention must begin during childhood rather than waiting until a child or adult has already been involved in criminal activity. Investment must be directed towards social and economic factors that encourage vulnerable individuals to engage in criminal behaviour.

Adverse childhood experiences (ACEs) are associated with a wide range of negative physical health, mental health, and social outcomes. It is not yet known what proportion of STPS recipients diverted by government policy have experienced trauma through ACEs because of neglect, physical abuse, verbal abuse, sexual abuse, and a range of other traumatic experiences in their past. However, research acknowledges that ACEs can cause profound negative effects on normal neurodevelopment, including negatively affecting mood and emotional regulation, learning, and the likelihood of engaging in a range of risk behaviours.[168]

---

[164] McIvor et al. (2004); Rumgay (2004a, b, c).

[165] Hedderman et al. (2008).

[166] Irish Penal Reform Trust (2010, 2012).

[167] National Crime Council (2002).

[168] Dermody et al. (2020).

Saxena and Messina's study involving over one thousand incarcerated women found a strong correlation between ACEs and violent behaviour.[169] Significantly, the study suggests that women who experience more ACEs are more likely to engage in violent behaviour than men. The study also found that the risk of women engaging in violence is increased by initial arrest prior to age 18 and polysubstance use. This is in line with previous research which has established a strong positive correlation between ACEs, earlier criminal involvement, and substance use.

For young people with trauma experiences, contact with the criminal justice system can be challenging to disengage from. Interactions with law enforcement and other actors of the criminal justice system can intensify fear, anxiety, and negative feelings in young people, possibly leading to re-traumatisation.[170] Although typically the young person will be supported by a professional to develop an action plan to decrease the likelihood of re-offending in the future,[171] a high prevalence of ACEs are still linked with increased chances of involvement with the criminal justice system and recidivism.[172] Young people, like women, tend to be disproportionately represented within the criminal justice system. Among women in custody, nearly one-third have previous experience of being in care, a figure notably higher than that for men, of whom approximately a quarter have similar backgrounds. Both young people and care-experienced women often face significant challenges, including mental health issues, substance misuse, disengagement from education, and adverse childhood experiences. These factors collectively increase the likelihood of involvement in the justice system, highlighting the critical overlap between childhood adversity and later criminal justice involvement.[173]

Olff notes how researchers have continually found that women also respond to stress differently than men and can have higher instances of PTSD.[174] She also notes how women are much more inclined to seek and rely upon social support to help them cope with their trauma than men. Lack of this support can be the most consistent predictor of negative outcomes for women in the criminal justice system.[175] Van der Meer observes that women are more likely to engage in emotionally-driven and avoidant coping styles, while men are more likely to utilise problem-focused coping.[176] In addition, as an extension of avoidant coping preferences, women are more likely than their male counterparts to self-medicate to cope with their trauma symptoms, making them much more vulnerable to subsequent trauma and possible re-offending.[177]

---

[169] Saxena et al. (2016).

[170] Dermody et al. (2020), p. 2.

[171] Department of Justice.

[172] Dermody et al. (2020).

[173] Masson and Booth (2022), Ch 10.

[174] Olff (2017).

[175] Ibid.

[176] van der Meer et al. (2017).

[177] Saxena et al. (2014).

Research has shown that women in the criminal justice system often have different responses to stress and trauma than men.[178] This is because their routes into offending and reasons for offending are often different from those of men.[179] Women are more likely to rely on social support to cope with their trauma.[180] A lack of this support can lead to negative outcomes. Additionally, women affected by ACEs may be more emotionally driven with avoidant coping styles and are more likely to self-medicate, which can make them vulnerable to subsequent trauma and re-offending.[181] These factors can negatively impact a woman's desistance from criminal behaviour. In the author's own research with five justice-involved women, all 'five participants documented adverse childhood experiences (ACEs) which they connected in a clear way to their offending pathway like childhood abuse, childhood poverty and growing up in deprived areas.'[182] The Inspector for Prisons recognised that unless there is some type of rehabilitative element, the woman will find desistance from offending difficult:[183]

> If a woman has not been able to avail of the rehabilitative programmes or engage with the services in the prison, which are designed to help her reintegrate into society, because of the short sentence that she is serving, the inevitable result will be that she goes back to the society that she has come from where drugs, alcohol and chaos in her life again becomes the order of the day. Petty crime feeds this chaos. The circle continues.[184]

Ongoing research continues on the effectiveness of trauma treatments that are evidence-based among justice-involved populations.[185] These studies are gender-responsive and measure ACEs to assess outcomes. They underscore the concept that women experience, perceive, and cope with trauma differently to men and require gender-specific responses and policies.[186] Thus far, the findings illustrate that women are more prone to heightened fear responses and negative cognitions after surviving traumatic experiences, and they require treatment that specifically addresses these factors to avoid negative interactions with the criminal justice system.[187]

---

[178] Jean Corston (2007); Hedderman (2004).

[179] Hedderman (2004).

[180] Rumgay (2004a, b, c).

[181] Merrington (2001).

[182] Duignan (2023), p. 254.

[183] Inspector of Prisons (2011).

[184] Office of the Inspector of Prisons (2013), p. 12 para 2.22.

[185] Messina and Schepps (2021).

[186] Ibid.

[187] Ibid.

7.7.2 Social Needs

In 2002, a report by the Social Exclusion Unit in the United Kingdom noted that any good work with offenders within prisons is sometimes quickly undone once offenders are released back into the community and face the difficult prospect of finding somewhere to live and having enough money to survive on.[188] The predominant demographic among incarcerated women consists of young individuals who possess limited criminal experience in comparison to their male counterparts.[189] The majority of incarcerated women are impoverished, burdened with debt, and have had minimal exposure to gainful employment. Their lives are frequently marked by encounters with homelessness and substance abuse, and when prompted to explain the motives behind their criminal activities, women offenders commonly cite drug and/or alcohol use, financial necessity to sustain their substance dependencies, or a general lack of financial support.[190] Gelsthorpe observes how the lives of women involved in criminal behaviour exhibit prevailing conditions of socioeconomic disadvantage, social marginalisation, and various psychological susceptibilities.[191]

Thus, to mitigate the risk of reoffending, it appears imperative that individuals who have been diverted from the criminal justice system engage in employment or training. Research highlights the significant role of unemployment in contributing to women's likelihood of being re-imprisoned. Research in Scotland by Cooke and Michie established a clear link between unemployment and higher rates of reconviction and reimprisonment among women.[192] A lack of employment opportunities further exacerbates the cycle of poverty and social exclusion, limiting women's prospects for stability and personal growth after release. O'Donnell et al.[193] also found a statistically significant relationship between unemployment and re-imprisonment, where low levels of educational attainment and poor literacy were also associated with an elevated risk of reimprisonment.

At the time of writing, there has been no review conducted of programmes in Ireland for offenders diverted under the government legislation. In the United Kingdom, a review of prison-based education and employment programmes and the role of employability-focused programmes post-release identifies only two studies which include women. However, studies by Hamlyn and Lewis[194] and Webster et al.[195] were prison-based, rather than community-based, and only the former focused exclusively on women. In their review of literature on the

[188] Social Exclusion Unit (2002).

[189] Gelsthorpe et al. (2007), p. 24.

[190] Ibid, p. 24.

[191] Gelsthorpe (2004).

[192] Cooke and Michie (1998).

[193] O'Donnell et al. (2008).

[194] Hamlyn and Lewis (2000).

[195] Webster et al. (2001).

effectiveness of community orders, Davis et al.[196] only make one reference to females. The accompanying report on the supervision of community orders in England and Wales[197] recognises that 'the provision of requirements needs to be sensitive to the needs of women'[198] and acknowledges that ongoing research into the effectiveness of requirements for women enhances the evidence base.

The only additional reference to women in the report highlights their increased likelihood of experiencing delays in the initiation of programs. The report recognises that such delays may detrimentally impact women's motivation, and thus requirements incorporated into the sentence may not be completed before expiration of the order. Literature focusing on the provision of community interventions for women, suggests that provision is often inappropriate, particularly in relation to the structure and delivery of interventions.[199] Patel and Stanley assert that the manner in which interventions are organised and executed holds equal significance to their content when considering the suitability of such interventions for women.[200]

The author's research underscored the significance of the 'female-centric' environment created by the program at the CBO. While the CBO itself was not exclusively for women, the programme they attended was. Within this space, many participants felt more comfortable and part of a familial community. The theme of peer support frequently emerged, highlighting both 'substitute family' and accountability. It was common for participants to refer to each other as 'sisters.' While not all explicitly mentioned it, descriptions of their circumstances revealed a high level of unmet needs from a young age.[201] 'Cara' recounts how she was abandoned by her only family member as a young child who 'just signed me into the care of the HSE and… didn't come down to visit me for 6 solid months.'[202] She describes how she uses the CBO to 'stay out of trouble': 'I'm coming here five years on and off. It's something to do in the day. It's not dossing on the corner and then getting arrested for loitering. A guard said to me last week, 'if I see you again on this street, I'm going to arrest you.'[203] Another participant acknowledged that without attendance at the programme, she would most likely resort to her familiar lifestyle which involved theft, indicating that the program instilled a sense of accountability within her.[204]

[196] Davis et al. (2008).

[197] National Audit Office (2008).

[198] Ibid.

[199] Clarke (2004); Gelsthorpe and Sharpe (2007); Gelsthorpe et al. (2007).

[200] Patel and Stanley (2008), p. 13.

[201] Duignan (2023), p. 257.

[202] Ibid, p. 245 'Cara'.

[203] Ibid, p. 245 'Cara'.

[204] Ibid, p. 249 'Kelly': 'I'd be out robbing if I wasn't in here.'

7.7.3 Situational Needs

The specific needs of offenders must be identified to prevent further offending, particularly those that may impede the success of community-based penalties. In the case of Irish women, the government lacks awareness of these needs due to the absence of large-scale research on the CBOs or programmes available for women diverted from custody. However, in the United Kingdom, Gelsthorpe et al. conducted research on both statutory and voluntary sector service providers of community-based provision for women offenders.[205] Case studies have been carried out on several community centres for women, and interviews were conducted with managers to identify 'a range of barriers to successful reintegration and desistance from further offending.'[206]

The complex and overlapping issues that women have been found dealing with included issues such as accommodation, childcare, education training and employment, substance misuse, victimisation, and mental health. The projects visited described the difficulties of 'unravelling' these problems, which are not always immediately obvious and may take some time to come to light.[207] One project manager described this process as being like 'a great big ball of wool, and they just throw these issues at you, and you have to unravel it.'[208]

Some actors within this space report feeling a sense of frustration with the criminal justice agencies. There are those, even from within the Probation Services themselves, who report a lack of referrals from probation officers and offender managers, with most referrals being made by a core group of committed (and usually female) officers.[209] The study noted that the low number of referrals was not a reflection of a low demand for services.

Geographically, the distribution of CBOs in Ireland is uneven. Over one-third of the CBOs in Ireland listed by The Probation Service are situated on the East Coast in the capital city, Dublin, with only three listed in Galway on the West coast.[210] The significance of CBOs lies in their role as the designated locations where individuals, diverted from custody and placed under supervision, are required to attend their appointments with the Probation Service. Where these locations are not centralised, they may pose difficulties for individuals in attending important appointments with their probation officers or attending court-mandated classes, such as parenting, drug treatment or anger-management classes. Accessibility is critical, given the serious consequences of non-compliance.

[205] Gelsthorpe et al. (2007).

[206] Ibid.

[207] Ibid.

[208] Ibid.

[209] Ibid.

[210] The Probation ServiceThe Probation Service website only lists 34 CBOs but state that there are 60 Community Based Organisations throughout the country.

There are three main projects that The Irish Probation Service focuses on. The first is the Irish Association for the Social Integration of Offenders (IASIO)[211] which organises work in the community for both male and female offenders. This initiative was set up in 2014 by the Department of Justice, through the Probation Service and the Irish Prison Service and it is one of the largest CBOs in the country. The two other projects are quite user- specific. The Cornmarket Project is an inter-agency community-based initiative which focuses on treatment and rehabilitation, specifically targeting offenders who struggle with substance misuse and Le Chéile ('together') operates in collaboration with the Young Persons' Probation division of the Probation Service. This scheme aims to support young individuals who have encountered legal issues.[212]

These CBOs are not female-only, unlike some in other jurisdictions, and therefore, they may feel intimidating to the women who attend them, given that they are in the minority.[213] Commentators have emphasised the necessity of women-only spaces due to the prevalent fears of abuse, violence, and coercion from males expressed by female clients.[214] Consequently, the specific needs of women are being overlooked in services that claim to cater to both genders, given the relatively small proportion of women within the adult offender population.[215]

In the author's primary research, two participants came from backgrounds of abusive relationships with a male. 'Emma' became involved in an abusive relationship and became addicted to drugs, eventually receiving an STPS for drugs offences. When she met a man who was also addicted to drugs and who mirrored the abuse of her childhood, her drug habit worsened, as did her offending. After a turbulent marriage where she was forced to leave, Emma found strength in seeking help to change her situation, even though she recognised she was unable to change the trauma of her past. This aligns with a key concept of how former offenders often need to believe they can change before they can benefit from assistance.[216]In order for this belief to be nurtured, they require support and encouragement.[217]

Emma's trajectory into criminal behaviour reflects a combination of indirect and direct criminogenic needs, including past traumas such as an unhappy childhood and deprivation, as well as present circumstances like addiction. She explains 'I never felt loved. I never ever got hugs as a child. I was never told that I was loved.'[218] Rather than perceiving these criminogenic needs as obstacles to desistance, Emma believes that the programs she participates in at the CBO assist her in overcoming her past traumas and ongoing struggles.[1032] She acknowledges her inability to

[211] 'Irish Association for Social Inclusion Opportunities' https://www.iasio.ie.

[212] 'The Probation Service' https://www.probation.ie.

[213] Gelsthorpe et al. (2007).

[214] Ibid.

[215] Sheehan et al. (2011).

[216] Woods (2020).

[217] Maruna (2001).

[218] Duignan (2023), 'Emma'. P240.

change the past, but as a member of a supportive group, she feels empowered to maintain sobriety and refrain from offending.

Female-only services that are not state-organised can present several challenges. These services may be localised and often rely on precarious funding arrangements, leaving project managers' time consumed by continual fundraising efforts. Staff contracts are frequently short-term or temporary, and employees may receive inadequate pay. Additionally, crèche and transport costs can be prohibitively expensive, particularly if the service location is not central. These logistical and financial challenges are crucial for the sustainability of women-only services. Without state involvement, the underlying criminogenic needs that contribute to offending behaviour may remain largely unaddressed for women.

7.8 Conclusion

Women offenders are being diverted into a community where their needs are frequently overlooked. Evaluations of community alternatives in other jurisdictions, along with small-scale research conducted in Ireland, demonstrate that as a vulnerable minority population, the impact of penal policies is reflected in their life stories. These life stories often include difficulties faced during childhood, socio-economic issues, periods of addiction, multiple offending, and ultimately, receiving convictions. The women become trapped in the revolving door of prison unless they, or someone else, help manage the direct and indirect criminogenic needs that initially led to their offending. If these needs are not identified, assessed, or addressed, many women may slip through the gaps in the criminal justice system, hindering their ability to achieve lasting desistance.

Law

Sex Offenders' Act (2000)
Children Act (2001)
Criminal Justice Act (2006)
Fines Act (2010)
Criminal Justice (Community Service) (Amendment) Act (2011)

References

Book

Andrews DA, Bonta J (1998) The psychology of criminal conduct. Routledge

Barry M (2006) Youth offending in transition: the search for social recognition. Routledge

Barry M (2007a) Effective approaches to risk assessment in social work: an international literature review. Scottish Executive Social Research, Edinburgh

Best D, Savic M (2014) Substance abuse and offending: pathways to recovery. Working within the forensic paradigm. Routledge

Bonta J, Wormith SJ (2007) Risk and needs assessment. In: McIvor G, Raynor P (eds) In developments in social work with offenders. Jessica Kingsley, pp 131–152

Brown SL, Blanchette K (2006) The assessment and treatment of women offenders: an integrative perspective. John Wiley & Sons

Carlen P (2002) Women and punishment: the struggle for justice. Willan

Cohen S (1985) Visions of social control: crime punishment and classification

Farrall S (2004) Social capital and offender reintegration: making probation desistance focused. In: Maruna S, Immarigeon R (eds) After crime and punishment. Willan Publishing, Cullompton

Garland D (1985) Punishment and welfare: a history of penal strategies. Gower, Aldershot

Garland D (2001) The culture of control. Oxford University Press, Oxford

Gelsthorpe L (2004) Female offending: a theoretical overview. In: McIvor G (ed) Women who offend. Jessica Kingsley

Gelsthorpe L, McIvor G (2007) Dealing with difference and diversity. In: Gelsthorpe L, Morgan R (eds) Handbook of probation. Willan Publishing, Cullompton

Gelsthorpe L, Sharpe G (2007) Women and resettlement. In: Hucklesby A, Hagley-Dickinson L (eds) Prisoner resettlement: policy and practice. Willan Publishing

Gottfredson MR, Hirschi T (2022) A general theory of crime. Stanford University Press

Hamlyn B, Lewis D (2000) Women prisoners: a survey of their work and training experiences in custody and on release. Home Office Research Study. ERIC

Hayles M (2006) Constructing safety. In: Parton N et al (eds) Constructive work with offenders. Jessica Kingsley Publishers

Healy D (2010) The dynamics of desistance: charting pathways through change. Willan Publishing Cullompton

Heidensohn F, Heidensohn F (1989) Gender and crime. Springer

Kemshall H (2004) Risk, dangerousness and female offenders. In: McIvor G, Malloch M, Gelsthorpe L (eds) Women who offend. Jessica Kingsley Publishers

Loucks N et al (2006) Evaluation of the 218 Centre. Scottish Executive Justice Department

Maruna S (2001) Making good. American Psychological Association, Washington, DC

Masson I, Booth N (eds) (2022) The Routledge handbook of women's experiences of criminal justice, 1st edn. Routledge. Care Experienced Women in the Criminal Justice System. Ch10

McIvor G, Malloch M, Gelsthorpe L (2004) Women who offend, vol 44. Jessica Kingsley Publishers

Monahan J (1981) 1981 predicting violent behavior: an assessment of clinical techniques. Sage

O'Donnell I, O'Sullivan E (2001) Crime control in Ireland: the politics of intolerance. Cork University Press

Patel S, Stanley S (2008) The use of the community order and the suspended sentence order for women. Centre for Crime and Justice Studies, London

Rumgay J (2004a) Living with paradox. In: Ivor GM (ed) Women who offend, vol 44

Sampson RJ, Laub JH (2003) Desistance from crime over the life course. Handbook of the life course. Springer

Sheehan R, McIvor G, Trotter C (2011) Working with women offenders in the community. Willan Publishing

Social Exclusion Unit (2002) Reducing re-offending by ex-prisoners. Social Exclusion Unit, London

Sparks R, Simon J (2012) The Sage handbook of punishment and society. Sage Publications Ltd

Walsh DP, Sexton P (2000) An empirical study of community service orders in Ireland. Stationery Office

Webster R et al (2001) Building bridges to employment for prisoners. Home Office, London

West DJ, Farrington DP (1973) Who becomes delinquent? Heinemann Educational, London

Worrall A (2002) Offending women: female lawbreakers and the criminal justice system. Routledge

Journal Article

Barry M (2007b) Youth offending and youth transitions: the power of capital in influencing change. Crit Criminol 15:185

Barry M (2013) Desistance by design: offenders' reflections on criminal justice theory, policy and practice. Eur J Probat 5:47

Beyens K (2010) From 'community service' to 'autonomous work penalty' in Belgium. What's in a name? Eur J Probat 2:4

Blanchette K (2004) Revisiting effective classification strategies for women offenders in Canada. Fem Psychol 14:231

Bottoms AE, McWilliams W (1979) A non-treatment paradigm for probation practice. Br J Social Work 9:159

Burnett R, Maruna S (2006) The kindness of prisoners: strengths-based resettlement in theory and in action. Criminol Crim Justice 6:83

Byrne CF, Trew KJ (2008) Pathways through crime: the development of crime and desistance in the accounts of men and women offenders. Howard J Crim Justice 47:238

Campbell L (2008) The culture of control in Ireland: theorising recent developments in criminal justice. Web J Curr Leg Issues 1

Carlton B, Segrave M (2016) Rethinking women's post-release reintegration and 'success'. Aust N Z J Criminol 49:281

Carr N, Robinson G (2021) A legitimate business? Representations of privatised probation in England and Wales. Crime Media Cult 17:235

Clarke RV, Cornish DB (1985) Modeling offenders' decisions: a framework for research and policy. Crime Justice 6:147

Clear TR, Rose DR, Ryder JA (2001) Incarceration and the community: the problem of removing and returning offenders. Crime Delinq 47:335

Convery U (2009) Addressing offending by women: a literature review

Cooke DJ, Michie C (1998) Predicting recidivism in a Scottish prison sample. Psychol Crime Law 4:169

Davies P (2007) The level of service inventory in the Republic of Ireland. Irish Probat J 4:93

Davis R et al (2008) A synthesis of literature on the effectiveness of community orders. RAND, Santa Monica

Feeley MM, Simon J (1992) The new penology: notes on the emerging strategy of corrections and its implications. Criminology 30:449

Fitzgibbon DW (2007) Risk analysis and the new practitioner: myth or reality? Punish Soc 9:87

Flew A (1954) The justification of punishment. Philosophy 29:291

Garland D (1996) The limits of the sovereign state- strategies of crime control in contemporary society. Br J Criminol 36

Garland D (2004) Beyond the culture of control. Crit Rev Int Soc Polit Philos 7:160

Gelsthorpe L, Hedderman C (2012) Providing for women offenders: the risks of adopting a payment by results approach. Probat J 59:374

Gelsthorpe L, Sharpe G, Roberts J (2007) Provision for women offenders in the community. Fawcett Society, London
Gendreau P, Goggin C, Smith P (2002) Is the PCL-R really the "unparalleled" measure of offender risk? A lesson in knowledge cumulation. Crim Justice Behav 29:397
Hannah-Moffat K (2005) Criminogenic needs and the transformative risk subject: hybridizations of risk/need in penality. Punish Soc 7:29
Hannah-Moffat K (2008) Re-imagining gendered penalities: the myth of gender responsivity. Imaginary Penalities 193
Healy D, O'Donnell I (2008) Calling time on crime: motivation, generativity and agency in Irish probationers. Probat J 55:25
Hedderman C (2004) The "criminogenic" needs of women offenders. Women who offend 227
Hedderman C et al (2008) Implementing services for women offenders and those 'at risk' of offending: action research with together women. Ministry of Justice Research Series
Hedderman C, Gunby C, Shelton N (2011) What women want: the importance of qualitative approaches in evaluating work with women offenders. Criminol Crim Justice 11:3
Heidensohn F (2006) New perspectives and established views. Gender Justice 1
Hirschi T (1969) Key idea: Hirschi's social bond/social control theory. 1969 Key Ideas in Criminology and Criminal Justice 55
Hollin CR, Palmer EJ (2006a) Criminogenic need and women offenders: a critique of the literature. Leg Criminol Psychol 11:179
Hollin CR, Palmer EJ (2006b) The Level of Service Inventory–Revised profile of English prisoners: risk and reconviction analysis. Crim Justice Behav 33:347
Holtfreter K, Cupp R (2007) Gender and risk assessment the empirical status of the LSI-R for women. J Contemp Crim Justice 23:363
Horsefield A (2003) Risk assessment: who needs it? Probat J 50:374
Kelly J, Bogue J (2014) Gender differences in criminogenic needs among Irish offenders. Irish Probat J 11:87
Kelly J, Egan V (2012) A case–control study of alcohol-related violent offending among Irish Probation Clients. 2012 Rehabilitation, Research, and Reform: Prison Policy in Ireland
Kemshall H, Wood J (2013) High-risk offenders and public protection. Handbook of probation 403
Kilcommins S (2005) Risk in Irish Society: moving to a crime control model of criminal justice. Irish Probat J 2:20
Maguire M, Raynor P (2006) How the resettlement of prisoners promotes desistance from crime: or does it? Criminol Crim Justice 6:19
Maruna S (2017) Desistance as a social movement. Irish Probat J 14:5
McCartan K, Kemshall H (2020) The potential role of recovery capital in stopping sexual offending: lessons from circles of support and accountability to enrich practice. Irish Probat J 17
McCarthy J (2014) Community service at the crossroads in Ireland. Irish Probat J 11:124
McNeill F (2006) A desistance paradigm for offender management. Criminol Crim Justice 6:39
Merrington S (2001) Ace profiles for female, ethnic minority and young offenders. Ace Practitioner Bull 4
Messina NP, Schepps M (2021) Opening the proverbial 'can of worms' on trauma-specific treatment in prison: the association of adverse childhood experiences to treatment outcomes. Clin Psychol Psychother 28:1210
Morash M et al (2019) Technical violations, treatment and punishment responses, and recidivism of women on probation and parole. Crim Justice Policy Rev 30:788
O'Donnell I, Baumer EP, Hughes N (2008) Recidivism in the Republic of Ireland. Criminol Crim Justice 8:123
Ogloff JR (2002) Offender rehabilitation: from "nothing works" to what next? Aust Psychol 37:245
Olff M (2017) Sex and gender differences in post-traumatic stress disorder: an update. Eur J Psychotraumatol 8
Padfield N, Maruna S (2006) The revolving door at the prison gate: exploring the dramatic increase in recalls to prison. Criminol Crim Justice 6:329

Prendergast M (2012) Practitioner perceptions on the merits, challenges and ethical dilemmas of LSI-R in practice. Irish Probat J 9:1

Radcliffe P, Hunter G (2015) 'It was a safe place for me to be': accounts of attending women's community services and moving beyond the offender identity. Br J Criminol 56:976

Rettinger LJ, Andrews DA (2010) General risk and need, gender specificity, and the recidivism of female offenders. Crim Justice Behav 37:29

Rex S (1999) Desistance from offending: experiences of probation. Howard J Crim Justice 38:366

Richardson M (2008) Risky business: an examination of probation officers' attitudes towards risk assessment. Dissertations 9

Roberson B, Radford E (2006) The reintegration needs of women prisoners in Northern Ireland. Irish Probat J 3:110

Rumgay J (2004b) Scripts for safer survival: pathways out of female crime. Howard J Crim Justice 43:405

Saxena P, Messina NP, Grella CE (2014) Who benefits from gender-responsive treatment? Accounting for abuse history on longitudinal outcomes for women in prison. Crim Justice Behav 41:417

Saxena P, Grella CE, Messina NP (2016) Continuing care and trauma in women offenders' substance use, psychiatric status, and self-efficacy outcomes. Women Crim Justice 26:99

van der Meer CA et al (2017) Gender and age differences in trauma and PTSD among Dutch treatment-seeking police officers. J Nervous Mental Dis 205:87

Weaver B et al (2012) The failure of recall to prison: early release, front-door and back-door sentencing and the revolving prison door in Scotland. Eur J Probat 4:85

Woods M (2020) 'Helping Others and Helping Myself': wounded healers as peer workers. Irish Probat J 17

Report

Barry M, McIvor G (2008) Chaotic lives: a profile of women in the criminal justice system in Lothian and Borders. Lothian & Borders Commnuity Justice Authority

Clarke R (2004) 'What works?' for women who offend: a service users' perspective exploring the synthesis between what women want and what women get (A Report for the Griffins Society Visiting Research Fellowship Programme). Griffins Society, London

Department of Justice (1985) Report of the Committee of Inquiry into the Penal System (The Whitaker Report). Dublin

Department of Justice Youth Justice Strategy 2021-2027

Dermody A et al (2020) Early life trauma and its implications for Garda Youth Diversion Services

Government of Ireland (1994) Five year action plan for the management of offenders. Department of Justice

Hough M, Jacobson J, Millie A (2003) The decision to imprison: sentencing and the prison population

Inspector of Prisons (2011) Standards for the Inspections of Prisons in Ireland- Women Prisoners' Supplement

Irish Penal Reform Trust (2010) From justice to welfare: the case for investment in prevention and early intervention

Irish Penal Reform Trust (2011) Briefing paper: women in detention

Irish Penal Reform Trust (2012) The vicious circle of social exclusion & crime: Ireland's disproportionate punishment of the poor (Shifting Focus)

Irish Penal Reform Trust (2013) Position Paper 10- Women in the Criminal Justice System: towards a non-custodial approach

Irish Penal Reform Trust (2021) Progress in the Penal System (PIPS)- The Need for Transparency. Dublin
Jean Corston B (2007) The Corston Report: a report of a review of women with particular vulnerabilities in the criminal justice system. London
Joint Committee on Justice DaE (2013) Report on Penal Reform. Houses of the Oireachtas
Ministry of Justice (2019) A whole system approach for female offenders
National Audit Office (2008) National Probation Service: The Supervision of Community Orders in England and Wales. The Stationery Office, London
Oberstown Children Detention Campus (2011) Key characteristics of young people in detention: a snapshot
Office of the Inspector of Prisons (2013) Interim Report on the Dochas Centre. Tipperary
Prison Reform Trust (2018) The rising numbers of women recalled to prison
Review Group for Penal Policy (2014) Strategic Review of Penal Policy- Final Report. Dublin
Rumgay J (2004c) The Asha Centre: Report of an Evaluation. Asha Centre, Worcester
Scottish Government (2008) Criminal Proceedings in Scottish Courts 2006/7. Edinburgh
The Probation Service (2009) Value for money and policy review of the community service scheme. Department of Justice, Equality and Law Reform
UK Home Office (2004) Women's Offending Reduction Programme. Home Office

Conference Paper

Bloom B, Covington S (1998) Gender-specific programming for female offenders: what is it and why is it important? 50th annual meeting of the American Society of Criminology, Washington, DC

Thesis

Duignan S (2023) Evaluation of the effect of Irish Penal Policy on female short-term prison sentence recipients: the need for gender-specific policy. University of Galway

Online Resource

Central Statistics Office (2022) Prison Re-Offending Statistics 2011-2018. CSO
Heidemann G, Cederbaum JA, Martinez S (2016) Beyond recidivism: how formerly incarcerated women define success
HM Inspectorate of Probation. The Risk-Need-Responsivity Model
IASIO, Irish Association for Social Inclusion Opportunities. <https://www.iasio.ie> accessed
Ministry of Justice/ NOMS (2008) National service framework: improving services to women offenders
National Crime Council (2002) Tackling the underlying causes of crime- a partnership approach
The Probation Service. Community Based Organisations
Webster C, MacDonald R, Simpson M (2006) Predicting criminality? Risk factors, neighbourhood influence and desistance
Work in the Community, The Probation Service. <https://www.probation.ie> accessed

Chapter 8
Transforming Justice: A Roadmap for the Criminal Justice System

8.1 Introduction

This chapter provides a strategic overview of how Irish penal policies affect female STPS recipients, synthesising insights from previous research on women offenders and current criminal justice practices. Through an examination of sentencing and diversion methods, it outlines the policies' broader implications for Irish penal reform. Rather than a conventional conclusion, this chapter aims to act as a roadmap, highlighting the essential insights and actionable outcomes of these policies, identifying their successes and limitations, and pinpointing areas for improvement.

The penal policy aimed at diverting STPS offenders from custody was less effective for women, primarily because it was implemented in response to a financial crisis rather than being grounded in one specific punishment philosophy. The introduction of new community penalties has inadvertently extended punishment to a cohort of offenders who would previously have received lesser sanctions.[1] The creation of these new penalties has potentially widened the net of social control. The impact of this in Ireland is that it has impacted the minority group of women offenders disproportionately.[2]

8.2 Key Lessons

8.2.1 Lack of Clear Philosophy

It is difficult to ascertain what, if any, underlying punishment philosophy grounds Ireland's policy of diversion from custody. Whilst a policy of diversion from custody

[1] Carmody and McEvoy (1996); Cohen (1985).

[2] Walsh and Sexton (2000); Duignan (2023).

S. Duignan, *Transforming Justice for Women*, Gender, Justice and Legal Feminism 3, https://doi.org/10.1007/978-3-031-82455-5_8

should be rehabilitative, because this policy did not do what it set out to do for women, it became retributive. This could be because the policy was not one that was made after thoughtful discussion but rather born out of economic necessity. There was relatively little parliamentary debate about how the general policy of diversion would be implemented, other than how the government would use legislation to save money after the economic crisis. The diversion of the most minor offenders away from expensive prison places into the community would claw back money from public expenditure. However, from the paucity of conversations regarding diverted offenders and their rehabilitation, it appears that little thought was given to the overall philosophy that would be the foundation of the government's scheme other than the avoidance of financial crisis.

When the Irish state gained independence from Britain, it retained all 'inherited' Westminster legislation that had been working effectively until the new Irish parliament saw the need to tailor these laws to better suit the Irish jurisdiction.[3] However, as the Irish parliament began adapting these laws to better fit the Irish jurisdiction, the emphasis often rested on their practical modification. Consequently, legislators at times overlooked the deeper philosophical foundations underpinning the original laws. As a result, there has been a notable absence of comprehensive discussions and debates regarding the penal philosophies behind this legislation. This lack of comprehensive discourse is particularly evident in the context of prison diversion policies.

The Wootton Committee in England and Wales engaged in extensive discussions and debates on this topic.[4] In Ireland, however, a culture of limited discussion constrained opportunities for a more nuanced, context-specific approach to policymaking. Although extensive parliamentary debate does not guarantee a policy's success, a clear guiding philosophy of punishment can foster coherent legislation aligned with that philosophy. When proposals diverge from this transparent framework, they can be effectively challenged and rejected during debates as the legislation progresses through the Oireachtas.

Without a large-scale review of the effects of diversion legislation in Ireland, it is impossible to determine conclusively whether in fact any net-widening has occurred. What is evident from statistics is that STPS did not reduce for women, nor did CSOs and it is also apparent that the level of female criminality did not increase during this period.[5] Thus, large-scale qualitative research is now required to evaluate the exact effect that the government's diversion policy has caused on female offenders on a large scale. Methodologically rigorous studies are required within the Irish context,

[3] A non-exhaustive example of Westminster legislation that was 'imported' for use in Ireland: UK Offences Against the Person Act (1861) and Offences against the Person Act 1861 (applied in Ireland). UK Criminal Justice Act (1967) and Criminal Justice Act 1967 (applied in Ireland). UK Misuse of Drugs Act (1971) led to Misuse of Drugs Act (1977) (adapted for use in Ireland). UK Theft Act (1968) led to Criminal Justice (Theft and Fraud Offences) Act (2001) which repealed and replaced earlier legislation.

[4] Wootton (1970).

[5] CSO.

considering its unique social, political, economic, and cultural characteristics, which considerably differ from the evidence base currently derived from Britain, the USA, and Canada.

There are circumstances which make women in the Irish jurisdiction particularly vulnerable:

8.2.2 Up-Tariffing in an Under Resourced Community

The introduction of the diversion policy has led to a significant shift towards using alternative measures such as CSOs and fines instead of custodial sentences. The Fines (Payment and Recovery) Act 2014, for example, allows for custodial sentences to be replaced with CSOs of up to 100 h for those defaulting on summary fines. Previously, defaulting on a summary fine might have resulted in a very brief STPS, sometimes lasting only a few hours. However, under the 2014 legislation, defaulting on a fine might now require several weeks of attendance at a worksite as part of a CSO and any other onerous conditions imposed by the court.

While a comprehensive list of work placements available through the main community service projects in Ireland is not provided, studies indicate that these placements can be limited and difficult for women to access.[6] The type of work mandated may not be suitable for women, particularly if they are unable to function in certain environments due to past trauma.[7] Additionally, certain work placements can present challenges for those with caring responsibilities or those dealing with physical, mental, or health care needs. The economic burden of traveling to a work site may also be insurmountable for some individuals. If the alternative work measures are not completed or are breached, the consequences can be more severe, potentially resulting in harsher sentences.

Instead of serving very brief prison sentences which may or may not have involved custodial stays, offenders might be asked to commit to more onerous community punishments, which they may refuse, fail to complete, or breach.[8] The Review of Policy Options for Prison and Penal Reform acknowledged that "the current low levels of alternative sanctions being imposed on defaulters undermines the success of the original goal, which was to reduce the level of imprisonment for non-payment."[9]

---

[6] Guilfoyle (2017); Duignan (2023).

[7] Woods (2020).

[8] Criminal Justice (Community Service) (Amendment) Act (2011), s3.

[9] There is no way to track how many CSOs are breached each year as this is at the Probation Officer's discretion. Where the offender appears again before the Court for resentencing, the specific charge will depend on the circumstances of the breach.

As a distinct minority cohort, women also exhibit criminogenic needs that differ significantly from those of men.[10] In under-resourced communities, minority groups face not only the intended consequences of alternative punishments but also additional unintended harms. Systemic inequalities often result in these groups having less access to resources, opportunities, and services that could mitigate the negative impact of policies. These inequities include less representation and implicit bias.

The Irish Prison Service did not publish data on female STPS recipients as a separate cohort until 2014. Consequently, the impact of the diversion policy on women was not immediately apparent. Notably, the number of female STPS recipients increased between 2011 and 2016 despite the implementation of the diversion policy. These unintended consequences exacerbate barriers to desistance, further marginalising women within their communities and perpetuating cycles of disadvantage.[11]

Interventions such as therapeutic programmes, social support, education and training, and childcare responsibilities that address indirect criminogenic factors all play a crucial role in addressing the barriers women face in achieving desistance from criminal behaviour. By incorporating these elements into diversion policies, a gender-responsive approach is adopted, which recognises and addresses the unique challenges women experience. This approach aims to minimise unintended negative consequences and promote more inclusive and supportive alternatives to custodial sentences. By focusing on these factors, interventions can help create a more effective and equitable system that supports women in their journey towards desistance from crime.

8.2.3 Poor Publication of Criminal Justice Data

Whilst the 2011 Act encourages greater use of CSOs, it fails to consider the wide range of offences within the STPS cohort, which includes both minor and serious cases. Following the implementation of the government's diversion policy in 2011, the proportion of male and female STPS recipients serving sentences of less than three months increased by 27% between 2013 and 2016.

Publishing criminal data is vital for the insights it provides, yet the Irish Prison Service reports STPS recipients as a single, homogeneous group, without distinguishing between different sentence lengths within this category. A more detailed breakdown—such as categorising STPS recipients into 0–3 months, 3–6 months, and 6–12 months—would be valuable, as it shows that the majority of Irish STPS cases fall within the 0–3 months range. This suggests that using CSOs as a direct alternative to 12-month sentences is ineffective, as most STPS recipients in Ireland, particularly women, are sentenced to terms of 0–3 months. Table 8.1 was

[10] Jean Corston (2007); Inspector of Prisons (2011).

[11] Department of Justice (2022), p. 53.

Table 8.1 Short term prison sentences of different levels changes from 2011 and 2020

STPS level	2011	2015	2020
<3 months	8070	10,229 (+2159)27% **increase**	796 (−9433)92% decrease
3–6 months	1786	1273 (−445)25% decrease	1023 (−250)20% decrease
6–12 months	1358	1028 (−330)24% decrease	778 (−250)24% decrease

Figures available from Irish Prison Service cf Duignan (2023)

created using figures from the Irish Prison Service to demonstrate how custodial alternatives in Ireland have not provided an effective diversion strategy, particularly for female offenders.[12]

8.3 One Single Diversion Policy

The single diversion policy, introduced from 2011, targets both male and female genders. However these two cohorts exhibit distinct offending patterns and possess diverse needs and pathways to criminal behaviour.[13] After policy was implemented, from 2013 to 2016, it is possible to see how the percentage of female STPS recipients increased from 19.9% to 22%.[14] The policy comprises two key pieces of legislation: the 2011 legislation,[15] which promotes the use of CSOs as an alternative to STPS, and the 2014 Act, which eliminates imprisonment for fine default.[16]

While the 2011 legislation does not effectively reduce the number of female STPS recipients, the fines legislation temporarily achieves this goal.[17] However, a more detailed investigation is necessary to address specific concerns. One such concern is the scenario where women originally sentenced to STPS after 2011 received a CSO as a substitute. If these CSOs were unsuccessful and subsequently led to an increase in the number of STPS, it may suggest a phenomenon known as 'net-widening'. Net widening occurs when the implementation of alternative measures works to increase the overall number of individuals subjected to custodial sentences rather than reduce them. To determine if net-widening is in fact occurring, comprehensive qualitative research is required to analyse individual cases where CSOs have been substituted for STPS and these CSOs were unsuccessful, resulting in custody. This analysis would provide valuable insights into the longer-term implications of the criminal justice system's response to this legislation.

Transparent publication of statistical data is required for the effective monitoring and evaluation of policies, enabling a comprehensive understanding of their impact

[12] Table 8.1 Duignan (2023).

[13] Jean Corston (2007); Inspector of Prisons (2011).

[14] See Table 8.2 below Duignan (2023).

[15] Criminal Justice (Community Service) (Amendment) Act (2011).

[16] Fines (Payment and Recovery) Act (2014).

[17] See Table 8.2.

Table 8.2 Female short term prison sentences changes from 2011 and 2020

Year	STPS male recipients	STPS female recipients	Total STPS recipients	% of female STPS recipients
2011	9603	1611	11,214	14.40
2012	9816	2028	11,844	17.10
2013	8953	2229	11,182	19.90
2014	8997	2554	11,551	22.10
2015	9601	2929	12,530	23.40
2016	8575	2421	10,996	22.00
2017	4082	818	4900	16.70
2018	3074	485	3559	13.60
2019	3687	618	4305	14.40
2020	2263	334	2597	12.90

Figures available from Irish Prison Service

on different genders. Table 8.2 presents data disaggregated by gender, as requested by the author from the Irish Prison Service. By examining gender-disaggregated data, policymakers and researchers can assess how policies specifically influence each gender, allowing for a more informed and targeted approach to addressing gender-specific needs and challenges.

The commissioning of a large-scale qualitative review similar to England and Wales would offer a deeper understanding of the lived experiences, perspectives, and complexities surrounding policy implementation. This would allow policymakers to gather valuable insights from individuals directly affected by the policies, leading to a more comprehensive assessment of their effectiveness and identify potential areas for improvement.[18] Transparent data publication enables a comprehensive comparison between the policy's stated objectives and its actual outcomes. If a policy fails to meet its objectives, it necessitates a prompt re-evaluation to ensure necessary revisions, aligning the policy goals with the outcomes. The government's policy of diversion appeared to lack any explicit philosophical punishment aims but was focused on cost-saving measures due to its implementation immediately after the financial crisis.

8.4 Implications

The lack of gender-aggregated data has had a negative impact, as the number of female STPS recipients did not decrease until after the introduction of fines legislation.[19] Where fines are imposed as an alternative to custodial sentences, the potential consequences can be far reaching, especially if the fines remain unpaid as persistent

[18] Hedderman et al. (2008).

[19] See Table 8.2.

non-payment will still ultimately lead to a custodial sentence. This highlights the importance of ensuring that alternatives to custody, such as fines, are accompanied by clear and comprehensive information regarding the associated obligations and duties.

Alternatives to custody may include additional requirements and conditions, such as licence conditions, reporting duties, or exclusion orders. These additional obligations can place a significant burden on the recipient. To protect the rights of individuals subject to these alternatives, it is essential to provide them with adequate information and ensure they are fully informed about their rights, obligations, and duties. This involves informing them about any additional requirements or conditions that may apply and providing support or resources to help them meet these obligations.

It is necessary to ensure that individuals are well-informed about their obligations and duties to protect procedural rights throughout. This includes providing clear explanations of the consequences of non-compliance or breach of the alternative to custody, as well as offering support or assistance to address any barriers or challenges they may encounter. A balance should be struck between providing alternatives to custody to reduce the use of custodial sentences and ensuring that individuals are fully aware of their rights, obligations, and duties, with the necessary support to fulfil them effectively.

Practical assistance might be achieved through a tailored support program that addresses specific needs. For example, if a CSO is given as an alternative to a custodial sentence individuals could be paired with a case manager who provides a clear breakdown of obligations and the potential consequences of non-compliance. This case manager could also help access services that address common barriers, such as childcare support where there are dependent children, mental health resources, or help with securing stable housing.

Furthermore, if employment is a condition of a CSO, the case manager might connect the individual with job training or educational programs. This targeted support would help ensure that they not only understand the obligations but also have practical tools and resources to overcome challenges, allowing them to successfully fulfil the conditions of the sentence.

8.5 Addressing Policy Shortcomings

8.5.1 Expansion of the Role of the Inspector for Prisons

Although the office of the Inspector for Prisons currently has the authority to monitor rights abuses within prison facilities, it still lacks jurisdiction to oversee such matters outside of them. However, the office is evolving into a more expansive and independent role, and there is potential for its jurisdiction to be extended to protect the rights of diverted women in the community.[20] The proposed Inspection of Places of Detention Bill introduces significant changes to Ireland's oversight of detention facilities.

This new legislation is important for Ireland's ratification of the Optional Protocol to the UN Convention against Torture (OPCAT),[21] creating a new Inspectorate of Places of Detention (IPD) as a National Preventive Mechanism (NPM).[22] Should this jurisdiction be extended to cover women subject to more intense supervision in the community, the office could then function as an effective rights protection system for CBOs that could then operate as 'places of detention' for women in the community.[23] The supervised women in the community could thus be effectively protected by a newly revitalised Office of Inspector of Places of Detention in the Community.

Community-based centres play a significant role in providing transparent supervision and cohesive services. Transparent supervision clarifies expectations and requirements for the diverted person and provides necessary resources and support for their desistance journey. Enhancing their availability, visibility, and public profile would make CBOs a viable option in judicial sentencing menus, thus promoting greater sentencing consistency at all levels.

The benefit of having transparent supervision practices in CBOs would create a consistent and accountable approach to monitoring and supporting individuals, helping them understand what is expected, reducing ambiguity, and promoting fairness. This transparency would also enable the identification of early indicators of disadvantage, particularly for minority groups, to prevent potential harm such as increased recidivism rates. Specific risk assessment tools tailored to individuals' needs and circumstances would be more effective than generic evaluative tools.

By employing such tools, CBOs could proactively address risk factors, provide appropriate resources, and develop personalised plans to mitigate potential harm and enhance successful reintegration into the community. Overall, standardised and transparent supervision, coupled with specific risk assessment tools, would foster a more effective and equitable approach to community-based diversion programmes, ensuring individuals receive the necessary support, resources, and interventions to promote desistance from offending and facilitate successful reintegration into society.

[20] Inspection of Places of Detention Bill (2022).

[21] Optional Protocol to the Convention Against Torture A/RES/57/199 (2002).

[22] NPMs are independent entities designed to prevent torture and other forms of cruel, inhuman, or degrading treatment. They are widely established across Europe and globally and play a key role in mitigating torture and abuse in detention settings.

[23] Inspection of Places of Detention Bill (2022).

8.5.2 Women-Only Spaces

Research shows that the establishment of women-only spaces within Community-Based Organisations (CBOs) yields substantial benefits for women involved in the criminal justice system.[24] These spaces enhance safety, foster a sense of community, and enable CBO staff to develop specialised expertise in supporting women. For women who have experienced abuse or dysfunction in their childhood homes or relationships, a unisex CBO can be intimidating and triggering. The presence of men in such settings may hinder their ability to feel comfortable and safe, thereby impeding their engagement and participation.

Creating women-only spaces acknowledges the unique challenges and traumas faced by women in the criminal justice system. It recognises that some women require mental and physical assistance and that their prior experiences with state institutions and personal relationships may have been marked by a lack of respect. By providing an environment exclusively for women, these programmes can help alleviate their reluctance to participate and increase their willingness to engage with the support and assistance offered. Women-only spaces allow for a more tailored and sensitive approach to meet the specific needs of women, promoting a greater sense of empowerment, trust, and overall success in their rehabilitation and reintegration journey.

A gender-specific Community-Based Organisation (CBO) facility functioning as a comprehensive 'one-stop-shop' can significantly benefit women in the criminal justice system. Such a facility would create a woman-centric environment where women can access essential resources and treatments tailored to their unique needs, thereby easing the challenges associated with community-based diversion.

This CBO could provide a range of services based on individual needs, including:

- Monitoring and compliance with probation conditions.
- Support in managing offending behaviours and promoting desistance.
- Assistance with securing accommodation or housing.

The establishment of these facilities has both specific benefits for female STPS recipients and broader societal advantages. For the female recipients, access to targeted support can enhance their rehabilitation and reintegration into society. For society, the economic cost of successful CSO completions is lower than that of prison sentences. Furthermore, persistently breached CSOs will inevitably lead to custodial sentences, underscoring the need for effective community support systems.

Promoting desistance and rehabilitation is beneficial both economically and altruistically, contributing to reduced recidivism and enhanced community safety. This dual benefit highlights the importance of investing in gender-specific CBO facilities to support female offenders effectively and sustainably.

---

[24] Hedderman (2004).

8.5.3 Integrating CBOs into State Oversight

The creation of gender-specific CBOs yields significant benefits for the criminal justice system. These facilities provide a woman-centric environment, offering the necessary resources and treatments to address the unique challenges associated with community-based diversion. Such centres cater to various levels of individual needs, ensure compliance with probation conditions, assist in managing offending and desistance, and support ex-offenders in securing housing and accommodation.[25]

The advantages of this approach are twofold. Firstly, for STPS recipients, successful completion of a CSO is more cost-effective than a custodial sentence. Persistent breaches of CSOs results in more costly custodial sentences. Secondly, for society, the focus on desistance and rehabilitation yields economic benefits and promotes societal well-being. In the 'what works paradigm,' which recommends the use of assessment tools, researchers agree that risk assessment instruments based on risk factors from general populations can lead to miscalculations of risk for minority groups.[26]

A common miscalculation might arise if a risk assessment tool evaluates a woman's criminal history or social stability without considering the context behind these factors. For instance, a woman who has experienced domestic violence, poverty, addiction or systemic discrimination may have a criminal record stemming from survival behaviours, like shoplifting to provide for her or her family, rather than a high propensity for violent or repeat offending. If the tool rates her as "high-risk" based solely on criminal history without accounting for these contextual factors, she may be directed towards intensive correctional programs rather than support-based interventions focused on rehabilitation, such as mental health counselling, housing assistance, or family support.

Such miscalculations not only misrepresent the actual risk she poses but also lead to interventions that are less effective for her unique situation, reducing the overall success of the "what works" approach for minority women offenders. In the long run, this can contribute to a cycle of reoffending if the root causes of her offending behaviour go unaddressed.

Implementing transparent supervision practices within CBOs establishes a consistent and accountable framework for monitoring and supporting individuals. This transparency reduces ambiguity, promotes fairness, and identifies early indicators of disadvantage, particularly for minority groups, thereby preventing potential harms such as increased recidivism rates. Specialised risk assessment tools tailored to individual needs enhances the effectiveness of interventions, facilitating targeted support and promotes successful reintegration into the community.[27]

By ensuring that CBOs are well-managed, adequately funded, and standardised, a more equitable approach to community-based diversion programmes can be

[25] Hedderman and Gunby (2013).

[26] Kemshall (2021); Raynor and Vanstone (1994); McNeill (2006).

[27] Una Convery (2009), Chapter 4; Gelsthorpe et al. (2007).

achieved, promoting desistance from offending and supporting successful reintegration into society. This aligns with international and European standards for gender-specific policies, ensuring that women's unique needs are addressed within the criminal justice system. Overall, a more comprehensive and structured approach to CBOs, focusing on transparency, standardisation, and gender-specific needs, significantly enhances the effectiveness of diversion policies, leading to better outcomes for female offenders and society.

The period between the enactment of the Criminal Justice (Community Service) (Amendment) Act 2011 and the Fines (Payment and Recovery) Act 2014 saw a significant rise in STPS for female offenders. Concurrently, there was a noticeable decline in the number of CSOs issued to women. The Fines Acts aimed to reduce the use of STPS by removing automatic imprisonment for fine defaulters. However, this approach may have inadvertently resulted in alternative sanctions merely substituting immediate custodial sentences. This method fails to address the root causes of offending behaviour but rather creates a type of 'holding pattern' for STPS recipients.

Considering these findings, confrontation of the root causes of custodial sentences is required to resolve the problem. For instance, current legislation limits the option of paying fines by instalment unless the amount exceeds €100. Removing Section 5(a)(i) of the Fines will enable individuals to address their financial obligations more effectively, avoiding unnecessary imprisonment and aligning with the goal of diverting individuals from STPS towards a more rehabilitative approach within the criminal justice system.

The 2011 and 2014 legislation introduced diversion policies aimed at providing alternatives to custody. However, these laws do not offer specific guidelines or instructions to the judiciary on how to effectively reduce the use of STPS or when it is appropriate to impose non-custodial alternatives for different categories of offenders. Instead, the judiciary is left to decide for themselves what each case merits within the overarching principle of proportionality. Typically, judges in the District Court will have their own rule of thumb, causing problems with consistency.[28] Thus, the criminal justice system requires increased transparency and structure.

8.5.4 *Solution-Focused Sanctions*

In Finland, statutory sentencing principles providing general and specific sentencing guidance were introduced in 1975, at a time when the prison population was almost twice the size of other Nordic countries. Since then, Finland has reduced its prison population to one of the lowest in Europe (66 per 100,000 of the general population). Finland provides a useful comparison for Ireland as a country on the fringes of

[28] Maguire (2008); Bacik (2000).

Europe with a similar population size. It has four times the crime rate of Ireland, yet it has a much lower use of custody.[29]

In Finland, there has been a mixture of decriminalising certain offences, such as public drunkenness, relaxing sentences, and reducing the minimum sentence.[30] In the 1990s, judges were allowed greater scope to impose conditional sentences as opposed to imprisonment, and the community sentence became popular. Finland employs a system known as 'dayfines'.[31] This system was adopted in 1921 and ensures the 'equal severity'[32] of the fine for offenders of different incomes and wealth. The number of dayfines is determined based on the seriousness of the offence while the amount depends on the financial situation of the offender. The amount of the dayfine equals roughly half of the offender's daily income after taxes. This fine is imposed by the police, and, in the case of non-payment, the penalty cannot be converted into imprisonment. This solution-focused sanction has reduced the use of custody.

A focus on desistance barriers represents a solution-focused paradigm for diverted STPS offenders. This paradigm acknowledges and incorporates feminist penological approaches that emphasise the unique pathways into offending experienced by women. In recent years, feminist penologists have highlighted a research blind spot regarding the specific needs and experiences of women in the criminal justice system.[33]

This gender-specific paradigm allows for a deeper understanding of the factors that contribute to women's involvement in crime and the challenges they encounter in the process of desistance. It recognises the importance of considering gender-sensitive approaches in policy development, program design, and interventions aimed at promoting rehabilitation and reducing reoffending among female offenders.[34]

By adopting this paradigm, researchers and practitioners can shed light on how certain factors disproportionately impact women involved in the criminal justice system, such as the impact of trauma, gender roles, caregiving responsibilities, and socioeconomic inequalities. This approach aims to rectify the historical neglect of gender-specific considerations in criminal justice research and practice, providing a more comprehensive understanding of female offenders and paving the way for more effective and equitable interventions.[35] Adopting this gender-specific paradigm not only illuminates the unique pathways into offending for women but also sheds light on how women experience state punishments differently from men.

---

[29] O'Donnell (2001).

[30] Sheehan et al. (2011), p. 13.

[31] Lappi-Seppälä (2009).

[32] Ibid, p. 336.

[33] McIvor et al. (2004); Hedderman et al. (2008).

[34] Gelsthorpe et al. (2007); Convery (2009).

[35] Carlen (1989); Gelsthorpe and Morris (1990); Maruska (2010).

By acknowledging the distinct ways in which women are affected by state sanctions, such as imprisonment or community-based alternatives, policymakers and practitioners can better understand and respond to the specific needs and challenges faced by female offenders. Even though in 2014 the Irish Joint Probation Service and Irish Prison Service Strategy in their strategy report recommended that 'a gender-specific approach to delivery of services will be developed,'[36] this is still outstanding. A Report by the IRPT in 2021 acknowledges that:

> [M]ore research needs to be carried out to understand why more women are not considered for CSOs, particularly when the Probation Service has made explicit commitments to the development and expansion of gender-specific community interventions.[37]

This study found aspects of the government's policy of diversion to be less effective for women, but regular policy evaluations serve to identify the parts of policy that are effective and ineffective on an ongoing basis. These evaluations should be designed to assess the advantages and disadvantages for all users, rather than the predominant male user, to ensure women are being catered for. It is essential to ensure that the CBO is efficiently managed and monitored to maintain consistency across the state. Any changes to the project should be evaluated using appropriate evaluative tools.[38]

By designating the Inspector for Places of Detention to monitor CBOs as part of a National Preventative Mechanism, this could potentially serve as a ground-breaking solution in effectively addressing the challenges faced by women in the community. This proposal gains further significance considering Ireland's ratification of the Optional Protocol to the Convention against Torture (OPCAT). With the Inspector's oversight, CBOs could be subjected to rigorous scrutiny, ensuring compliance with human rights standards and providing accountability.[39]

Implementing this approach would allow for a comprehensive assessment of CBOs, ensuring their adherence to appropriate guidelines, protocols, and regulations. This monitoring mechanism would help identify any shortcomings, areas for improvement, or systemic issues within the CBOs. Additionally, it would facilitate ongoing evaluation and feedback to promote consistent and high-quality services across different CBOs throughout the country. The inclusion of CBOs under the purview of the Inspector for Places of Detention as part of a National Preventative Mechanism aligns with Ireland's commitment to respect the rights of female offenders as a signatory of the Bangkok Rules.[40] It provides an opportunity to establish a robust framework that ensures the well-being, rehabilitation, and successful reintegration of women, while also safeguarding their rights and dignity.

---

[36] Irish Prison Service and The Probation Service (2014), p. 9.

[37] Irish Penal Reform Trust (2021), p. 45.

[38] Hedderman and Hough (2004).

[39] United Nations Rules for the Treatment of Women Prisoners and Non-custodial Measures for Women Offenders: Vienna: UNODC (2011) 2010. United Nations Office on Drugs and Crime (UNODC).

[40] Ibid.

Overall, this initiative has the potential to transform the landscape of women's rehabilitation within the community.

International and European laws provide for gender-specific policies for women.[41] However, implementing specific legislative policies for a small minority of the penal system, who are often invisible both statistically and as a physical group, may not be a priority for governments. In Ireland, the small minority of women was deprioritised in an increasingly unmanageable prison system in the early 2010s, where financial considerations and a functioning criminal justice system were higher priorities.

However, it now appears that diverted STPS offenders have proliferated in the under-resourced community, re-offended, and are being returned to prison.[42] A former IPS governor remarked on how 'diverting people from prison should focus on those sentenced to 12 months or less, but would rely on having proper resources at the community level and for the Probation Service.'[43] Irish Prison Service statistics illustrate both male and female prisons operating over one hundred percent over capacity at the time of writing in 2023.[44] If the community fails to foster desistance, there is a significant likelihood of reoffending. This will lead to cumulative offending and subsequent sentencing, ultimately rendering an offender ineligible for community-based alternatives. Such alternatives are typically available only for offences that would generally warrant a maximum sentence of twelve months imprisonment or less.

8.6 Conclusion

The community holds the key to the solution. By resourcing the community with CBOs that function as one-stop shops and programmes that adequately cater to all levels of diverted STPS females, individuals will then be able to fulfil all community alternative obligations and address any outstanding responsibilities required of them by law. Locations will be equipped to evaluate any existing needs and support ex-offenders in maintaining their desistance from offending. This should be delivered in a female-cantered space, where direct and indirect needs are addressed and not confused with risks.[45]

Since the CBO caters to women who have been sentenced to direct alternatives to detention under the 2011 or 2014 legislation, it should be categorised for monitoring under the 'places of detention' category in the Inspection of Places of Detention Bill

[41] International Covenant on Civil and Political Rights (1976) United Nations General Assembly Convention on the Elimination of all Forms of Discrimination Against Women (1979).

[42] Jack Power (2023).

[43] RTE (2023).

[44] Irish Prison Service.

[45] Convery (2009), p. 1.

2022.[46] This would mean that any Centre will be subject to consistent monitoring and subject to reporting as a prison visiting committee would be empowered to visit and inspect the treatment and conditions of those persons in such places each year.[47]

While the Optional Protocol to the Convention against Torture (OPCAT) stipulates that 'sufficient resources should be provided and these should be independent,'[48] the proposal suggests that funding for this office will remain within the Department of Justice. While this arrangement may constrain the office's independence, it would establish the office on a statutory footing. Consequently, this designation would make the option of sentencing women to women-only CBOs a highly visible option for the judiciary, presenting an alternative approach for women convicted of less serious offences. This approach promotes fair sentencing within a gender-resourced community that prioritises balanced rehabilitative principles.

Law

Offences Against the Person Act (1861)
Criminal Justice Act (1967)
Theft Act (1968)
Misuse of Drugs Act (1971)
International Covenant on Civil and Political Rights (1976)
Misuse of Drugs Act (1977)
Criminal Justice (Theft and Fraud Offences) Act (2001)
United Nations Rules for the Treatment of Women Prisoners and Non-custodial Measures for Women Offenders: Vienna: UNODC (2011)
Optional Protocol to the Convention Against Torture A/RES/57/199 (2002)
Convention on the Elimination of all Forms of Discrimination Against Women (1979)
Criminal Justice (Community Service) (Amendment) Act (2011)
Fines (Payment and Recovery) Act (2014)
Inspection of Places of Detention Bill (2022)

References

Book

Cohen S (1985) Visions of social control: crime punishment and classification

---

[46] Inspection of Places of Detention Bill (2022).
[47] Ibid, Head 17 The functions of a National Preventive Mechanism (NPM).
[48] Ibid, Head 3 - Expenses.

Maruska JH (2010) Feminist ontologies, epistemologies, methodologies, and methods in international relations. Oxford Research Encyclopedia of International Studies
McIvor G, Malloch M, Gelsthorpe L (2004) Women who offend, vol 44. Jessica Kingsley Publishers
Sheehan R, McIvor G, Trotter C (2011) Working with women offenders in the community. Willan Publishing
Walsh DP, Sexton P (2000) An empirical study of community service orders in Ireland. Stationery Office

Journal Article

Bacik I (2000) The practice of sentencing in the Irish courts. Criminal Justice in Ireland 348
Carlen P (1989) Feminist jurisprudence-or women-wise penology? Prob J 36:110
Convery U (2009) Addressing offending by women: a literature review
Gelsthorpe L, Morris A (1990) Feminist perspectives in criminology
Gelsthorpe L, Sharpe G, Roberts J (2007) Provision for women offenders in the community. Fawcett Society, London
Guilfoyle E (2017) An exploration of the potential negative effects of using Community Service Orders as an alternative to imprisonment for fine defaulters. Irish Crim Law J 26:94
Hedderman C (2004) The "criminogenic" needs of women offenders. Women who offend 227
Hedderman C, Gunby C (2013) Diverting women from custody. Probat J 60:425
Hedderman C, Hough M (2004) Getting tough or being effective: what matters? In: What matters in probation. Willan, Cullompton, p 146
Hedderman C et al (2008) Implementing services for women offenders and those 'at risk' of offending: action research with together women. Ministry of Justice Research Series
Kemshall H (2021) Risk and desistance: a blended approach to risk management. HM Inspectorate of Probation Academic Insights 7
Lappi-Seppälä T (2009) Imprisonment and penal policy in Finland. Scand Stud Law 54:333
McNeill F (2006) A desistance paradigm for offender management. Criminol Crim Justice 6:39
O'Donnell I (2001) Prison matters. Irish Jurist 36:153
Raynor P, Vanstone M (1994) Probation practice, effectiveness and the non-treatment paradigm. Br J Soc Work 24:387
Woods M (2020) 'Helping others and helping myself': wounded healers as peer workers. Irish Probat J 17

Media

Jack Power (2023) Prison overcrowding: 120 prisoners without beds as system reaches full capacity. The Irish Times (3rd February 2023). <https://www.irishtimes.com/ireland/2023/02/03/irish-penal-reform-trust-concerned-as-prison-system-reaches-full-capacity/>
RTE (2023) Irish prison service confirms overcrowding issues. https://www.rteie/news/2023/0423/1378662-irish-prison-service-confirms-overcrowding-issues/ (23rd April 2023). Accessed 1st May 2023

Report

Carmody P, McEvoy M (1996) A study of Irish female prisoners. Dublin

Department of Justice (2022) Criminal Justice Policy Review of Policy Options for Prison and Penal Reform 2022-2024. gov.ie/en/collection/

Inspector of Prisons (2011) Standards for the Inspections of Prisons in Ireland- Women Prisoners' Supplement

Irish Penal Reform Trust (2021) Progress in the Penal System (PIPS)- The Need for Transparency. Dublin

Jean Corston B (2007) The Corston Report: a report of a review of women with particular vulnerabilities in the criminal justice system. London

Wootton B (1970) Report on Non-Custodial and Semi-Custodial Treatment of Offenders (Probation). Penal Advisory Council Sub Committee on Non-Custodial Treatment

Thesis

Duignan S (2023) Evaluation of the effect of Irish Penal Policy on female short-term prison sentence recipients: the need for gender-specific policy. University of Galway

Maguire N (2008) Sentencing in Ireland: an exploration of the views, rationales, and sentencing practices of district and circuit court judges. Trinity College, Dublin

Online Resource

CSO, CSO Crime and Justice Statistics

Irish Prison Service and The Probation Service (2014) Community return: a unique opportunity- a descriptive evaluation of the first twenty-six months. Irish Prison Service/Irish Probation Service

Irish Prison Service, Daily Prisoner Population

The manufacturer's authorised representative in the EU is Springer Nature Customer Service Centre GmbH, Europaplatz 3, 69115 Heidelberg, Germany. If you have any concerns regarding our products, please contact ProductSafety@springernature.com

Printed and bound by CPI Group (UK) Ltd, Croydon, CR0 4YY
01/10/2026
02225982-0016